THE FAMILY
CREATIVE WORKSHOP

Index

Plenary Publications International, Inc.
New York and Amsterdam

Published by Plenary Publications International Incorporated 300 East 40th Street, New York, New York, 10016 for the Blue Mountain Crafts Council.

Library of Congress Catalog Card Number: 73-89331. Complete set International Standard Book Number: 0-88459-021-6. Index International Standard Book Number: 0-88459-024-0.

Manufactured in the United States of America. Printed and bound by the W. A. Krueger Company, Brookfield, Wisconsin.

Printing preparation by Lanman Lithoplate Company.

Plenary Publications International, Incorporated 300 East 40th Street New York, New York 10016

Publishers:
Plenary Publications International, Incorporated 300 East 40th Street New York, New York 10016

Steven R. Schepp
EDITOR-IN-CHIEF

Jo Springer
VOLUME EDITOR

Joanne Delaney
Ellen Foley
EDITORIAL ASSISTANTS

Jerry Curcio
PRODUCTION MANAGER

Photo and illustration credits:
COVER PHOTOGRAPH: Steven Mays. MATERIALS REFERENCE GUIDE (FOOD): Specialized cooking equipment, page mi-22, courtesy of Hubert DesForges, New York, N.Y. MATERIALS REFERENCE GUIDE (PLANTS): Illustration, page mi-34, adapted from salad garden plans featured in the 1975 and 1976 Burpee Seeds Catalogs, with permission of the W. Atlee Burpee Company, Warminster, Pa.

Acknowledgements:
BASIC REFERENCE GUIDE (COLOR AND COLORANTS): Aljo Manufacturing Co., Inc., New York, N. Y.; Colonial Printing Ink Co., East Rutherford, N. J.; Fezandie and Sperrle, Inc., New York, N. Y.; Edith Gecker, ASID, New York, N. Y.; Higgins, Inc. (Division, Faber-Castell Corporation), Newark, N.J.; Hunt Manufacturing Co. Statesville, N.C.; Talbot A. Love, Representative, Benjamin Moore & Co.,

New York, N.Y.; Minwax Company, Inc., Clifton, N.J.; Winsor & Newton, Secaucus, N.J.; Jack D. Wolfe, Brooklyn, N.Y.

Editorial preparation:
Tree Communications, Inc. 250 Park Avenue South New York, New York 10003

Rodney Friedman
EDITORIAL DIRECTOR

Ronald Gross
DESIGN DIRECTOR

Paul Levin
DIRECTOR OF PHOTOGRAPHY

Donal Dinwiddie
CONSULTING EDITOR

Jill Munves
TEXT EDITOR

Sonja Douglas
ART DIRECTOR

Marsha Gold
DESIGNER

Lucille O'Brien
EDITORIAL PRODUCTION

Ruth Forst Michel
COPYREADER

Eva Gold
ADMINISTRATIVE MANAGER

Editors:
Andrea DiNoto, Donal Dinwiddie, Michael Donner, Linda Hetzer, Nancy Bruning Levine, Marilyn Nierenberg, Mary Grace Skurka.

Originating editor of the series:
Allen Davenport Bragdon

Contributing illustrators:
Marina Givotovsky, Patricia Lee, Lynn Matus, Alan A. Okada, Sally Shimizu.

Contributing photographer:
Steven Mays

Production:
Thom Augusta, Christopher Jones, Patricia Lee, Patrick O'Connell, Douglas Porcaro, Sylvia Sherwin, Leslie Strong.

Indexer:
Bernd Metz

Note:
The small **mi** preceding each page number in this volume stands for **master index**.

Contents

Basic Reference Guide mi-5

Weights, Measures, and Metric Conversion Tables mi-6
Increments of U. S. customary and metric measurement systems; tables of U. S. customary and metric equivalents; metric prefixes; conversion charts for frequently used values; conversion formulas; converting fractions to decimals and metric equivalents; temperature conversions.

Color and Colorants mi-8
Chroma, value, and warm-cool color charts; color guidelines; colorants for wood, metal, and stone; printing inks, studio paints, and dyes.

Abrasives and Polishes mi-12
Abrasive papers and cloths: grit designations, descriptions, and uses; steel wool and wire brushes: descriptions, grades, and uses; grinding and buffing wheels: types and uses; buffing compounds: list and uses.

Adhesives mi-15
Listings of glues, cements, and adhesive tapes with descriptions and uses; joining of metal by soldering, brazing, and welding.

Materials Reference Guide mi-17

Clay mi-18
Glossary of potter's terms.

Fibers and fabrics mi-19
Properties and care; needle types; thread glossary; stain removal.

Foods mi-21
Kitchen planning; basic kitchen equipment; glossary of cooking terms; specialized utensils; equivalent measures; yields from measured amounts of foods; emergency substitutions.

Glass mi-25
Stained-glass; blown-glass; glass enamels and glazes.

Leather mi-26
Cleaning and care; cutting and measuring tools; stitching; decorating; dyeing and finishing; glossary of leather terms; chart of leather uses.

Metals mi-28
Glossary of metals, tools, and materials; metal-working terms; charts of heat colors, gauge numbers, annealing temperatures, ductility, melting temperatures, malleability, tensile strength, and troy equivalents.

Minerals mi-31
Lapidary minerals and associated gemstones; charts of hardness, specific gravity, surface luster, weights and dimensions; charts of tumbling, sawing, grinding, sanding, and polishing; mineral terminology.

Plants mi-34
Plan for a small garden; plants listed for special purposes; house plants charted by requirements of soil, light, food and water, and temperature.

Plastics mi-36
Types of plastic; materials, tools, and processes of plastics work.

Wood mi-38
Charts of hardwood and softwood quality grades and lumber sizes; plywood grades; nail sizes and weights; screw types and dimensions.

Patterns mi-41
A discriminating selection of patterns both traditional and modern, applicable to a wide variety of crafts projects in many media. Instructions for enlarging the patterns to any size are included.

Master Index and Project Evaluation Lists mi-73
In the master index for **The Family Creative Workshop** encyclopedia, individual projects are grouped and listed alphabetically under craft-category headings and by groups of related projects. Following the master index are three alphabetical project-evaluation lists, based on cost, time required, and level of skill needed.

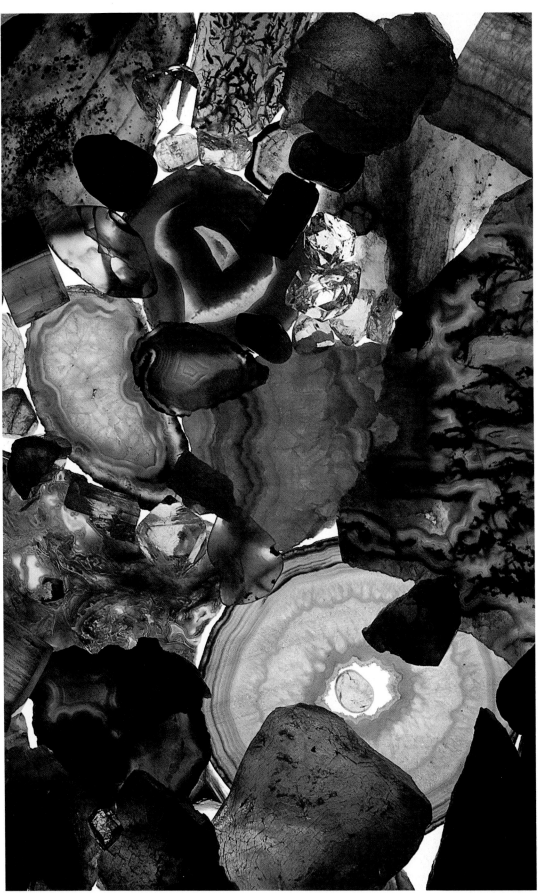

Basic reference guide

Weights, measures, and metric conversion tables   mi-6

Colors and colorants   mi-8

Abrasives and polishes   mi-12

Adhesives   mi-15

For easy reference, general information applicable to a variety of crafts is summarized in the charts, tables, glossaries, and lists on the pages that follow. Included in this section are four universal craft processes—measuring, selecting colors and finishes, smoothing and shaping, and assembling.

METRIC AND U.S. CUSTOMARY MEASUREMENTS

┌Table of equivalents┐

U.S. customary measure

Approximate equivalent metric measure

LINEAR VALUES

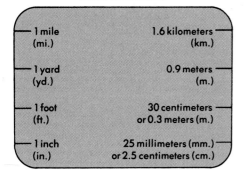

1 mile (mi.)	1.6 kilometers (km.)
1 yard (yd.)	0.9 meters (m.)
1 foot (ft.)	30 centimeters or 0.3 meters (m.)
1 inch (in.)	25 millimeters (mm.) or 2.5 centimeters (cm.)

UNITS OF WEIGHT

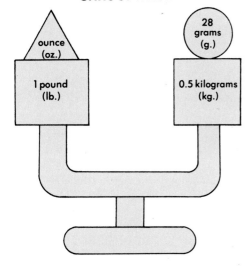

ounce (oz.)	28 grams (g.)
1 pound (lb.)	0.5 kilograms (kg.)

UNITS OF CAPACITY

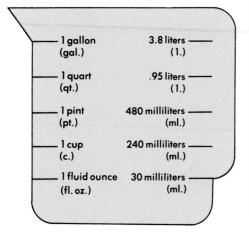

1 gallon (gal.)	3.8 liters (l.)
1 quart (qt.)	.95 liters (l.)
1 pint (pt.)	480 milliliters (ml.)
1 cup (c.)	240 milliliters (ml.)
1 fluid ounce (fl. oz.)	30 milliliters (ml.)

Weights, measures, and metric conversion tables

United States customary weights and measures are matched with their metric counterparts in the chart at left. Incremental measures of each system are listed below. At the bottom of the page are formulas for converting measurements from one system to the other. Opposite are charts showing conversions of frequently used values. Additional measurement data also appear opposite.

U.S. CUSTOMARY WEIGHTS AND MEASURES

Linear measure	Area measure	Cubic measure
12 inches = 1 foot 3 feet = 1 yard	144 square inches = 1 square foot 9 square feet = 1 square yard	1,728 cubic inches = 1 cubic foot 27 cubic feet = 1 cubic yard

Capacity

Dry measure	Liquid measure	Weight avoirdupois
2 pints = 1 quart 8 quarts = 1 peck 4 pecks = 1 bushel	3 teaspoons = 1 tablespoon 16 tablespoons = 1 cup 2 cups = 1 pint 2 pints = 1 quart 4 quarts = 1 gallon	16 drams = 1 ounce 16 ounces = 1 pound

METRIC MEASURES

The values above can be rendered into three basic metric units: the meter (linear measurement), the liter (capacity), and the gram (weight). Each unit can be expressed in a number of ways by multiplying or dividing it by ten or a multiple of ten, indicated by the prefix given the word. For example, kilo means 1000. Thus a kilogram is 1000 grams. Milli means one thousandth of, so a milligram is a thousandth of a gram. The table lists the most common metric increments.

Metric system prefixes

milli=1000th of	**deca**=10 times
centi=100th of	**hecto**=100 times
deci=10th of	**kilo**=1000 times

The same prefixes are used for all three units. A decagram is 10 grams; a decaliter is 10 liters; a decameter is 10 meters. Area and cubic measures are derived by squaring or cubing the linear measure. Ten millimeters = 1 centimeter; therefore, 100 square millimeters = 1 square centimeter, and 1000 cubic millimeters = 1 cubic centimeter.

CONVERSION FORMULAS

When you know a measurement or quantity in either the metric or U.S. customary system, you can convert it to the other system by multiplying it by a given number. The table below lists the multiplication factors for converting measurements from one system to the other. All abbreviations used are defined at left.

Linear		Area		Volume		Capacity	
To convert:	**Multiply by:**	**To convert:**	**Multiply by:**	**To convert:**	**Multiply by:**	**To convert:**	**Multiply by:**
in. to cm.	2.5	sq. in. to sq. cm.	6.5	cu. in. to cu. cm.	16.4	fl. oz. to ml.	30
cm. to in.	0.4	sq. cm. to sq. in.	0.16	cu. cm. to cu. in.	0.06	c. to l.	0.24
ft. to cm.	30	sq. ft. to sq. m.	0.09	cu. ft. to cu. m.	0.03	pt. to l.	0.47
cm. to ft.	0.03	sq. yds. to sq. m.	0.8	cu. m. to cu. ft.	35	qts. to l.	0.95
yds. to m.	0.9	sq. m. to sq. yds.	1.2	cu. yds. to cu. m.	0.76	gals. to l.	3.8
m. to yds.	1.1			cu. m. to cu. yds.	1.3	ml. to fl. oz.	0.03
Weight						l. to pt.	2.1
oz. to g.	28					l. to qts.	1.06
g. to oz.	0.035					l. to gals.	0.26
lb. to kg.	0.45						
kg. to lb.	2.2						

METRIC CONVERSION CHARTS AND TABLES

Inches to millimeters		Inches to centimeters				Yards to meters	
in.	mm.	in.	cm.	in.	cm.	yd.	m.
1/8	3	1	2.5	11	28.0	1/8	0.15
1/4	6	2	5.0	12	30.5	1/4	0.25
3/8	10	3	7.5	13	33.0	3/8	0.35
1/2	13	4	10.0	14	35.5	1/2	0.50
5/8	15	5	12.5	15	38.0	5/8	0.60
3/4	20	6	15.0	16	40.5	3/4	0.70
7/8	22	7	18.0	17	43.0	7/8	0.80
1	25	8	20.5	18	46.0	1	0.95
2	50	9	23.0	19	48.5	2	1.85
3	75	10	25.5	20	51.0	3	2.75

Fractions and decimals of an inch converted to millimeters

Fraction	Decimal	Millimeters
1/16	.063	1.6
1/8	.125	3.2
3/16	.188	4.8
1/4	.25	6.4
5/16	.31	7.9
3/8	.375	9.5
7/16	.438	11.1
1/2	.500	12.7
9/16	.563	14.3
5/8	.625	15.9
11/16	.688	17.5
3/4	.75	19.1
13/16	.813	20.6
7/8	.875	22.2
15/16	.938	23.8
1	1.000	25.4

(All figures have been rounded off.)

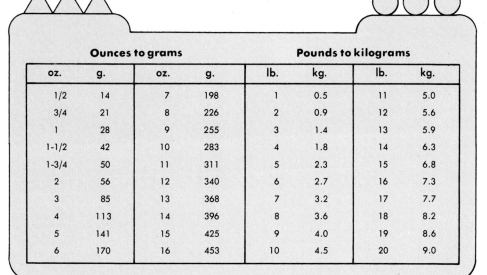

Ounces to grams				Pounds to kilograms			
oz.	g.	oz.	g.	lb.	kg.	lb.	kg.
1/2	14	7	198	1	0.5	11	5.0
3/4	21	8	226	2	0.9	12	5.6
1	28	9	255	3	1.4	13	5.9
1-1/2	42	10	283	4	1.8	14	6.3
1-3/4	50	11	311	5	2.3	15	6.8
2	56	12	340	6	2.7	16	7.3
3	85	13	368	7	3.2	17	7.7
4	113	14	396	8	3.6	18	8.2
5	141	15	425	9	4.0	19	8.6
6	170	16	453	10	4.5	20	9.0

Temperature conversions

The following table lists various temperatures on the Centigrade scale and their Fahrenheit equivalents. For values not shown, use the formulas following the table to convert one temperature to the other.

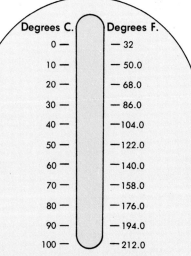

Degrees C.	Degrees F.
0	32
10	50.0
20	68.0
30	86.0
40	104.0
50	122.0
60	140.0
70	158.0
80	176.0
90	194.0
100	212.0

Fluid ounces to milliliters				Pints to liters		Gallons to liters	
fl. oz.	ml.	fl. oz.	ml.	pt.	l.	gal.	lit.
1	30	11	325	1/4	0.1	1	3.8
2	59	12	355	1/2	0.24	2	7.6
3	89	13	384	1	0.47	3	11.3
4	118	14	414	2	0.95	4	15
5	148	15	444	3	1.5	5	19
6	177	16	473	4	1.9	6	23
7	207	17	503	5	2.4	7	26
8	237	18	532	6	2.8	8	30
9	266	19	562	7	3.3	9	34
10	296	20	591	8	3.8	10	38

To convert a Fahrenheit temperature to its Centigrade equivalent, subtract 32 from the Fahrenheit temperature, multiply by 5, and divide by 9. To convert a Centigrade temperature into Fahrenheit, multiply the Centigrade temperature by 9, divide by 5, and add 32.

(Figures have been rounded off to simplify the tables.)

Color and colorants

Color coordination guide

Mixing color

For the craftsman, colorants come in many forms. Regardless of the medium, the relationship between colors and the rules for mixing them remain the same. The color wheel at right is a valuable guide for establishing color relationships. Red, yellow, and blue are the primary colors. By mixing equal amounts of any two primaries, you can form a secondary color as shown. A primary and a secondary color that lie opposite each other on the color wheel are known as complementary colors. By mixing any two, such as red and green or yellow and purple, you can neutralize both and form a gray tone. By mixing equal amounts of a primary color and a neighboring secondary color, you can create an intermediary color. Six such colors are shown on the color wheel: red-orange, red-purple, yellow-green, yellow-orange, blue-green, and blue-purple. You can form many others by varying the proportions of the primary and secondary color.

Colorant charts

The vast array of coloring materials available to the craftsman ranges from common house paints used as covering agents to studio paints, inks, and dyes. In addition, there are stains and finishes which, while not colorants, add to the richness or gloss of the final product. In the following charts are colorants used to cover finished projects and colorants used in the studio arts—painting, textile work, and print making.

Cautions: Paints, finishes, and solvents can be hazardous. Follow all instructions on the labels of the products you use, paying special attention to precautionary measures. Work in a well ventilated area, and dispose of solvent-soaked rags promptly.

In addition to the color, which is known as the hue, every color has three other properties: the amount of brightness of the hue, known as chroma; the coolness or warmth of the hue; and the value of the hue, which is the pureness of the color. These factors are shown in the charts at right.

Using these guidelines, you can create many colors from a few. A tint of a color is produced by adding a small amount of white. A shade is made by adding small amounts of black. When you mix colors, gradually add a

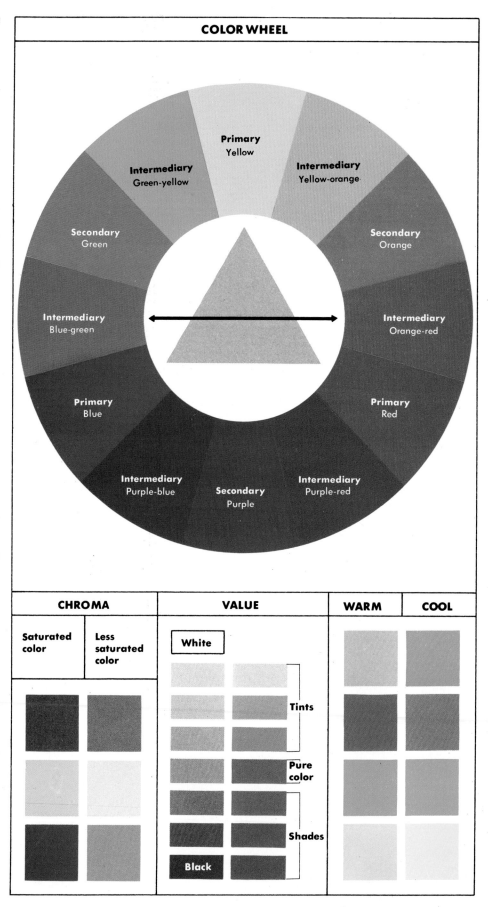

COLOR WHEEL

EXTERIOR SURFACES

Material	Desired finish	Recommended covering
Wood	Paint	Two coats of exterior quality oil or water-based house paint over one coat of the recommended primer
	Clear glossy finish	Exterior quality polyurethane
	Clear matte finish	Spar varnish
Iron	Paint	Two or three coats of rust-inhibitive primer plus two coats of exterior quality house paint or enamel
Aluminum	Paint	One coat of primer plus two coats of weatherproof aluminum paint
Galvanized metal	Paint	One coat of galvanized metal primer plus two coats of exterior-quality house paint
Stone	Paint	Any desired paint protected with three or four coats of polyurethane varnish, either matte or glossy, exterior quality

INTERIOR SURFACES

Material	Desired finish	Recommended covering
Wood	Paint	Two coats of oil- or water-based house paint over one coat of the recommended primer
	Clear, glossy finish	Two coats of shellac, lacquer, or polyurethane
	Clear matte finish	Two coats of varnish
Metal	Paint	One coat of rust-inhibitive primer plus one coat of house paint or enamel
Galvanized metal	Paint	One coat of galvanized metal primer (thinner) plus one coat of house paint
Stone	As for exterior	

little of the darker color to the lighter one. In addition, start with the brightest, purest primaries you can find.

Color selection

There are no absolute rules for using color. You should use whatever colors you like. There are, however, principles for determining what colors and color combinations will fulfill your purpose. The color wheel can be used in many ways for this. First, it can be divided to determine warm and cool colors, for despite the fact that every hue comes in a warm and cool tone, certain colors are generally considered psychologically cool (green and blue), while others such as orange, red, and yellow suggest warmth.

Another way to use the color wheel is to put a triangle in its center. No matter how you shift the triangle, you will create a **triadic** color harmony, a color scheme in which three colors, equally spaced on the color wheel, are used. You can create a similar color harmony by choosing any two complementary colors and combining them with the gray formed by mixing them together. Other popular color combinations include: analogous harmonies (using two or three colors lying next to each other on the color wheel) and monochromatic harmonies (using varying proportions of white, black, or gray with one color).

Studio paints

Studio paints are those colorants an artist uses to create a picture. All such paints consist of pigment—ground-up organic or inorganic color—suspended in a medium called a vehicle. The vehicle may be oil, glue, gum, or any substance that will hold the pigment particles in even suspension. There are two major categories of studio paints: water-soluble and oil-soluble. The charts that follow list the major paints within each group; the surfaces for which they are suitable; methods of modifying the paints; and the solvent for clean up. A basic palette should include white, black, a selection of earth colors, and a warm and cool value of each of the primaries (see color chart opposite).

Cautions: Paints and solvents can be hazardous. Some paint pigments contain lead, and the solvents used for thinning oil paints give off fumes that may be harmful and are flammable. Use paint thinners in a well-ventilated room and dispose of used rags promptly in a closed container. Store all paints and solvents well out of children's reach.

Print-making inks

Like studio paints, printing inks are in two categories: water-soluble and oil-based. Some inks are especially formulated for silk-screen printing, others for block printing, still others for either purpose. Block-printing inks must be tacky enough not to run.

Inks for serigraphy must also be tacky but not so thick they cannot pass through the mesh of the screen. The type of ink must be matched to the type of stencil or mesh-blocking material used.

Cautions: Fumes from turpentine or mineral spirits can cause irritation to skin and eyes. Work in a well-ventilated area away from flame or sparks.

Dyes

Inexpensive and readily available dyes can be used in many ways: to change the color of an entire piece of fabric; to create patterns in it; even to color wax, bone, and wood. The chart that follows lists the major types of dyes, materials they can be used with, what form they come in, and the way in which a typical dyebath is formed. Also included is information on color modifiers and on whether mordants are needed to make the dye colorfast.

WATER-SOLUBLE PRINTING INK

Ink description	Suitable surfaces	Ink selection	Modifiers	Solvent
Water-soluble block-printing ink: a tacky ink recommended for beginning projects in linoleum-, wood-, and vinyl-block printing.	Paper and cardboard.	Available in a large assortment of colors, in tubes and cans.	Water to thin ink, drying reducer to speed drying time.	Water
Water-soluble textile ink: an opaque ink recommended for silk-screening synthetic fabrics.	Polyester, polyester-cotton blends, rayon, Fiberglas, and other synthetic fabrics.	Available in cans in a wide range of colors.	Water to thin ink and dilute color, extender-base to increase the quantity of ink without affecting color or consistency; and ink thickener.	Water

OIL-BASED PRINTING INK

Oil-based printing ink: permanent and waterproof, recommended for advanced block printing.	Paper, wood, cardboard, cloth.	Available in tubes and cans in many colors.	Turpentine to thin ink, transparent medium to render colors translucent	Turpentine
Flat-finish poster ink for silk-screen printing	Paper and cardboard.	Poster inks come in cans in a variety of colors.	Mineral spirits to thin ink; extender base to increase ink quantity without affecting color or consistency; transparency base to render color translucent.	Mineral spirits or benzine
Gloss-finish inks for silkscreening.	Paper, cardboard, wood, hardboard, polystyrene and some foils.	Canned gloss inks come in many colors and have good opacity.	Mineral spirits and extender base as above; retarder base to slow drying.	Mineral spirits
Synthetic lacquer ink for screen-printing	Cotton and synthetic fabrics and non-waterproof nylon.	All ink colors have good opacity on light-colored grounds.	Lacquer ink reducer to thin inks.	Lacquer thinner

WATER-SOLUBLE STUDIO PAINT

Paint description	Suitable surfaces	Paint selection	Modifiers	Solvent
Watercolors: pigment mixed with water-soluble vehicle, such as glue, casein, or gum.	Paper, canvas, wood, or stone. One hundred percent rag watercolor paper is recommended to preserve the finished painting.	Watercolors are available in dry cake form in tins and in semifluid paste form in tubes. Poster paint and tempera paint are opaque watercolors available in powdered and liquid forms.	Water, used to make paint translucent or transparent, and white watercolor, used to make paint opaque.	Water
Acrylic paint: pigment carried in an acrylic polymer resin. The resin makes the paint dry waterproof, noncracking, and non-yellowing.	Paper, canvas, wood, stone, metal, or plastic. For canvases and other highly absorbent surfaces at least two coats of primer are recommended.	Available in paste and liquid form.	A small amount of water mixed with the paint yields opaque color; transparent gloss medium mixed with the paint yields transparent color.	Water

OIL-BASED STUDIO PAINT

Artist's oil paint: pigments carried in a pure drying oil, such as linseed or poppy oil.	Canvas, paper, wood, stone, or metal. Oil paint primer is recommended as a base coat.	Available in paste form in tubes.	Turpentine and linseed oil in varying proportions.	Turpentine

DYE COLORINGS

Dye	Compatible materials	Selection	Typical dyebath	Modifiers	Maintenance
Household dyes are blends of several kinds of dyes, mordants, and salts. Nothing need be added but fabric and water.	Natural fibers, nylon, acetate, and rayon.	Available in powdered and liquid form, in a wide range of colors. Dyes can be mixed to increase color selection. Color can also be modified by using less dye than recommended on package.	Full packet of dye dissolved in recommended amount of water.	Color remover.	Dyed garments should be hand laundered or washed separately several times before they are washed with other clothes.
Vegetable or natural dyes are made by extracting color from organic materials. Some yield dyes that are colorfast, but most require the use of a chemical mordant to color permanence. Consult a dyebook about mordants; some are hazardous, so handle with extreme care.	Natural fibers such as wool, cotton, silk, and linen, and cellulosic fibers like wood, paper and bone.	Almost any organic substance can be converted to dye form.	3/4 pound fresh marigolds simmered in 4 gallons water for one hour.	Premordant for colorfastness, postmordant to modify or brighten color.	Treat as regularly dyed garments.
Candle dye is designed for coloring wax.	Unrefined paraffin wax and beeswax.	Liquid and cake candle dye comes in many colors. Colored crayons can be used but may contain chemicals that impair burning.	Candle dye added to melted paraffin wax according to package directions.	Once colored wax hardens it can be dipped in another color. It will take many applications to make the new exterior color opaque.	
Acid dye is especially designed for coloring silk and wool. Salt and acetic acid or vinegar must be added to the dye for colorfastness.	Silk, nylon, and wool.	Available in dry form, and in many bright colors.	2 or 3 ounces of dry color, depending on the depth of shade desired, added to one gallon of hot water plus 1 cup of vinegar and 1 tablespoon salt.	Sodium hyposulphite or bath of half bleach and half water to lighten color.	Acid dyes resist fading from light but gradually fade when washed. Dry cleaning is recommended.
Direct dyes are made to color cotton fabric. They are characterized by exceedingly bright, lasting colors. This dye requires the addition of salt to help dye penetrate the fabric.	Viscose rayon and vegetable fibers such as cotton, linen, and hemp.	Available in dry form, in many colors.	2 to 3 ounces of dry color added to one gallon of hot water along with 4 to 6 ounces of salt.	Sodium hyposulphite or household bleach, following package directions.	Direct dyes gradually fade after repeated washing. Dry clean to obtain better colorfastness.

Cautions: When working with dye, protect your hands with rubber gloves. Wear a plastic apron, and cover the work surface with a plastic covering or drop cloth. Prepare dyes and mordants in chemically neutral containers fabricated of stainless steel, enamel, or glass. Fumes may be caustic; so work in a well-ventilated room. Store dyes and additives in tightly sealed glass jars out of the reach of children. Clean all utensils with scouring powder. Do not use dyeing equipment to prepare food.

Glossary:

Colorfast: A color that retains its original hue and will not fade or run due to washing, cleaning, wearing, or long exposure to light.

Dyebath: The liquid in which the material to be dyed is soaked; normally, it consists of dye, water, and various mordants or fixatives.

Mordant: A chemical such as salt, vinegar, or alum that serves to make the bond between a dye and the fabric permanent.

Resist-dyeing: Dyeing a fabric in such a way that the dye is prevented from penetrating parts of a fabric. Resist-dying techniques include batik (applying hot wax on fabric); tie dyeing (knotting and sewing fabric); fold dyeing (pleating and binding fabric); and block dyeing (inserting fabric between identical wood-block patterns and securing them in place with clamps).

Abrasives and polishes

Abrasives and polishes for craft work include: sandpapers and cloths, steel wool, wire brushes, grinding wheels, and polishing and buffing wheels with the compounds used on them. The charts that follow indicate the abrasives best suited for specific uses.

Abrasive papers and cloths

Sandpapers and cloths have flint, garnet, aluminum-oxide, silicon-carbide, zirconia-alumina, emery, or iron-oxide abrasive grains bonded to paper or cloth backings. Grit sizes range from extra coarse for rough work to extra fine for finishing. In addition to grit size and type, abrasive cloths and papers can be classified by whether the grit is spread sparsely or tightly on the backing (open- or closed-coat); what form the abrasive comes in (belt, sheet, disk); and the weight of the backing material. The open-coat papers are less likely to clog than are closed-coat papers. They are used for machine-sanding painted surfaces and soft woods. Closed-coat papers are used on hardwoods, for hand-sanding wood, and for belt-sanding rough metals.

Abrasive papers and cloths are available in sheets for hand sanding or polishing; in sheet, belt, or disk form for power sanding or polishing. Labels on the backing indicate whether they are open-coat, whether they can be used for wet sanding, and the weight of the paper or cloth. The letters A, C, D, E, and F on paper backings, and J, X, S, and Y on cloth indicate increasing weights. Use grade A for greatest flexibility on wood, grade C or D for light machine-sanding of wood, E for drum-or belt-sanding on wood projects and floors, J for light power sanding and contour sanding, and X for heavy-duty power sanding such as belt-sanding burrs and scale from metal.

Steel wool is available in grades from coarse No. 3 grade (above, right) to very fine 0000 grade (above left).

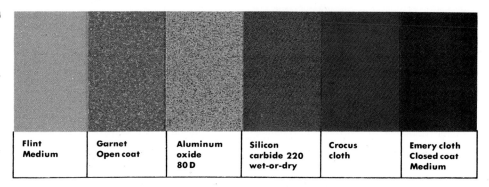

Flint Medium	Garnet Open coat	Aluminum oxide 80 D	Silicon carbide 220 wet-or-dry	Crocus cloth	Emery cloth Closed coat Medium

ABRASIVE SANDPAPERS AND CLOTHS

Grit description	Grit designation	Recommended abrasive use
Extra coarse	12 through 30 (or 4½ through 2½)	Machine-sanding rough surfaces or removing heavy paint: use aluminum oxide on metal. Use flint or garnet for light-pressure wood sanding, aluminum oxide for heavy power sanding of wood.
Coarse	26 through 60 (or 2 through ½)	Removing gouges or substantial amounts of wood or metal: Aluminum oxide, flint, or garnet can be used for hand-sanding wood.
Medium	80, 100 (or 1/0, 2/0)	Sanding new wood and removing scratches and other small imperfections: On wood use aluminum oxide for power sanding, garnet or aluminum oxide for hand sanding, silicon carbide for floor sanders. On metals, use aluminum oxide or silicon carbide. On plastics or other heat-sensitive materials, use only wet-or-dry silicon carbide, and then only on deep scratches, used wet.
Fine	120, 150, 180 (or 3/0, 4/0, 5/0)	Final sanding of raw wood before priming or sealing; smoothing old plaster or paint; removing light rust or discoloration from metals: Use aluminum oxide on wood or metal, emery cloth on unplated metals lightly rusted or discolored, wet-or-dry silicon carbide used wet on plastics.
Extra fine	220, 240, 280 320, 360, 400, 500, 600 (or 6/0, 7/0, 8/0) 9/0, 10/0)	Sanding fine woods to be given a natural finish; dry or wet sanding of sealers and finishes between coats: Use finish grits (320 to 600) for wet sanding and polishing wood finishes, metal, stone, and plastic before final polishing or buffing. Use silicon carbide for wet sanding glass, stones, plastics; aluminum oxide or emery cloth for fine-sanding or polishing metals, crocus cloth for a scratch-free finish on metals and glossy-finished woods.

STEEL WOOL

Description	Grade	Recommended use
Coarse	3 to 1	Used with paint remover to remove thick finishes from wood; on metal, used to produce a matte finish.
Medium	0 to 00	Used with linseed oil on wood to satinize a high-gloss finish; used on metal as described above.
Fine to very fine	000 to 0000	Used with mineral oil to polish final coats of finish and to remove dust mars on wood or metal.

WIRE BRUSHES

Coarse	35 to 18 gauge	Removing rust, dirt, or scale from metal; finishing metal with a scratch-brushed surface.
Fine	50 to 36 gauge	Eliminating pits, scratches, and burrs from metal surfaces; blending surface irregularities prior to finishing or polishing.

For matte finish on hard alloys, stainless steel, or aluminum, use crimped stainless-steel brushes. For soft matte finish on softer metals, use crimped soft-brass brushes.

Sandpapers come in sheet, disk, or continuous belt form. Cut sheets fit onto hand sanders (red and blue models above) or orbital power sanders (the pale-green model). Opposite page, papers and cloths in their characteristic colors.

The small bench grinder (rear) has a stitched buffing wheel beside it (top, at right). In center are cupped and straight grinding wheels with a variety of stones for sharpening by hand at center right. Small stemmed wheels (lower left) are called mounted grinding wheels. Beside them is a cutoff wheel.

Steel wool

Steel wool comes in several grades and has many uses. For applications listed opposite (below), use soapless steel wool.

Wire brushes

Wire brushes (with metal bristles) have many uses, but their chief use, as indicated opposite (below), is cleaning and polishing metal.

Grinding wheels

Grinding wheels are molded from abrasive grits or grains fused with a bonding agent. The common straight grinding wheels are wheel shaped with a hole in the center that slips over the shaft of a bench grinder. Mounted grinding wheels consist of small abrasive tips in various shapes bonded to the end of a metal stem that fits into the chuck of an electric drill or other small motor tool. They are good for intricate, hard-to-get-at grinding, deburring, and finishing jobs on metal or plastics. The following chart (page mi-14) indicates which abrasives should be used with which materials. For rough abrading jobs, choose a coarse grit. For materials that tend to clog, use an open-grain structure. Hard-grade wheels cut and wear slowly. They are used for grinding soft metals. Soft-grade wheels cut quickly but wear rapidly; they are used for grinding harder metals and gemstones. To save money, many lapidaries use grades ranging from medium soft to medium hard. In terms of bonds, vitrified bonds are most

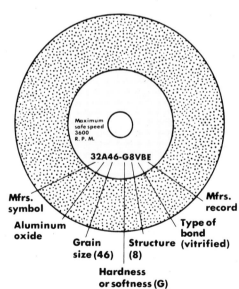

Label on a grinding wheel reveals its maximum safe operating speed and the characteristics of the abrasive, explained in the table on page mi-14.

widely used. Impervious to acid, oil, water, or normal temperature ranges, such wheels are used for most hand-held grinding.

Wheels with diamond abrasives (marked D) are available for cutting, edging, grinding and finishing of granite, glass, gemstones, ceramics, and other hard-to-work nonmetallic materials.

Cautions: Grinding wheels sometimes break; never exceed the maximum safe speed marked on the wheel. Tighten the nut only enough to hold the wheel firmly, and never alter the hole in the wheel or force it on the spindle. Wear safety goggles, and if you are using a bench-mounted grinder, adjust the work rest before you start the wheel. Let the wheel run one full minute before you start grinding. Apply the work to the wheel without impact. Grind on the face rather than the side of a straight wheel, and do not force grinding so the motor slows or the work gets hot.

Buffing wheels

Polishing and buffing wheels, used with the same tools as grinding wheels, are made of or covered with cotton flannel, muslin, canvas, felt, leather, cork, rubber, plastic, wood, or metal. Compounds spread on the working surface of the wheel do the polishing and buffing. For preliminary polishing, use rock-hard pressed felt or hard, closely stitched cloth wheels, coated with the proper abrasive. To remove scratches, use rubber wheels in which emery is embedded. For buffing to a high luster and color or a mirror finish, use unstitched or loosely stitched wheels of muslin or cotton, or disk wheels covered with soft leathers to carry the compound.

The compounds come in bar, stick, brick, powder, slurry, and liquid form, and in grit sizes ranging from about 12 to an extremely fine 3000. As with sandpapers and grinding wheels, grits with lower numbers are for grinding and smoothing surfaces; higher numbers (220 and up) are for final polishing and buffing.

GRINDING WHEELS

Abrasive types	Range of grit sizes	Grade	Grain structure	Recommended uses
Aluminum oxide (Labeled A)	8-24 (coarse) 30-60 (medium) 70-180 (fine) 220-600 (very fine)	A-H (soft) I-P (medium) Q-Z (hard)	1 (dense) through 6 (open)	For grinding wrought iron, cutlery, pocketknives, and tool steel.
Silicon carbide (Labeled C)				For grinding hard, brittle metal alloys, brass, aluminum, copper, ceramics, marble, and gemstones.

BUFFING COMPOUNDS

Compound	Recommended uses
Aluminum oxide	For fine grinding and smoothing the relatively soft low-carbon steel, known as mild steel, and bronze. In the form labeled levigated alumina, it is used for medium polishing of hardened metals and gemstones.
Silicon carbide	For fine-grinding, tumbling, smoothing, and polishing hard, brittle materials, such as hardened steels, alloys, and gemstones.
Garnet	For fine grinding and smoothing of glass and plastics.
Black rouge	For smoothing and polishing soft to medium-hard materials.
Red rouge (jeweler's rouge)	For polishing soft materials.
White rouge	For finishing medium-hard materials as well as gold and platinum.
Tripoli (silicon dioxide)	For removing scratches and for medium polishing of metals and some gemstones.
Cerium oxide	For polishing glass and most minerals.
Tin oxide	For polishing all metals. Not recommended for lapidary work.
Chrome oxide	For polishing stainless steel, chrome, hard metals, and plastics.
Pumice	For cleaning and fine-polishing softer metals. The type designated 4/F can be used with mineral oil or raw linseed oil to rub down finishes on wood between coats and after the final coat.
Zirconium oxide	For smoothing and polishing stainless steel and aluminum. Also for polishing gemstones.
Crocus powder or compound	For grinding, smoothing, and polishing copper, brass, aluminum.
Boron carbide	For smoothing and polishing ceramics and exotic metals.
Rottenstone	Used with mineral oil or raw linseed oil for wood finishes (as pumice is) but leaves a finer finish.
Whiting	As a powder, used with water to hand-polish metals.
Diamond powder	For cutting and polishing such metals as brass, copper, and aluminum.

Terminology of abrasives

Arbor: The shaft or spindle of the machine on which a grinding wheel is mounted.

Blotter: A disk of compressible paper around the center of a grinding wheel, carrying the label.

Bond: Material that binds abrasives together.

Burning: Surface discoloration on work caused by heat of grinding or sanding.

Chatter marks: Surface marks on work caused by vibrations of wheel or work.

Chuck: Device for holding grinding wheels and sanding disks in power tool.

Cone wheel: Small wheel with bullet-shaped nose for use in portable grinding.

Coolant: Liquid used to cool the work or to keep it from rusting.

Cup wheel: Grinding wheel shaped like a cup or bowl.

Cutoff wheel: A thin wheel used like a saw to cut material.

Cutting compound: Abrasive mixture applied to wheels for grinding or surfacing.

Cutting rate: The amount of material removed by a grinding wheel in a unit of time.

Disk sander, disk grinder: Machines that use circular abrasive disks.

Dressers: Tools used to true up grinding wheels and improve cutting action.

Dressing: Using a dresser to improve or alter cutting action of a grinding wheel.

Finish: Surface quality or appearance of the work.

Fluting: Grinding the grooves of a twist drill.

Freehand grinding: Grinding by holding the work against a wheel by hand, also known as offhand grinding.

Glazing: Dulling of cutting particles of abrasive resulting in slower cutting.

Grain spacing: Relative density of cutting particles on a grinding wheel.

Grindstone: A flat circular grinding wheel cut from sandstone, sometimes used for sharpening tools.

Lapping: A surface finishing process using loose abrasive grains or bonded abrasive wheels or coated abrasives.

Loading: Clogging pores of sanding or grinding surface with material being ground, resulting in slowed abrasive action and poor finish.

Lubricant: Liquid for lubricating a grinding wheel for more efficient cutting action.

Mandrel: Solid cylindrical metal core surrounded by abrasive portion of grinding wheel.

Oilstone: Abrasive stone impregnated with oil and used for sharpening tools.

Operating speed: Speed of abrasive wheel expressed either in revolutions per minute or in surface feet per minute.

Polishing: Smoothing off rough surface or putting on a high final finish.

Rest: That part of the grinding-wheel stand that supports the work or tool being ground.

Rough grinding: First grinding that removes stock rapidly without regard to finish produced.

Rubber bond: Natural or synthetic rubber used to bond abrasives into grinding wheel.

Scratches: Marks left on ground or sanded surface caused by using the wrong abrasive or a dirty coolant.

Sharpening stone: Natural or manufactured abrasive stone, usually oblong, used for sharpening or whetting tools.

Straight wheel: A grinding wheel of any size with straight sides, a straight face, and a straight or tapered arbor hole.

Tapered wheel: A grinding wheel that tapers from hub to face, hence is thicker at the hub.

Truing: Restoring the cutting face of a wheel so it produces perfectly round, flat, or smooth work; also altering the cutting face for grinding special contours.

Tumbling: Deburring, breaking sharp edges, finishing, or polishing by putting material in a rotating or vibrating barrel with water and abrasives.

Wet-or-dry: Abrasive papers that can be used wet as well as dry.

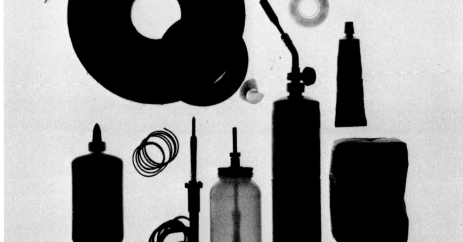

The broad range of modern adhesive techniques is suggested by these familiar shapes (clockwise from top): tapes, epoxies, pastes, a torch for welding, paper cements, soldering equipment, and glues.

Adhesives

Glues and cements

The great variety of glues and cements available can be classified as follows. Some are dangerous. Hazards are noted in the listing, but read all labels carefully and follow all precautions of the manufacturer.

White glue (polyvinyl acetate) is useful for light- and medium-weight joining of paper, wood, rigid plastic foam, cloth, some other porous and semiporous materials, and some nonporous substances such as glass and ceramic. It should not be used on photographs, metal, or surfaces that will be exposed to water or heat. White glue is non-flammable, nontoxic, resists dampness, and has no harmful vapors; it dries strong and clear.

Two-component epoxy resin is a heavy-duty adhesive. One type contains stainless-steel filings for use in rigorous circumstances. It can be used on wood and stone and can take the place of solder in joining metal. Epoxy resin is flammable and toxic.

Rubber cement is used for temporary or

permanent joining of paper and other lightweight substances. It retains a tacky bond and any excess can be removed with a rubber eraser or by hand. Rubber cement contains naphtha and is very flammable as well as toxic in vapor form. Its solvent, acetone, is also hazardous.

Clear plastic glue (acetate cement) is used for making small household repairs on china, glass, wood, metal, leather, paper, some plastics, and other porous and nonporous surfaces. Some types result in a rigid bond, while others remain flexible after drying. The fumes are flammable and toxic; solvents are acetone and nail-polish remover.

Contact cement is suited for use on light- and medium-weight surface additions, such as laminates or veneers, on a variety of porous and nonporous surfaces (metal, china, rubber, wood, masonry, leather, and wallboard, among others). It cannot be used with some plastics because it may disfigure or dissolve them. If in doubt, test the adhesive first. Contact cement bonds instantly, leaving no leeway for error. This flammable, toxic adhesive can also be a skin irritant.

Spray adhesives of various modern chemicals are used for joining paper and other lightweight materials. In addition to the dangers of all aerosol products, most forms of this adhesive are highly flammable and toxic.

White school paste, water soluble, harmless, and strong, is a heavy organic paste that can be used for joining paper and other lightweight substances.

Mucilage, amber in color and of a syrupy consistency, is good for light- to medium-weight joining of cardboard and wood. It is strong and resists climate changes. Presenting no hazards, it is a good glue for children to use.

Rabbit-skin glue is a traditional adhesive used as a binder in the preparation of gesso and canvas panels and is preferred by many woodworkers to modern synthetics. It is nontoxic and provides a strong bond.

Cyanoacrylates are as effective for household uses as they claim to be, but the glue dries so fast and is so strong that people have been known to glue their fingers together inadvertently, necessitating medical assistance. It must be used with extreme care and never by children.

Wallpaper paste, containing methyl cellulose, is nontoxic and nonstaining. It is usually sold in powder form, for mixing with cold water. It is inexpensive and can be used for papier-mâché and collage work as well as wallpapering.

Hot-melt adhesives, requiring an electric glue gun, are used on wood, metal, leather, flexible plastic, and fabrics, especially in large-scale industrial applications. A second type of hot-melt glue, used with a heated press, is designed for mounting photographic prints.

Model cement, containing toluol and oil of mustard, is limited to joining polystyrene parts together. Model cement is flammable and its fumes are toxic. Many other plastics, such as acrylics and vinyls, have specific solvents which act as adhesives by melting and fusing the pieces together. These solvents, usually containing noxious chemicals, are also highly flammable and toxic. They should be used with extreme care and in a well-ventilated area.

Shellac is sometimes used as an adhesive, especially in paper crafts such as decoupage.

Adhesive Tapes

Numerous adhesive tapes are available for general use and for a wide range of special jobs. **Masking tape** has moderate strength and is useful for holding glued parts together while they dry. It is also used for masking—or striping—surface areas during painting. **Drawing tape,** less tacky than masking tape, is used for holding paper on a drawing board; it leaves no remnants when removed. **Cellophane tape,** transparent and shiny, is primarily for use on paper. It has been replaced to some extent by low-glare **transparent tapes,** all but invisible when in place, moisture resistant, and more permanent. **Surgical tape** is flexible and porous but leaves an adhesive residue when peeled away. Costlier **cloth tapes,** used by photographers and others for heavy-duty joining, are less flexible but strong enough to hold metal parts together under stress. Cloth tapes are available in many colors with a plastic finish for use in decoration. Nonconductive **electrical tape** is available with plain or glossy finish. The plain type provides a stronger hold and hence

tighter connections, but the glossy coating is used when the work will be visible. **Sealing tape,** for mailroom use, comes in long brown strips or on a roll. One variety has a dry gum that must be moistened before use; another is tacky and ready to use, a third is reinforced with fiber or plastic strips for extra strength. **Foam tapes,** sticky on both sides and strong, are costly but useful for hanging lightweight pictures on walls. Many other two-sided adhesive tapes are available.

Joining Metals with Heat

Metal parts are generally joined by means of heated alloys called solders, which melt at a lower temperature than the metals themselves. Solders are usually applied with the heat of a soldering iron or gun or a propane torch. They are used in combination with a flux, which cleans the metal and promotes adhesion. Some metals, especially the more precious ones, require special solders, which are designated by the metal they are used with. Thus for joining gold, a gold solder is used. For work on base metals, the most common solders are 60-40 (tin to lead ratio) for electrical work and 70-30 for nonelectrical work. These solders are usually sold in wire form, though bar, sheet, and paste forms also exist. Wire solder with a hollow core is filled with flux to make soldering a one-step operation. When solid-core solder is used, the flux must be applied separately just before the solder is melted. Acid and chloride fluxes leave a residue and are only used when a later cleaning step is feasible or when appearance is unimportant. (Acid flux is never used on electrical work.) Pure rosin fluxes are less efficient but noncorrosive and leave no residue.

Brazing is a form of soldering in which metals are joined by means of brass solder or other alloys that melt at a high temperature.

Welding refers to the joining of two metal parts, without the help of a solder, by heating them in a forge or with an acetylene torch until they are fusible.

Materials reference guide

Clay mi-18

Fabrics and fibers mi-19

Foods mi-21

Glass mi-25

Leather mi-26

Metals mi-28

Minerals mi-31

Plants mi-34

Plastics mi-36

Wood mi-38

In this section is specific information of use to craftspeople working with any one of the ten popular crafts materials listed above. The information is summarized for easy reference in charts, tables, glossaries, plans, and lists.

Most of the pottery in the foreground, above, was thrown or formed on a potter's wheel by Nessa Darren (left) and Deborah Ackerman (center). The potters are shown in their New York City studio.

Clay

Ball clay: A type of clay used as an ingredient in most clay bodies to impart plasticity.

Bat: A plaster disk used by potters as a surface for throwing or drying pottery.

Bisque ware: Pottery that has been fired once, unglazed.

Bisque firing: The first firing of pottery at a low temperature to harden it and make it ready for glazing.

Centering: The first step in forming clay on a potter's wheel.

Ceramics: Descriptive of any fire-hardened claylike substance that includes pottery, glass, enamels, even cement and bricks.

Clay: A natural earthlike substance, formed from rock by the constant weathering, erosion, and aging of the earth's surface.

Clay body: A formula composed of different types of clays that in combination produce specific desired results in regards to plasticity, firing temperature, and evenness of color. There are many different clay bodies within the three general categories of pottery clay: earthenware, stoneware, and porcelain.

Coiling: A method of building pottery by hand in which long coils of clay are stacked one upon the other to build up a form.

Cones (pyrometric): Slender clay pyramids with a specific chemical composition that are placed inside a kiln during firing as a temperature gauge. They can be observed through a peephole by the potter. When cones melt and bend, it indicates that the proper time and temperature needed to mature the ware has been achieved. Cones are numbered (e. g., cone 4) according to their specific melting temperature.

Crackle: A fine network of cracks that forms in a glaze, especially characteristic of raku ware.

Earthenware: A low-fired coarse clay characterized by a reddish color and used most often to make crockery.

Fire bricks: Bricks made of heat-resistant materials used in the construction of kilns.

Firing: The process whereby pottery is fired, or baked, in a kiln for the purpose of making the pottery hard and durable.

Flux: An ingredient in glaze that aids melting.

Frit: Sometimes added to clay bodies and glazes, frit is glass that has been melted and ground to a powder. In glazes, a frit renders poisonous oxides (such as lead) insoluble and thus nonpoisonous.

Glaze: A glassy coating melted onto a ceramic body making it nonporous and often of a desirable texture and color.

Greenware: Unfired pottery sometimes called raw ware.

Oxides: Compounds composed of oxygen and one or more elements, frequently used by potters as coloring agents in clays and glazes.

Oxidation firing: A firing condition in which complete combustion with sufficient oxygen occurs.

Plasticity: A quality of clay that implies a moist, workable consistency.

Porcelain: A fine, white, high-fired clay which, when fired, can be both translucent and resonant.

Potter's wheel: A disk on which potters place a lump of unformed clay. When the wheel is made to spin, it aids the potter in drawing cylindrical shapes quickly and easily.

Raku: A method of low-firing pottery quickly under reduction-firing conditions. Raku ware is characterized by a fine crackle in the glaze.

Reduction firing: A firing condition in which the supply of oxygen is reduced, thus causing incomplete combustion. In pottery, this results in changes in color and texture to clay and glaze. Used in raku firing.

Refractory: Heat resistant. Refractory materials such as fire bricks and saggers are used in the construction and outfitting of kilns.

Sgraffito: A technique used to decorate slip-glazed pottery in which a line is scratched through a layer of slip to expose the clay beneath.

Slip: A liquid mix of clay and water.

Stoneware: A high-fired, fine-grained clay used extensively to make dinnerware similar to, but more plastic than, porcelain.

Throwing: The process of forming pottery on a wheel.

Tooling: The technique of embellishing leather-hard pottery by means of small hand tools.

Wedging: The act of kneading clay to rid it of air bubbles and bring it to a plastic, workable state.

Fabrics and fibers

Fiber	Fabrics	Properties	Care
Cotton (a natural fiber from the cotton plant)	Available in fabrics of very different weights, textures, and construction, ranging from sheer organdy to heavy corduroy.	Very strong. Free from static electricity. Comfortable; absorbent. Cool in summer; warm in winter. Takes dyes well. Fabric will shrink unless treated. Tends to wrinkle (often blended with synthetics to increase wrinkle resistence). Will deteriorate from mildew. Can be weakened by sunlight.	Wash cotton garments in hot water with detergent. Use chlorine bleach on white cottons unless the label states otherwise. Fabric softener will reduce wrinkling. Tumble dry but remove garment while still damp and press with a hot steam iron. Or use dampened pressing cloth.
Wool (a natural fiber from sheep)	Available in fabrics in a variety of weights, textures, and weaves.	Wrinkle resistant; elastic; very absorbent; does not abrade; takes dyes well. Traps air in the fibers, thus providing warmth. Weakens and stretches when wet; weakened by sunlight; susceptible to moths and mildew.	Dry-clean woven wool fabric and brush it between cleanings. Dry-clean knitted wool unless labeled washable. If washable, hand-wash in cool water with mild soap; block it to shape and dry on a flat surface away from heat. Do not use bleach; it will weaken and yellow the fibers.
Silk (a natural fiber from silkworms)	Available in a variety of weights and textures, ranging from sheer chiffon to stiff brocade. Has deep luster.	Wrinkle resistant; very strong; absorbent; takes dyes well; resistant to moths and mildew. Weakened by sunlight and perspiration; may yellow or fade with age; builds up static electricity and may cling.	Dry-clean. If labeled washable, hand-wash in cool water with mild soap. Do not bleach. Hang up to dry, away from direct sunlight. While damp, iron on wrong side with low to medium heat. Use a pressing cloth to avoid water spots.
Linen (a natural fiber from the flax plant)	Fabric can be sheer, medium- or heavyweight; durable; lustrous.	Very strong but stiff; absorbent; lint-free; moth resistant. Tends to wrinkle; shows wear at the edges and folds, does not take dyes well; tends to shrink; susceptible to mildew.	Dry-clean to retain shape and color. If labeled washable, machine-wash in hot water with detergent. Bleach can be used, but it weakens the fibers. Tumble-dry but remove while still damp; iron damp fabric at high setting.
Acrylic (man-made)	Available in sheer fabrics, knits, fur-like pile fabrics; often blended with natural fabrics.	Wrinkle resistant; strong; takes dyes well; elastic; moth and mildew resistant; does not soil easily, texture and shape can be heat-set. Low absorbency; holds in body heat; fades in sunlight; may pill; will melt under high heat.	Dry-clean or hand-launder in warm water with mild detergent. Gently squeeze out water; do not wring. Hang up to dry. If labeled machine-washable, use regular cycle. Tumble-dry at low setting and remove immediately. If necessary, iron on wrong side with iron on low setting.
Nylon (man-made)	Available in many textures and weights, from soft to crisp, from lightweight to bulky. Used for lingerie, stretch fabrics, and thread.	Wrinkle resistant; strong; takes dyes well; elastic; moth and mildew resistant; does not soil easily, texture and shape can be heat-set. Low absorbency; holds in body heat; fades in sunlight; may pill; will melt under high heat	Machine-wash in warm water. Use bleach with white fabrics. A fabric softener in the rinse will reduce static electricity. Tumble-dry at low setting. Remove immediately. If necessary, iron on wrong side, with iron on low setting.
Polyester (man-made)	Available in a range of weights and textures; often used in blends. Used for permanent-press and knit fabrics.	Wrinkle resistant, strong; easily washed, dries quickly. Does not stretch or shrink; colorfast; retains heat-set pleats and creases; resistant to abrasion, mildew, moths. Accumulates electricity; low absorbency; holds body heat; picks up lint; may pill; white fabrics yellow.	Machine-wash in warm water. Tumble-dry at low setting; remove from dryer immediately to avoid wrinkling. If necessary iron on wrong side at medium iron setting. Some white fabrics pick up color from other fabrics, so wash separately. Dry-clean polyesters only if so labeled.
Rayon (man-made)	Available in a wide range of woven and nonwoven fabrics, from light to heavyweight, from smooth to bulky. Can be made to resemble natural fibers; drapes well. Used in blends.	Soft and comfortable; absorbent; takes dyes well; colorfast. Susceptible to mildew; a fragile fabric, weaker when wet; wrinkles; shrinks and stretches if not specially treated; weakened by sunlight.	Dry-clean. If labeled washable, hand-wash in warm water; do not wring or twist; do not use chlorine bleach. Hang to dry away from sunlight. Press on wrong side while still damp with iron at moderate setting.

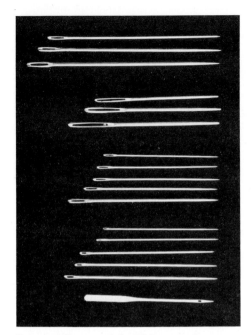

Various needles are made for different types of sewing. Most needles come in several sizes for use with specific threads and fabrics. Above, from top to bottom, are three graduated darning needles; three tapestry needles used for needlepoint; five embroidery or crewel needles with long eyes for use with more than one strand of thread; five hand-stitching needles, called sharps; and a sewing-machine needle.

Thread Glossary

Mercerized cotton sewing thread: For machine and hand stitching of light- and medium-weight fabrics of any fiber content.

Heavy-duty mercerized cotton thread: A heavier thread suitable for coat and suit fabrics, draperies, and slipcovers; can be used for machine- and hand-stitching.

Button and carpet thread: A very heavy, very strong thread with a lustrous finish. Can be used only for hand-stitching.

Quilting thread: A fine, strong thread with a lustrous finish used for hand- and machine-quilting.

Cotton-covered polyester thread: Has a silicone finish for smoother stitching; used for permanent-press, stretch, and knit fabrics; handles like cotton but has the durability of synthetic thread.

Silk sewing thread: For silk and lightweight wool fabrics.

Buttonhole twist: A strong, twisted silk thread for hand-stitching and decorative stitching by hand and machine.

Polyester thread: For hand-and machine-stitching of woven synthetics, knits, and stretch fabrics. Has a silicone finish for smoother stitching.

Nylon thread: A strong, elastic, durable thread made of one continuous filament; used for synthetic fabrics.

STAIN REMOVAL CHART

Stain	On washable fabrics	On dry-clean fabrics
Alcoholic beverage	soak in cold water, then wash in warm, soapy water.	Sprinkle immediately with talcum powder or cornstarch until liquid is absorbed.
Ball-point pen	Soak in solution of detergent and warm water. Rinse in cold water. Wash normally. If fabric can be bleached, use mild bleach.	At dry cleaner's, specify stain was made by a ball-point pen.
Berry and other fruit	Launder. If stain remains, apply white vinegar; rinse.	Apply white vinegar; rinse.
Blood	Soak in cold water. Launder. If fabric is white, use bleach.	Sponge with cold water and salt (one tablespoon to one quart water). Rinse and blot with a towel.
Candle wax	Rub wax with an ice cube until hard; then scrape off with a blunt knife. Or, place paper towels under and over the wax; press with a warm iron.	Follow method for washable fabrics.
Chewing gum	Rub with an ice cube; then scrape off with a blunt knife.	Follow method for washable fabrics.
Cosmetics	Pretreat by rubbing detergent dissolved in lukewarm water into the spot. Launder.	Use a greasy stain solvent; dry-clean.
Grass	Work detergent into the stain; then rinse and launder. If fabric can be bleached, use bleach in the laundry.	Follow method for washable fabrics.
Grease	Sprinkle liberally with talcum powder or cornstarch. Let powder absorb the grease, then brush off.	Follow method for washable fabrics.
Hemline ridge	Rub the line with white vinegar; rinse with water. Launder.	Follow method for washable fabrics.
Ink	Pour water through stain until it runs clear. Then apply detergent and white vinegar; rinse.	Follow method for washable fabrics.
Milk or cream	Soak immediately in cold water; rinse and launder.	Sprinkle immediately with talcum powder or cornstarch. Allow to dry thoroughly; then brush powder away.
Nail polish	Sponge with alcohol mixed with a few drops of ammonia. Use nail polish remover only after testing it in an inconspicuous place.	Follow method for washable fabrics.
Paint (oil based) and varnish	Sponge immediately with turpentine. Then rub detergent into the stain and launder.	Follow method for washable fabrics.
Paint (water based)	Remove with water.	Sponge with water, then dry-clean.
Paint (acrylic)	Remove with water while still wet.	Sponge with water; then dry-clean.
Pencil	Erase with a soft eraser. Work detergent into remaining stain; rinse and launder.	Erase with a soft eraser, then dry-clean.
Perspiration	If garment color has been affected, sponge a fresh stain with ammonia, an old stain with white vinegar. Rinse and launder. If color has not been affected, rub with detergent and launder.	Follow method for washable fabrics.
Scorch	Sponge with hydrogen peroxide or ammonia. Rinse well and launder.	Dampen with hydrogen peroxide until stain is removed.
Shirt-collar ring	Sprinkle with talcum powder or cornstarch to absorb dirt and body oil; launder.	Follow method for washable fabrics.

Foods

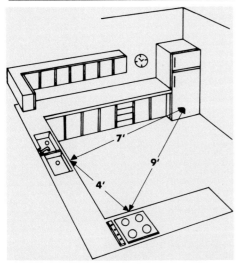

To locate major kitchen appliances, professionals advise that you measure from the center front of your sink to the center front of your range and refrigerator, then back to the sink. The distance between any two points should be at least 4 feet (to allow adequate counter and storage space at each center) but not more than 7 feet (to save needless steps). The exception is the distance between the refrigerator and the range, which can be up to 9 feet. These three distances added together should not be more than 22 feet nor less than 12 feet.

Planning a kitchen

Whether or not you want to remodel an existing kitchen, you often can move major appliances to make meal preparation more convenient and efficient. Begin by planning three major work areas, each with counter space to serve it. The location of the first work area—the sink—is determined by existing plumbing. If you have a choice, however, it is traditionally placed under a window. The second work area is the refrigerator, and its door should be hinged on the side opposite the counter serving it. The refrigerator should not be next to the range, the center of the third work area. Each of these work areas can be conceived of as the point of a triangle formed as you walk from one to another. The drawing above shows a well-planned kitchen and suggests workable distances between these three points.

Basic kitchen equipment

Good cooking is easier, more pleasant, and more efficient if you work with the right equipment. Good utensils save time and effort. The best way to assemble kitchen equipment is to buy each piece as you try a recipe that calls for it.

Baking pans: one or two cake and pie tins, a spring-type pan, muffin pan, a baking (cookie) sheet, and a sifter.

Blender: you will not need an elaborate one for most recipes.

Casseroles: 3-quart and 6-quart capacity, with lids, and an open baking (au gratin) dish, all pretty enough to go from stove to table.

Colander

Double boiler: made of flameproof glass so you do not run the risk of water boiling away without your knowing it.

Electric beater: for whipping egg whites.

Grater/shredder

Implements: ladle, slotted spoon, tongs, a metal spatula (for turning pancakes and hamburgers), a rubber spatula (for scraping bowls).

Knives: a carbon-steel knife takes the best edge but will rust if not dried immediately after it is used or washed. Stainless steel is easier to care for and more attractive, but only the most expensive keeps a good edge. Sharpen knives regularly with a steel or stone; dull knives smash rather than cut food. Get two paring knives, a serrated knife for slicing bread, a large chef's knife for chopping, a narrow-bladed boning knife, and a chopping board to protect your counter top.

Measuring spoons and cup

Mixing bowls: 1-, 2-, and 3-quart capacity that nest to save space.

Roasting pan

Saucepans: heavy-bottomed so they will not tip. The best all-purpose saucepans are the heavyweight type made of enameled cast iron. Those of heavy aluminum or aluminum lined with stainless steel are good too, but unlined aluminum or iron will discolor foods containing white wine, egg yolks, or lemon juice. A good selection includes 2-, 3-, and 4-quart saucepans with tight lids (they should nest, one inside the other, to save space) and a few smaller pans for heating soups and gravies or melting butter.

Skillets or frying pans: with their own covers, fitted with removable handles or handles that can go into the oven.

Soup or spaghetti pot: at least 6-quart capacity, made of aluminum.

Strainer

Thermometers: one for meat and one for the oven.

Whisk: a wire whisk for blending sauces and gravies.

A glossary of cooking terms

The following cooking terms, many of them in foreign languages, are those most frequently encountered in recipes.

Al dente: Pasta cooked to the point at which it is tender but still slightly resistant to the bite

Amandine: Served with sliced or finely chopped almonds

À point: Beef or steak cooked to medium-rare stage

Aspic: Molded jellied dish

Au gratin: Cooked with a topping of buttered crumbs or grated cheese that forms a brown crust

Au jus: Served with natural juices or gravy

Au naturel: Simply boiled

Bake: Cook by dry heat in an oven

Ballottine: Meat, fowl, or fish that has been boned, stuffed, and rolled into the shape of a bundle

Baste: To spoon melted butter, fat, or liquid over foods

Béarnaise sauce: Made with egg yolks, butter, shallots, lemon juice, and tarragon

Beat: To mix foods or liquids thoroughly and vigorously with a spoon, fork, whisk, or electric beater

Béchamel: A basic white sauce of flour and butter

Beurre: Butter

Bien cuit: Well done (meat)

Bifteck: Steak

Bisque: Creamed soup, usually with a shellfish base

Blanch: To plunge food into boiling water in order to whiten it, soften it, or make removal of the skin easier

Blend: To mix foods together with a fork, spoon, or spatula (less vigorous than beating)

Boil: To cook in a liquid that has been heated to the bubbling point

Braise: To brown foods in fat, then cook them in a covered casserole with a small amount of liquid

Broil: To cook by dry heat, exposing one side of the food at a time to the heat

Cacciatora: Hunter's style, with tomatoes and wine

Canapé: Small, decorative, open-faced sandwich served with cocktails

Carve: To slice meat, usually against the grain, into serving pieces

Chantilly: Sweetened, flavored whipped cream

EQUIVALENT MEASURES

1 tablespoon	3 teaspoons
¼ cup	4 tablespoons
1 cup	16 tablespoons
1 cup	8 ounces
1 pint	2 cups
1 quart	4 cups
1 gallon	4 quarts

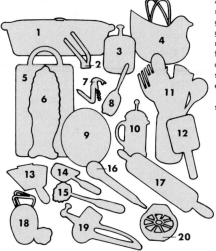

After you stock your kitchen with the basics listed on page mi-21, you'll want a few specialized utensils and gadgets. Pictured above and keyed at left are 1) fish poacher, 2) garlic press, 3) mortar and pestle for crushing herbs, spices, and nuts, 4) deocrative storage basket 5) chopping board, 6) copper fish mold, 7) cork screw, 8) pastry feather, 9) steaming basket, 10) demitasse coffeepot, 11) an assortment of wooden spoons for stirring, turning, and tasting food 12) a wooden scoop, 13) expanding spatula, 14) cheese slicer, 15) meat mallet, 16) baster, 17) rolling pin, 18) garlic basket, 19) cheese grater, and 20) apple slicer and corer.

Chaud-froid: Foods cooked but served cold

Chutney: Spicy Indian relish of fruit seasoned with garlic, mustard, brown sugar, and vinegar

Compote: Stewed fruit

Cordon bleu: Stuffed with ham and cheese

Créme fraîche Heavy cream

Crêpe: A thin pancake

Croutons: Diced bread, sautéed in a pan or browned in an oven, used as a garnish for soups and salads

Dashi: A light, clear fish stock used in Japanese cooking

Deep-fat frying: To cook food by immersing it in fat that is hot enough to cause a golden brown crust to form immediately

Dice: To cut foods into cubes usually about 1/8 inch in size

Dredge: To coat food before cooking, usually with flour or fine bread crumbs

En brochette: Cut-up pieces of meat, tomatoes, onions, and other similar foods roasted on a skewer

Fettuccine: Cooked noodles to which butter and cheese are added

Fillet: To cut meat or fish into boneless pieces

Flambé: Served with flaming brandy or other liqueurs

Florentine: With spinach

Fold: To blend a fragile mixture delicately into a heavier one or to mix ingredients gently without breaking or mashing them

Fricassee: Poultry stewed in a white sauce

Glaze: To coat food with a liquid that becomes hard and glossy

Hollandaise: Egg yolk and butter sauce flavored with lemon juice

Julienne: Cut into long, thin strips

Légumes: Vegetables

Linguine: Long, thin, flat noodles

Lyonnaise: Prepared with onions

Macédoine: Mixed vegetables or fruit

Manicotti: Tube-shaped pasta stuffed with a meat or cheese mixture, covered with a sauce and Parmesan cheese, and baked

Marinara: Sailor style, with tomato, garlic, oil, and oregano

Marrons: Chestnuts

Matzoh: Flat, crisp, unleavened bread

Meringues: Stiffly beaten egg white blended with sugar

Meunière: Made or served with melted butter, lemon juice, and parsley

Milanaise: Food dipped in egg, breaded with crumbs mixed with grated Parmesan cheese, and fried in clarified butter

Mince: To chop foods very fine

Moules: Mussels

Mull: To heat, sweeten, and flavor with spices (usually cider or wine)

Nicoise: Dishes with tomatoes and usually garlic

Noisette: Small round slice of meat

Paella: Saffron rice with seafood and chicken

Pan fry: To cook and brown food, sometimes coated with breading or flour, in a small amount of fat, turning it only once in the pan

Parboil: To boil briefly as a preliminary cooking procedure

Parfait: Frozen dessert

Parmigiana: Made or seasoned with parmesan cheese

Pasta: Any type of noodle, including spaghetti

Pasta é fagioli: Pasta and beans in a spicy tomato sauce

Pastitsio: Alternating layers of egg noodles and chopped meat in a white sauce, with a cheese topping

Pâté: Meat paste

Pâté de foie gras: Finely ground goose livers

Pâté en croûte: Pâté covered with pastry

Pâtisseries: Pastries

Pesto: A mixture of basil, garlic, Parmesan cheese, and olive oil

Petit fours: Rich, small, individual cakes

Petits pois: Young, tender green peas

Piccata: Prepared with lemon juice

Pilaf: Middle Eastern rice, steamed and sautéed

Pisto: Cooked vegetables into which beaten eggs are added

Poach: To submerge and cook food in a liquid that is kept barely simmering

Poisson: Fish

Pollo: Chicken

Polonaise: Served with bread crumbs which have been browned in butter

Pomme: Apple

Pommes de terre: Potatoes

Pommes frites: French-fried potatoes

Potage: Soup

Pot-au-feu: Beef and vegetable soup or stew

Poulet rôti: Roast chicken

Poulet sauté: Sautéed chicken

Prosciutto: Dry-cured ham

Provencale: Cooked or prepared with garlic, tomatoes, and olive oil

Purée: To render solid food into a paste with a mortar and pestle, food mill, electric beater, or sieve

Quenelle: Minced or puréed fish, veal, or poultry formed into small oval shapes, poached in stock, and served hot in a rich sauce

Reduce: To boil down a liquid (usually a sauce), reducing its quantity and concentrating its taste

Ricotta: Fresh white cheese that resembles cottage cheese

Risotto: Rice

Rôti: Food cooked or roasted in the oven or on a spit

Sake: Japanese white wine

Salsa: Sauce

Saltimbocca: Prosciutto (or ham) and veal sautéed in butter

Sashimi: Raw fish

Saumon: Salmon

Sauté: To cook and brown food rapidly in a small quantity of very hot fat, usually in an open skillet

Scald: To cook at a temperature just below boiling (usually milk)

Scaloppine: Thin slices of meat sautéed and served with a seasoned sauce

Scampi: Large shrimp from the Adriatic Sea

Simmer: To cook food in a liquid that has been heated to the point where small bubbles come gently to the surface and barely break

Spätzle: Small dumpling

Steam: To cook or heat food by exposing it to steam, usually by placing it directly over boiling water

Stollen: Christmas fruitcake

Sukiyaki: Beef and vegetables simmered in soy sauce and sake

Tempura: Shrimp or vegetables dipped in a batter, then deep fried

Teriyaki: Fish, shellfish, meat, and/or chicken marinated and grilled on skewers

Tournedos: Filet steaks

Vichyssoise: Leek and potato soup, served cold

Vinaigrette sauce: Oil and vinegar dressing

Wonton: Chinese noodle dough with a filling, may be deep fried, steamed, or boiled in soup

Zuppa inglese: Cake soaked in rum, covered with a light custard or whipped cream, and garnished with candied fruit

FOOD EQUIVALENCIES

Food	Amount	Yield	Food	Amount	Yield
Beans			Orange	1 medium	6 to 8 tablespoons juice, 2 to 3 tablespoons grated rind
Kidney	1 pound (1-1/2 cups)	9 cups, cooked			
Lima or navy	1 pound (2-1/3 cups)	6 cups, cooked	Pineapple	1 medium	2-1/2 cups, cubed
Beef (raw)	1 pound	2 cups, ground	**Gelatin**	1/4-ounce envelope	1 tablespoon
Breadcrumbs			**Graham crackers**	12 squares	1 cup crumbs
Dry	1 slice dry bread	1/3 cup crumbs	**Macaroni**	1 pound (5 cups)	12 cups, cooked
Soft	1 slice soft bread	3/4 cup crumbs	**Noodles**	1 pound (5-1/2 cups)	10 cups, cooked
Butter	1 stick	1/2 cup (8 tablespoons)	**Nuts**		
Cheese			Almonds, whole	1 pound	2-2/3 cups, grated
Cottage	1/2 pound	1 cup	Coconut	1 pound	5 cups, shredded
Grated	1 pound	4 to 5 cups	Coconut, grated	3-1/2 ounces	1 cup
Chicken	3-1/2 pounds (raw, drawn)	2 cups, cooked and diced	Coconut, fresh	1-1/2 tablespoons	1 tablespoon dried, chopped
Chocolate	1 square (1 ounce)	4 tablespoons, grated	Peanuts, shelled	1 pound	2-1/4 cups
Coffee			Pecans, shelled	1 pound	4 cups
Ground, fresh	1 pound (80 tablespoons)	40 cups, brewed	Walnuts (unshelled)	1 pound	2-1/2 cups, shelled
Instant	2 ounces	25 cups, brewed	**Rice**	1 pound (2-1/2 cups)	8 cups, cooked
Cream (heavy)	1 cup	2 cups, whipped	**Sugar**		
Eggs			Brown	1 pound	2-1/4 cups, packed
Whites	1 egg white	1-1/2 tablespoons	Confectioners'	1 pound	3-1/2 cups, packed
Yolks	1 egg yolk	1 tablespoon	Granulated	1 pound	2 cups
Flour	1 pound	4 cups, sifted	**Tea**	1 pound (loose)	125 cups, brewed
Fresh fruit			**Fresh vegetables**		
Apples	1 pound (3 medium)	2 cups, sliced	Beets	1 pound (4 medium)	2 cups, diced and cooked
Bananas	1 pound (3 or 4 medium)	2 cups, mashed	Cabbage	1 pound	4 cups, shredded
Berries	1 pint	2 cups	Carrots	1 pound (7 or 8 medium)	4 cups, diced
Cherries	1 quart	2 cups, pitted	Corn	12 ears	3 cups, cut
Cranberries	1 pound	3 to 3-1/2 cups sauce	Mushrooms	1 pound (36 medium)	5 cups, sliced, raw
Grapefruit	1 medium	1-1/3 cups pulp	Peas (in pod)	1 pound	1 cup, shelled and cooked
Lemon	1 medium	3 tablespoons juice, 2 teaspoons grated rind	Potatoes	1 pound (4 medium)	2-1/2 cups, diced and cooked
			Spinach	1 pound	1-1/2 to 2 cups, cooked

EMERGENCY SUBSTITUTIONS

For	Substitute	For	Substitute
1 tablespoon flour	1-1/2 teaspoons cornstarch, arrowroot, potato starch, or rice starch	1 teaspoon baking powder	1 teaspoon baking soda plus 1/2 teaspoon cream of tartar
1 whole egg	2 egg yolks plus 1 tablespoon water (in cookies) or 2 egg yolks (in custard)	1 small clove garlic	1/8 teaspoon garlic powder
1 cup fresh whole milk	1/2 cup evaporated milk plus 1/2 cup water, or 1 cup reconstituted nonfat dry milk solids plus 2 tablespoons butter	1 tablespoon fresh grated ginger	1/8 teaspoon powdered ginger
		1 tablespoon fresh herbs	1/3 to 1/2 teaspoon dried herbs
1 ounce unsweetened chocolate	3 tablespoons cocoa plus 1 tablespoon butter	1 tablespoon fresh horseradish	2 tablespoons, bottled
1-2/3 ounce semisweet chocolate	1 ounce unsweetened chocolate plus 4 teaspoons sugar	1/2 cup maple sugar	1 cup maple syrup
		1/8 teaspoon noncaloric sweetener, liquid	1 teaspoon sugar
1 cup honey	1-1/4 cups sugar plus 1/4 cup liquid	20 mgs saccharin	1 teaspoon sugar

Glass

The craftsman uses glass in three major ways. In glassblowing, it is melted down and re-formed. In stained glass, bits of colored glass are rimmed in lead and soldered to one another. As a surface covering agent, glass is applied to metal (enamels) and pottery (glazes).

Stained-glass glossary

Antique glass: Glass made by hand blowing—an antique method.

Beading: The process of applying additional solder to provide a rounded rather than a flattened surface. This makes the soldering look better and increases its stability.

Cartoon: The full-sized drawing for a stained glass design, containing all the cut lines.

Cathedral glass: Glass made by machine.

Copper sulfate: A chemical that reacts with solder to form a dark, coppery tone on the surface, giving it an antique appearance. It is toxic and should be handled with care and kept out of the reach of children.

Dalle: A thick glass which may be employed as is or may be cut to chunks with the proper tools. Since cutting such glass is a dangerous process (it is usually 1 inch thick), many stained-glass workers buy scraps from their suppliers. This type of glass is also known as **dalle-de-verre** or slab glass.

Double rolled: A term used to define the manufacture of stained glass that is not blown. The glass comes out in large sheets between two rollers which gives the sheet a uniform thickness not found in most antique glass. The rollers may also texture the surface of the glass.

Flux: A material used in the soldering process. The best flux is a liquid called oleic acid. It is used to clean the material to be soldered.

Glass cutter: A tool with a small wheel on one end which makes a score or scratch on the surface of the glass so the glass can be broken on the desired line.

Glass pliers: Instruments with wide, toothed jaws that are good for snapping off small pieces of glass.

Grozing pliers: Small-jawed pliers used for removing rough edges from a cut piece of glass.

Joint: The meeting place for two or more lead cames. Soldering takes place here.

Laminate: To fuse several layers of glass, either by using an adhesive or melting the layers in a kiln, thus forming a single piece.

Lathkin: An instrument made of wood, bone, plastic, or metal which is used for opening the channel of lead came.

Lead came: Channeled lengths of lead (usually 6 feet) used for joining pieces of glass.

Leaded glass: A glass object that consists of pieces of glass that are held together with lead. Originally lead came and solder were used to join glass. Now, strips of copper foil are also used.

Lead knife: A weighted, sharp, usually curved knife used to cut lead came.

Lead stretcher: A small vise that holds one end of a piece of lead came while it is stretched to remove curls and kinks.

Opalescent glass: Sheet glass that is translucent and so diffuses light.

Score: The scratch on the surface of a piece of glass left by a glass cutter so the glass can be snapped apart at that point.

Solder: A mixture of lead and tin that comes in the form of wire wound on a spool. It is used to join metal-rimmed glass pieces (solder does not stick to glass).

Soldering iron: A tool used to melt solder.

Tinning: The act of coating lead with solder all along its length or coating the tip of a soldering iron to prepare it for use.

Transparent glass: Clear glass (it may be colored) that permits the passage of light so objects may be seen through it.

Whiting: A white chalky powder used to clean the completed leaded glass project.

Blown-glass glossary

Blowpipe: A long tube that enables a glass worker to blow into a glob of molten glass to form an object without using a mold.

Blown glass: A glass object formed with a blowpipe.

Combing: A method of combing coils of molten colored glass into decorative shapes over the surface of a glass object.

Free-blown glass: A glass object that has been formed only with a blowpipe and hand tools, not with a mold. The process of making it is also known as offhand glassblowing.

Gather: A glob of molten glass taken from the glory hole on the end of the blowpipe.

Glass: Technically, a supercooled fluid formed by a fusion of three major oxides—silica, soda, and lime.

Glory hole: The mouth of the glass furnace from which molten glass is gathered.

Knit glass: Glass of a very soft composition used to make small glass animals and ornaments by the lamp-work method, also called spun glass.

Lamp work: A method of working glass on a small scale that utilizes preblown glass rods and tubes melted by a blowtorch instead of molten glass from a furnace.

Marver: A flat carbon surface used by lamp-workers to smooth and form molten glass.

Mold-blown glass: Glass that is formed by being blown into a mold.

Oxides: Compounds composed of oxygen and one or more elements, used in glass work as colorants.

Pontil: A long metal rod used by a glass-blower to support a piece of blown glass during the forming process.

Silica: Sand, the main ingredient in glass.

Glossary of glass enamels and glazes

Champlevé: An enameling technique in which depressions are formed in the metal backing and then filled with enamel.

Clay: A basic ingredient in making glazes that holds and fuses the glaze to the clay object.

Cloisonné: An enameling technique in which metal wires, called cloisons, are used to separate different sections of enamel on a metal background.

Counterenamel: To put enamel on the back of the metal, a step taken to forestall warping.

Enamel binder: An adhesive that holds powdered enamel to metal.

Firing stilt: A cross that holds the metal while enamel is applied and during the firing so the fused enamel will not stick the metal to the kiln.

Flux: The major ingredient in enamel—a clear glass that consists of silica and other minerals. Also, one of the three basic ingredients in glaze that helps cause the clay to melt at the proper temperature.

Glaze: A glassy coating melted onto pottery during a second firing, imparting a non-porous, often colorful surface and texture to the pottery.

Kiln: An insulated, electrically heated oven where glass is transformed into a smooth, hard finish.

Mesh: A term that designates the fineness of the powdered enamel. The mesh number of the enamel is matched to the mesh number of the strainer through which it is applied to the metal.

Metal oxides: Oxides of various colors added to flux to impart color to the enamel.

Opaque enamel: An enamel that cannot be seen through.

Planche: A steel mesh firing platform used to hold the enamel work before, during, and after firing.

Plique-à-jour: A style of enameling similar in effect to stained glass. The enamel has no metal backing but is held between fine wires joined to each other.

Screening paste: A type of enamel used on steel that has been specially prepared for enameling.

Silica: A basic glaze ingredient used as a glass former and hardening agent.

Transparent and translucent enamel: Enamels that are either completely or partially transparent.

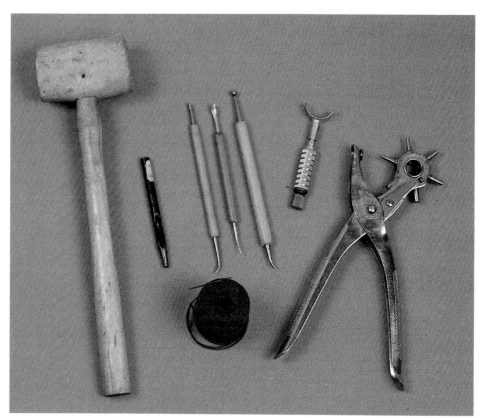

These are some of the tools used in leather working. From left to right are: a synthetic-headed mallet, a single-hole punch, three modeling tools, a swivel knife, a rotary punch. At center bottom are waxed linen thread and a harness needle.

Leather

Cleaning and care of leather

Smooth-surfaced leather: Smooth leathers resist soiling, but marks and spills should be wiped off immediately with a damp cloth or sponge. If garments, bags, or shoes become wet with rain, dry off most of the moisture with an absorbent cloth or paper towels. Then allow the leather to dry slowly, away from direct heat. If you try to speed the drying process by placing the leather near a heat source, it may become brittle and hard, aging prematurely.

To store leather, keep it in a bag made of porous material such as cloth or paper. Leather stored in plastic cannot breathe and is prone to mildew.

Saddle soap is probably the best known cleaning, conditioning, and polishing agent. It comes in cake form in a small tin. To use it, apply the soap to the leather with a damp sponge, and wipe off the excess. Let the soap dry, and then buff the leather with a soft, dry cloth. There are many other products available for cleaning, conditioning, and polishing leather. Before using any, test it on a small inconspicuous patch of leather, following the manufacturer's directions.

Suede: Because it has a nap, suede soils quite easily and so should be worn and handled with care. Brush off surface dirt with a suede brush. Remove small marks with a pencil eraser (test on an inconspicuous place, and don't rub so vigorously that you damage the suede). Blot up liquids immediately. If it is only water or rain, let the article dry away from direct heat; then brush up the nap with a suede brush. If another liquid, take the article to a leather and suede cleaning specialist.

Cutting and measuring tools

Cutting Board: A board of soft wood used to protect the work surface from the blade of the cutting knife. Hardboard makes a good substitute but must be replaced more often as it becomes scarred.

Cutting knife or replaceable-blade craft knife: Used for cutting shapes from heavy leather. Lightweight leather can be cut with leather shears or ordinary fabric shears.

Edger or beveler: Used to smooth and round cut leather edges.

Fine-point felt-tipped pen: For marking leather.

Skiving knife: Used to shave away unwanted thickness, such as at seams, to reduce the bulk of the leather; it resembles a short chisel with a rounded, slanted blade.

Steel rulers: Used for measuring leather and as a straightedge guide for cutting it. A steel square or right-angled triangle is used to obtain accurate corners.

Stitching leather

Awl and thonging chisel: Used for making the sewing holes. The awl pierces single holes; the thonging chisel makes multiple slits. Both are used with a mallet.

Bone folder or seam marker: To impress guidelines along which the stitches will be made.

Cork block: Used to back leather when holes are pierced in it.

Mallet: Used for pounding the awl or thonging chisel into leather; may have a leather, synthetic, or wooden head. Also for pounding sewn seams flat.

USES FOR LEATHER

Project	Type of leather
Garments	Smooth-surfaced leather, sueded leather, and firm (usually chrome-tanned) leather, such as cowhide, pigskin, sheepskin, deerskin, and chamois.
Belts, straps, bands	Usually smooth-surfaced vegetable-tanned cowhide; occasionally suede.
Hats	Almost any leather, vegetable- or chrome-tanned, depending upon the effect desired. Cowhide is most common.
Handbags and luggage	Any type of leather, depending upon the design and function. Smooth-surfaced leather is easier to keep clean. Vegetable-tanned leather, because of its stiffness, is most desirable for luggage.
Moccasins	Almost any leather, including fur. If they are to be worn outdoors, chrome-tanned leather is used for the sole.
Sandals	Top sole: vegetable- or chrome-tanned cowhide. Bottom sole: oak-tanned cowhide. Straps: vegetable-tanned cowhide, or latigo.

Needles: Blunt needles are used to stitch leather, since the holes have already been made. Harness needles are commonly used, but tapestry needles, usually used for needlework, can be substituted.

Rotary punch: A plierslike tool with six revolving punch tubes in graduated sizes—used to make single round holes for stitching. The larger-sized tubes are used for punching holes in belts and straps.

Rubber cement or leather contact cement: Used for holding leather in place temporarily while the stitching is done, or for keeping sewn seam allowances flat. Leather contact cement can replace stitching altogether.

Stitch marker or hole spacer: Used to make evenly spaced stitch marks along the seam guideline. As the wheel is run along the stitching line, its teeth (similar to those on a dressmaker's tracing wheel) leave impressions in the leather, which indicate where the sewing holes should be made.

Thread and lacing: Special nylon or linen thread or leather lace is used for making the stitches that hold leather pieces together. Commercial wax-coated thread is available at leather shops. It can be made at home by running strong, heavy thread over a cake of beeswax. Leather thonging or lacing is sold on spools.

Decorating leather

Decorative stamps: Small instruments made of brass or steel are available in many designs. They are used on dampened leather to form repeat patterns, borders, and to impart a texture to a large design area.

Modeling tools: Various types of tools are used on dampened leather to press down certain areas of a design, leaving others raised.

Dyeing and finishing

Dye: Aniline dye in powdered form, mixed with methylated spirits, is used for dyeing leather. If aniline dyes are not available, woodworking stains can be used.

Finishes: Used to protect dyed or undyed smooth-surfaced leather. Colorless wax-type shoe, floor, or furniture polish can be used. Other finishes include oils, conditioners, creams, jellies, and leather butters.

Shearling pad: Used to apply dye to leather. A piece of sponge placed inside cotton cloth can be substituted.

Glossary of leather terms

(Leather is sold by the square foot in the form of a whole hide, half hide, back, and belly.)

Back: The center part of a hide when the two bellies have been trimmed away from the sides.

Belly: The two sides of a hide or skin (usually the thinnest and weakest part).

Buckskin: Soft suede leather, made from the skin of a deer.

Calfskin: Leather made from the hide of a calf; it has a fine grain and is very supple and durable.

Chamois: Originally the leather made from the skin of the chamois goat; more recently, sheepskin processed with oil to keep it supple.

Cowhide: Leather made from the hide of a cow; it is available in many types and thicknesses.

Doeskin: Very fine, soft leather, usually white or cream colored, made from a lamb or sheepskin split.

Goatskin: Leather made from the skin of a goat; it is very tough and has a tight grain.

Grain: The outer or hair side of a skin or hide.

Hide: Leather made from the skin of a full-grown bovine animal, such as a cow.

Kid: Soft leather from the skin of a young goat.

Lamb: Leather made from the skin of a young sheep; it is very soft.

Latigo: Cowhide that has been tanned in animal oils; it is strong and flexible.

Pigskin: Leather made from the skin of a domestic pig; it has a characteristic pattern of tiny holes in groups of three all over the skin and a firm, attractive grain.

Shearling: The skin of a sheep with short wool left on.

Sheepskin: Leather made from the skin of a sheep; it is porous and open textured.

Side: Half a hide.

Skin: Leather from a small animal such as a goat, sheep, or deer.

Split: Leather that has been obtained by slicing a thick hide into layers. Such leather is usually sueded on both sides. **Top grain** leather is the topmost layer and includes the grain side of the leather; only the flesh side of top grain leather is sueded.

Suede: Leather that has been buffed or sanded to produce a velvety texture; it is made from lamb or sheepskin. Sheer suede is soft, supple, and so lightweight it handles almost like fabric and can be sewn by machine.

Tanning: The process of impregnating a cleaned animal skin or hide with any of several special solutions to preserve it and keep it supple. Vegetable-tanned leather is dry and stiff and so is the best type to use for tooling, modeling, and stamping. Chrome-tanned leather is tough, firm, and water-resistant (not waterproof).

Metals

Aluminum: A silver-white metal with a blue cast, notable for its lightness, malleability, ductility, reflectivity, and resistance to rust; usually used in the form of alloys and foil.

Antimony: A silvery white, brittle, yet soft metal, used primarily in alloys to improve the working qualities of other metals.

Brass: An alloy of copper (50-95%), zinc (5-50%), and sometimes other metals, malleable, ductile, and harder and stronger than copper alone.

Britannia: A silver-white alloy of tin, antimony, copper, and sometimes other metals, similar to pewter and once widely used in domestic utensils.

Bronze: An alloy of copper and tin, and sometimes other elements, harder and stronger than brass and used in cast products.

Cast iron: A hard, brittle, nonmalleable alloy of iron, silicon, and 2 to 4½% carbon, used primarily for casting in a mold.

Chromium (chrome): A hard, brittle, bluish-white metal used chiefly in stainless steel and for planting other metals.

Copper: A ductile, malleable reddish metal that conducts heat and electricity well, used in the pure state as well as in alloys.

Electrum: An alloy of gold and silver, pale yellow in color.

Gold: A malleable, ductile metal, impervious to most chemicals, usually alloyed with copper, silver, zinc, or other metal to improve its working properties.

Iron: A heavy, malleable, ductile, magnetic metal subject to rust; the chief component of steel; silver white when pure.

Lead: A heavy, soft, malleable, barely ductile metal, bluish-white to dull gray, usually in alloys; a major component in most solders. Caution: contact with lead can contaminate food with poison.

Nickel: A silver-white, hard, malleable, ductile, rust-resistant metal, used mainly in alloys and for plating.

Palladium: A ductile, malleable, tarnish-resistant metal, resembling platinum, used primarily in silver alloys for jewelry.

Pewter: Any of various alloys with tin as the main component; bright modern pewter contains antimony (6-7%) and copper (1-2%); the dull metal of the past contained up to 25% copper, antimony, or lead.

Pig iron: Crude iron produced by smelting ore; the raw material for making steel, wrought iron, and cast iron.

Platinum: A heavy, precious, noncorroding, ductile, malleable metal, usually grayish-white, used mainly in jewelry in the form of alloys.

Silver: A ductile, malleable, noble metal; the best conductor of heat and electricity known; usually alloyed with copper to increase its hardness; often used to plate baser metals.

Stainless steel: A steel alloy, virtually impervious to rust and corrosion, containing about one-eighth chromium.

Steel: An alloy of iron with no more than 1.7% carbon, noted for strength and malleability.

Sterling: An alloy of silver (92½%) and copper (7½%); harder and more workable than pure silver.

Tin: A soft, malleable, somewhat ductile, low-melting metal, bluish-white in color, used chiefly in foils, solders, bronze, pewter, and casting alloys.

Wrought iron: A soft but tough, malleable, ductile form of iron containing less than .3% carbon and 1 to 2% slag, used primarily in forging.

Zinc: A bluish-white, moderately soft metal, ductile when heated but ordinarily brittle, used chiefly in alloys and to plate iron and steel.

Tools and Materials

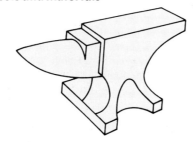

Anvil: A heavy, usually steel-faced iron block on which a smith holds metal while shaping it with a hammer.

Asbestos: A fibrous, fireproof mineral used in gloves, aprons, and mats for its heat resistance. Caution: Prolonged contact with asbestos is a health hazard; wear a protective mask when you work with it.

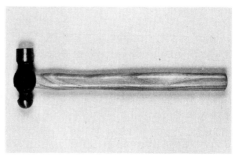

Ball peen hammer: A hammer with a rounded head on one side and a flat or slightly convex head on the other, used to drive other tools or, by itself, to shape surfaces.

Burgundy pitch: A viscous, slightly yielding, easy-to-melt resin used in repoussé to hold the work steady while it is being struck.

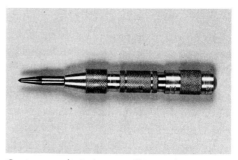

Center punch: A short steel bar with a point at one end, used to mark holes to be drilled.

Flux: A substance, largely borax, that is applied to surfaces being soldered, brazed, or welded—to dissolve impurities—and to sterling during annealing—to prevent fire scale.

Forge: A place where iron and other metals are worked by heating and hammering; the furnace where the metal is heated; to form by heating and hammering.

HEAT COLORS IN DEGREES FAHRENHEIT:	
Faint red	650-700
Dull red	700-900
Medium red	900-1300
Bright red	1300-1600
Cherry red	1600-1750
Orange	1750-1850
Bright yellow	1850-1950
Light yellow	1950-2200
White	2200-2350
Blinding white	above 2350

Gauge: A device used to measure the thickness of sheet metal or wire; the thickness of metal expressed in terms of a standard system.

THICKNESS IN INCHES OF STANDARD (BROWN AND SHARPE) GAUGE NUMBERS:	
Gauge number	Thickness in inches
000000	0.580000
00000	0.516500
0000	0.460000
000	0.409642
00	0.364796
0	0.324861
1	0.289297
2	0.257627
3	0.229423
4	0.204307
5	0.181940
6	0.162023
7	0.144285
8	0.128490
9	0.114423
10	0.101895
11	0.090742
12	0.080808
13	0.071962
14	0.064084
15	0.057068
16	0.050821
17	0.045257
18	0.040303
19	0.035890
20	0.031961
21	0.028462
22	0.025346
23	0.022572
24	0.020101
25	0.017900
26	0.015941
27	0.014195
28	0.012641
29	0.011257
30	0.010025
31	0.008928
32	0.007950
33	0.007080
34	0.006305
35	0.005615
36	0.005000
37	0.004453
38	0.003965
39	0.003531
40	0.003144

Graver: A hard, sharp-pointed tool used to engrave metals; also called burin or scorper.

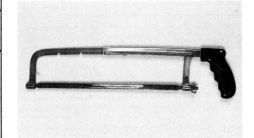

Hacksaw: A fine-toothed saw with a blade under tension in a frame, used to cut metal.

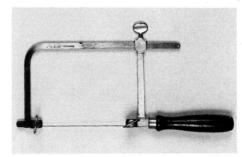

Jeweler's saw: A saw consisting of a fine blade under tension in an adjustable frame, used for cutting curves in soft, thin metal.

Jig: Any device used to hold a piece of metal being worked in a certain position.

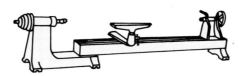

Lathe: A machine on which work can be rotated on an axis while being shaped.

Machine bolt: A metal fastener with a square or hexagonal head on one end and threads to hold a nut on the other.

Machine screw: A screw with a slotted or socket head and narrow threads, used for holding metal parts together.

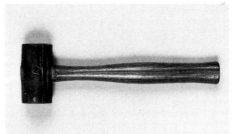

Mallet: A pounding tool with a barrel-shaped head of wood, leather, paper, or other soft material, used for shaping a metal surface without marring it.

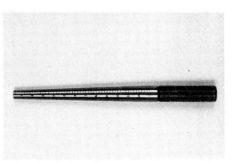

Mandrel: A gently tapered cylinder around which rings or bracelets can be shaped.

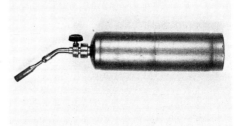

Propane torch: A blow torch for heating metals, fueled by flammable gas and capable of producing a temperature of 6000 degrees Fahrenheit.

Punch: A sharp-pointed rod driven by a hammer, to perforate or emboss metal.

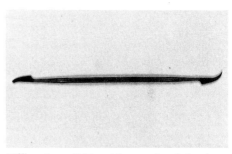

Riffler: A small file with curved ends for shaping and smoothing hard-to-reach areas.

Rivet: A headed bolt of malleable metal, used to join pieces by passing the shank through a hole in each piece, then beating down the plain end to form a second head.

Sandbag: A yielding backing used in shaping sheet metal into hollow ware.

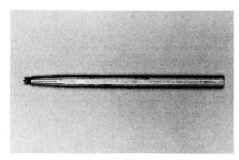

Scriber: A sharp-pointed tool for marking metal to be cut.

Size: An adhesive substance used to attach metallic leaf (especially gold leaf) to surfaces.

Solder: An alloy with a low melting temperature, frequently lead and tin, used to join metals.

Stove bolt: A bolt with a flat or round slotted head at one end and a square nut at the other, used for joining metal parts.

Tapping screw: A hardened screw that cuts threads as it is driven into the pieces it secures.

Processes

Anneal: To soften a metal by heating it so as to renew its capacity to be worked.

ANNEALING TEMPERATURES IN DEGREES FAHRENHEIT	
Aluminum	650
Brass	1100
Bronze	1100
Copper	1200
Gold (fine)	No annealing required
Nickel	1700
Pewter	No annealing required
Platinum	1200
Silver (fine)	570
Silver (sterling)	1200
Steel	1450
Zinc	212

Braze: To solder with an alloy such as brass that melts at a higher temperature than common solder and thus creates a stronger bond.

Cast: To shape a metal by pouring it in molten form into a mold and letting it harden there.

Chase: To ornament a metal surface by indenting it with blunt tools driven by a hammer.

Emboss: To raise an ornament in relief from a metal surface, usually by stamping the metal with a design from the rear.

Engrave: To produce designs on a metal surface by incising with a hard, pointed tool.

Etch: To produce a design on a metal surface by coating it with an acid-resistant substance, scratching a design through the coating, then covering the surface with acid.

Gild: To coat with a thin covering of gold.

Lost-wax process: A casting process consisting of coating a wax model with clay or plaster to form a mold, melting and draining the wax away, and pouring molten metal into the empty mold.

Niello: Decorating metal with incised designs filled with a black alloy of sulfur and silver or other metals.

Pickle: To soak metal in a chemical solution, usually acid, to remove surface impurities.

Planish: To condense, toughen, and polish a metal surface by tapping it with a smooth-faced hammer.

Plate: To cover a metal surface with a second metal, mechanically, chemically, or electrically, for protection or adornment.

Quench: To cool a heated metal quickly by immersing it in water or oil.

Raise: To form sheet metal into hollow ware by alternately hammering and annealing.

Repoussé: Metalwork shaped or ornamented with relief patterns made by hammering the reverse side.

Roll: To spread a metal into a sheet with a roller.

Sink: To raise the edges of a piece of metal by directing hammer blows at the middle while holding the metal over a sandbag or rigid form.

Smelt: To melt ore in a furnace to separate metal from unwanted material.

Spin: To form metal hollow ware on a lathe.

Temper: To soften hardened steel or cast iron by reheating it to a temperature well below that at which it was previously quenched.

Tool: To ornament the surface of a metal object with hand tools.

Upset: To compress the end of a length of metal by heating it and pounding on it.

Weld: To unite two or more metallic surfaces by heating them to a plastic state and hammering them together or to a fluid state and letting them flow together.

Terms

Alloy: A substance such as pewter, brass, or sterling consisting of a mixture of two or more metals.

Base metal: A metal or alloy such as lead or iron of low value and inferior properties, as opposed to noble metal.

Burr: A small roughness that usually occurs on the edge of metal that has been cut, drilled, or engraved.

Carbon: A nonmetallic element in coal that combines with iron during smelting to form steel, wrought iron, and cast iron.

Dap: To produce hollows in sheet metal with a hammer and punch.

Ductility: The relative ability of a metal to be drawn into a wire without breaking.

COMMON METALS ARRANGED IN DESCENDING ORDER OF DUCTILITY	
1. Gold	6. Aluminum
2. Silver	7. Nickel
3. Platinum	8. Zinc
4. Iron	9. Tin
5. Copper	10. Lead

Half-round: Having one side flat, the other round; said of certain files, wires, and pliers.

Hallmark: A mark stamped on metal articles (usually gold or silver) attesting to their purity or identifying their maker.

Hardening: The effect on any metal of continued hammering; reversed by annealing.

Hollow ware: Articles such as cups, bowls, and pots that have volume and depth.

Karat: A unit for measuring the fineness of gold equal to 1/24th part of pure gold in an alloy; 24-karat gold is pure, 12-karat is a half-and-half mixture with another metal.

Leaf: Metal, usually gold, used in a thin layer for surface decoration of other metals and wood.

COMMON METALS ARRANGED IN DESCENDING ORDER OF MALLEABILITY	
1. Gold	8. Zinc
2. Silver	9. Wrought Iron
3. Copper	10. Soft steel
4. Aluminum	11. Nickel
5. Tin	12. Hard steel
6. Platinum	13. Cast iron
7. Lead	

Malleability: The relative capacity of a metal for being extended or shaped by hammering.

Molten: Fused or liquefied by heat; melted.

MELTING TEMPERATURES OF METALS IN DEGREES FAHRENHEIT			
Aluminum	1220	Lead	621
Antimony	1167	Nickel	2651
Chromium	3209	Platinum	3224
Copper	1981	Silver	1761
Gold	1945	Tin	449
Iron	2802	Zinc	787

Nobility: The relative resistance of a metal to corrosion and other chemical action or foreign matter.

Ore: A natural mineral that can be mined and reduced to pure metal by smelting.

Oxidation: Chemical combination of a metal with oxygen; rust or corrosion.

Runner: A channel for conducting molten metal into a mold.

Sprue: The hole through which molten metal is poured into a casting mold.

Tarnish: The altered luster or surface color of a metal caused by chemical action or foreign matter.

Tensile strength: A metal's ability to resist elongation before finally breaking.

COMMON METALS ARRANGED IN DESCENDING ORDER OF TENSILE STRENGTH		
1. Iron	4. Silver	7. Aluminum
2. Copper	5. Zinc	8. Tin
3. Platinum	6. Gold	9. Lead

Troy weight: Units of weight used in measuring precious metals and stones.

TROY WEIGHT TABLE OF EQUIVALENTS
24 grains = 1 pennyweight
20 pennyweights = 1 troy ounce
12 troy ounces = 1 troy pound
1 troy ounce = 31.103 grams
1 kilogram = 32.151 troy ounces
1 troy ounce = 1.10 avoirdupois ounces
14.58 troy ounces = 1 avoirdupois pound

Wire: Metal in the form of a continuous, uniform, flexible thread, produced by pulling larger pieces of metal through progressively smaller holes in a steel plate.

Minerals

The minerals that qualify as craft material can be divided into two groups: the gem minerals that lapidaries use in making jewelry, and the metals. The data that follow relate primarily to lapidary minerals and the ores from which metals are extracted. For additional information about metals, see page mi-28.

Minerals in natural form rarely reveal what they are to the eye. There are several methods of identifying them. Three which do not require professional equipment are in the charts that follow: relative hardness, relative weight, and surface luster. The Mohs' scale of hardness lists ten minerals in ascending order of hardness. Each mineral listed will scratch those minerals that are numerically lower than it on the sacle. The specific gravity chart ranks minerals according to their weight relative to the weight of an equal volume of water. The formula for deriving specific gravity is in that chart. The surface luster chart lists and describes the terms used to identify minerals by their surface appearance, including examples of minerals that typify each type of luster.

MAJOR LAPIDARY MINERALS	
Mineral	Associated gemstones
Beryl	Aquamarine, emerald, golden beryl, morganite
Chrysoberyl	Alexandrite, cat's-eye
Corundum	Ruby, sapphire
Diamond	Diamond
Feldspar	Amazonite, labradorite, moonstone, peristerite, sunstone
Garnet	Varieties: almandine, andradite, grossularite, pyrope, rhodolite, spessartite
Jade	Varieties: Jadeite, nephrite
Lapis lazuli	Lapis lazuli
Malachite	Malachite
Olivine	Peridot
Opal	Varieties: precious, white, black, fire, jelly, hyalite, common, wood
Quartz	Agate, amethyst, bloodstone or heliotrope, cairngorm, carnelian, chalcedony, chrysoprase, citrine, jasper, onyx, petrified wood, rock crystal, sard
Sphene	Titanite
Spinel	Spinel
Spodumene	Hiddenite, kunzite
Topaz	Varieties: golden, imperial
Tourmaline	Varieties: Indicolite, rubellite; pink, green, brown, and mixed-color tourmalines
Turquoise	Turquoise

MOHS' SCALE OF HARDNESS	
1. Talc	6. Orthoclase feldspar
2. Gypsum	7. Quartz
3. Calcite	8. Topaz
4. Fluorite	9. Corundum
5. Apatite	10. Diamond

Soft minerals are generally considered to be those below 6 in hardness.

SPECIFIC GRAVITY OF FAMILIAR MINERALS

Formula: $\dfrac{\text{weight in air}}{\text{weight in air minus weight in water}}$ = specific gravity

Mineral	Specific gravity (about how many times heavier than water)	Feel in the hand
Gold	19	very heavy
Silver	10-1/2	very heavy
Copper	9	very heavy
Lead	7-1/2	very heavy
Iron	5	heavy
Ruby	4	heavy
Diamond	3-1/2	heavy
Topaz	3-1/2	heavy
Emerald	2-3/4	fairly light
Quartz	2-1/2	fairly light
Gypsum	2-1/2	fairly light
Aluminum	2	light

SURFACE LUSTER

Surface appearance	Sample minerals
Adamantine or brilliant	Diamond
Dull	Coral
Earthy	Carnotite
Glassy or vitreous	Opal, quartz
Greasy	Serpentine
Metallic	Gold, silver
Pearly	Feldspar
Resinous	Rhodonite, smithsonite
Silky	Satin spar, malachite
Waxy	Chiastolite

WEIGHTS AND DIMENSIONS IN LAPIDARY WORK

Carat is the unit of weight used for gemstones

One gram equals 5 carats

One avoirdupois ounce equals 141.75 carats

One pound equals 453.60 grams

The "grain" is the unit of weight used for pearls

One grain equals 1/4 carat

For troy weight, used for precious metals, see page mi-31.

Dimensions of gemstones are given in millimeters

One millimeter equals .001 meter or about 1/25 inch

LAPIDARY PROCESSES

Tumbling minerals and gemstones		Length of time	
Process	Abrasive or polish used	Hard stones	Soft stones
First grind	80-grit silicon carbide and water	5 days	4 days
Second grind	220-grit silicon carbide and water	4 days	2 days
Third grind	400-grit silicon carbide and water	4 days	3 days
Fourth grind	600-grit silicon carbide and water	4 days	3 days
Polish	cerium oxide and water	2 weeks	5 days

SAWING MINERALS AND GEMSTONES

Size of specimen	Size and type of saw blade	Coolant
Small	6-inch continuous rim diamond saw blade, .015 to .036 inch thick	Water
Large	10-inch notched rim diamond saw blade, .055 to .065 inch thick	50 percent flushing oil and 50 percent deodorized white kerosene

(For this operation the saw used is a trim or slab saw and the mineral is fed into it at a rate of 1/4 inch per minute for hard minerals, 1/2 inch per minute for soft minerals.)

GRINDING AND SHAPING GEMSTONES

Process	Size of grinding wheel	Grit of grinder or sander		
		Hard stones	Soft stones	Coolant
1st grind	1-1/2 inches wide, 8 or 10 inches in diameter	100-grit wheel	200-grit wheel	Water
2nd grind	as above	220-grit wheel	400-grit sanding drum	Water

SANDING AND POLISHING GEMSTONES

Process	Sander or polisher	Abrasive or polish	Coolant
First sanding	3- or 4-inch-wide sanding drum 8 or 10 inches in diameter	400-grit circular sanding belt	Water
Second sanding	same as above	600-grit circular sanding belt	Water
Polishing	8- or 10-inch leather-covered polishing wheel with 1/4-inch convex curvature	Cerium oxide and water mix applied to wheel	

GRINDING AND POLISHING MINERAL SLABS AND FLAT SURFACES

Process	Grinder or polisher	Abrasive or polish
First grind	Steel or cast-iron lap wheel or vibrating lap machine	100-grit silicon carbide and water
Second grind	Steel or cast-iron lap wheel or vibrating lap machine	220-grit silicon carbide and water
Third grind	Steel or cast-iron lap wheel or vibrating lap machine	400-grit silicon carbide and water
Fourth grind	Steel or cast-iron lap wheel or vibrating lap machine	600-grit silicon carbide and water
Fifth grind	Steel or cast-iron lap wheel or vibrating lap machine	1000-grit silicon carbide and water
Polish	Pellon disk fixed to lap wheel	Cerium oxide and water

(Other polishes may be used for lapidary work; see page mi-14.)

Terminology of minerals

Aluminum pencil: A tool for marking minerals to be cut.

Asteriated: Reflected light in four- or six-rayed star pattern, characteristic of some forms of sapphire, ruby, quartz, spinel, garnet, and others.

Barrel liner: A replacable lining for a tumbler barrel used in polishing minerals.

Belt sander: A machine with a continuous abrasive belt that conforms to the rounded contours of gemstones.

Bezel: The top part of a gemstone mounting which surrounds and holds the stone.

Black light: The popular name for light from filtered ultraviolet ray lamps, used to determine fluorescence or phosphorescence in minerals.

Black sand: Dark magnetic sand associated with gold flakes; it can be separated from the gold with a magnet.

Brilliant cut: The familiar round-cut gemstone with 56 facets.

Cabochon: A round or oval gem with rounded top, flat bottom, and no facets.

Cerium oxide: A polishing agent for minerals and gems.

Chatoyancy: A mineral's ability to reflect a silky sheen.

Cleavage: The planes along which a mineral will naturally separate when split.

Color: The prospector's term for dirt containing small flakes of gold.

Conchoidal: A curved concave shape, like the inside of a seashell, that occurs when minerals like quartz, opal, and glass are chipped or fractured.

Crown: The upper angled portion of a faceted gemstone, extending from the widest part of the stone to the flat top.

Crystal: A symmetrical shape established by plane surfaces that meet at particular angles, which vary according to the mineral.

Culet: The bottom point of a faceted gemstone.

Diamond blade: A saw blade with diamond fragments embedded in its edge, used for cutting minerals.

Dop or dop stick: A dowel or metal rod to which a gemstone is mounted (with wax) for shaping and polishing.

Dopping stove: The unit with which the stone and wax are heated before the stone is mounted on the dop stick.

Double refraction: The ability of some minerals such as Iceland spar calcite to divide one ray of light into two rays.

Dredge: A machine that draws up stream-bottom material and then runs it through a sluice to separate heavy minerals from gold.

Drum sander: A power-driven flexible drum to which abrasive belts are mounted for sanding and polishing gemstones.

Dry placer: Dirt or a gravelly area such as an old stream bed where gold has been and is likely to be found.

Facet: A flat-plane cut on the face of a gem at a specific angle to help it refract light.

Fibrous or splintery: The appearance of a fractured or broken surface, characteristic of certain minerals.

Findings: Small metal parts used by lapidaries for mounting gemstones.

Flat: A thin slice of mineral sawed from a thicker chunk of mineral.

Flour gold: Tiny flecks or flakes of gold, frequently found mixed with black sand.

Fluorescence: A glowing color reaction of a mineral while it is exposed to invisible ultraviolet rays.

Fool's gold: Any of various forms of pyrite that are mistaken for real gold.

Fracture: A mineral's chipped or broken surface.

Gemstone: Any stone used for lapidary work.

Girdle: The widest part of a cut gem separating the top from the base.

Gold pan: A shallow pan used by prospectors to separate gold from dirt and gravel.

Goniometer: A protractor with a pivoting head used for measuring the interfacial angles of mineral crystals.

Hackly: Jagged appearance of some minerals, such as copper or silver, when fractured.

Hardness: The resistance a mineral has to surface scratching.

Igneous: Rock formed from the solidification of molten material.

Interfacial angle: The angle formed by the meeting of two faces of a crystal.

Iridescent: Showing a rainbow play of colors as a mineral is turned.

Lap or lap wheel: A rotating wheel used for smoothing and polishing flat gem materials.

Lapidary: One who fashions or works with gem minerals.

Lode: A mineral vein or mass of ore embedded in rock.

Luster: The surface appearance of an unbroken mineral.

Matrix: The rock a mineral is attached to or embedded in.

Metamorphic: Rock that has been changed from its original state by pressure, heat, gases, or solutions.

Mineral: An inorganic substance with a specific chemical composition and an orderly internal atomic structure.

Mounting: Shaped material in which a gemstone is held.

Needle rod: Steel rod to which abrasives are applied for carving and engraving gem minerals.

Nodule: A small rounded mineral lump that may form in a cavity in rock.

Nugget: A small lump of precious metal as found in its natural state.

Opalescent: Having a milky iridescence.

Pavilion: The lower part of a cut gem, extending from the girdle to the cutlet.

Phosphorescence: A glowing color reaction a mineral retains after it has been exposed to ultraviolet rays and the light source has been removed.

Placer gold: Loose ore deposits found in dirt and gravel at the bottom of river beds and streams.

Precious stones: The gems that have the greatest value, such as diamonds, rubies, sapphires, emeralds, and opals.

Prospector's pick: A hammerlike tool with one blunt end and one pointed end.

Resinous: Having a surface luster like that of resin.

Riffle box: A metal chute lined with removable slats that catch heavy metal particles and let them fall through mesh.

Rock: Natural inorganic solid made up primarily of a mixture of minerals.

Sedimentary: Rock formed from the remains of other rocks or organisms.

Semiprecious stones: Stones cut and worn as gems, but of lesser value than precious stones..

Slab: A flat slice of mineral.

Sloughing off: Spilling water and light debris over the edge of a gold pan to separate it from the heavier gold.

Sniping tool: A metal rod with bent ends, one pointed, the other shaped like a shallow spoon; used for digging in crevices and spooning up dirt samples that might contain gold.

Splintery: The appearance of fractured surfaces of some minerals like jade.

Streak: A powdery mark left by a mineral when scratched across unglazed tile or frosted glass; the color of the mark helps in identifying the mineral.

Table: The flat surface on top of a faceted gemstone.

Tumbling: Rotating gemstones in a small barrel with abrasives and water to smooth and polish them.

Plants

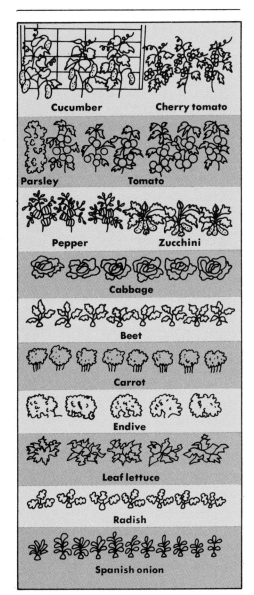

Cucumber   **Cherry tomato**

Parsley   **Tomato**

Pepper   **Zucchini**

Cabbage

Beet

Carrot

Endive

Leaf lettuce

Radish

Spanish onion

In a space only 10 feet wide and 15 feet deep, you can plant a garden that will provide an abundance of fresh salads all summer long (above). This plan includes 13 kinds of vegetables, the total cost of the seed is less than ten dollars. Note that the plants are graduated in height from the onions and radishes in front to the cucumber vines climbing on a wire fence at the rear. In a south facing garden, the various heights let sunlight reach all the plants.

Annual: A plant that grows, blooms, seeds, and dies in one season.

Perennial: A hardy plant that will live and bloom every year for a long period, and once established requires less care than an annual.

Biennial: Plants that bloom the second year from seed, then die.

PLANTS FOR EVERY PURPOSE

Annuals for hot, dry places

California bluebells
California poppy
Cape marigold
Cleome
Cornflower
Cosmos
Dahlia
Dusty miller
Four o'clock
Gaillardia
Gazania
Geranium
Ice plant
Nasturtium
Poppy
Portulaca
Prickly poppy

Flowers for fragrance

Carnation
Clematis
Flowering tobacco
Gardenia
Heliotrope
Hyacinth
Jasmine
Lavender
Lilac
Lily-of-the-valley
Mignonette
Mock orange
Moonflower
Nasturtium
Peony
Petunia
Phlox
Rose
Stock
Strawflower
Sweet alyssum
Sweet pea
Tuberose
Verbena
Wisteria

Perennials to grow from seed

Columbia
Coreopsis
Delphinium
English daisy
Forget-me-not
Foxglove
Gloriosa daisy
Hollyhock
Iceland poppy
Marguerite
Pansy
Red-hot poker
Sweet William

Plants for moist places

Astilbe
Bee balm
Canterbury bells
Columbine
English daisy
Forget-me-not
Foxglove
Pansy
Phlox
Plantain lily
Primrose
Rose mallow
Sweet pea
Viola
Wax begonia

Dwarf plants for edgings

Ageratum
Alyssum
Celosia (dwarf)
Daisy (English)
Lobelia
Marigold (dwarf)
Pansy
Portulaca
Viola
Wax begonia
Zinnia (dwarf)

Plants for bedding

Aster
Balsam
Begonia
Dahlia
Geranium
Impatiens
Iris
Marigold
Nicotinia
Pansy
Petunia
Portulaca
Snapdragon
Verbena
Viola
Zinnia

Windowbox plants

Alyssum
California poppy
Celosia (dwarf)
Coleus
Geranium
Ivy
Lobelia
Marigold (dwarf)
Petunia
Verbena
Wax begonia

Plants for partial shade

Azalea
Bleeding heart
Caladium
Coleus
Columbine
English ivy
Ferns
Foxglove
Lily-of-the-valley
Pachysandra
Periwinkle
Violet
Tuberous begonia
Wax begonia

Easy-to-grow annuals

Alyssum
Calendula
California poppy
Cornflower
Cosmos
Evening stock
Garden balsam
Larkspur
Marigold
Phlox
Portulaca
Strawflower
Sunflower
Zinnia

Rock-garden plants

Ageratum
Alyssum
Bearberry cotoneaster
California poppy
Candytuft
Corsican pearlwort
Dianthus
Forget-me-not
Gazania
Helianthemum
Linaria
Lobelia
Marigold (dwarf)
Moss phlox
Mother-of-thyme
Portulaca
Sedum
Sun rose
Verbena
Yerba buena
Zinnia (dwarf)

Flowers for cutting

Aster
Bells of Ireland
Calendula
Carnation
Chrysanthemum
Cornflower
Cosmos
Delphinium
English daisy
Gladiolus
Iris
Marigold
Peony
Poppy
Rose
Snapdragon
Stock
Sweet sultan
Sweet William
Zinnia

Tall flowers for backgrounds

Babies' breath
Canna
Canterbury bell
Cleome
Chrysanthemum (tall)
Day lily
Delphinium
Foxglove
Gladiolus
Gloriosa daisy
Hibiscus
Hollyhock
Lupine
Peony
Poppy
Red-hot poker
Rose mallow
Shasta daisy
Snapdragon (tall)
Sunflower
Yarrow (fern-leaved)
Zinnia (tall)

Plants for hanging baskets

Begonia
Donkey-tail sedum
Ferns
Fuchsia
Ivy geranium
Lobelia
Nasturtium
Petunia
Philodendron
Rosary vine
Spider plant
Tuberous begonia
Wandering jew

THE POPULAR HOUSE PLANTS

Name	Type	Potting medium	Light needs	Care and feeding	Ideal temperatures
African violet (Saintpaulia)	Flowering	2 parts peat moss to 1 part general-purpose potting soil and 1 part perlite.	Bright indirect or curtain-filtered sunlight or 14 to 16 hours of artificial light.	Keep soil barely moist. Do not allow water to touch leaves; water from saucer beneath pot. Feed monthly.	75° day; 65° to 70° night. Needs high humidity.
Heart-leaved philodendron (Philodendron oxycardium)	Foliage	General-purpose potting soil. Can grow in plain water.	Bright indirect or curtain-filtered sunlight or strong artificial light.	Keep soil barely moist at all times. Feed every 3 or 4 months.	75° to 85° day; 65° to 70° night.
Piggyback plant (Tolmiea menziesii)	Foliage	General-purpose potting soil.	Bright indirect or curtain-filtered sunlight or strong artificial light.	Keep soil constantly moist. Feed every 2 months.	55° to 70° day; 40° to 55° night.
Dumb cane (Dieffenbachia)	Foliage	General-purpose potting soil.	Bright indirect or curtain-filtered sunlight or strong artificial light.	Leaves and stems are poisonous—keep away from children and pets. Let soil become moderately dry between thorough waterings. Feed every 2 or 3 months with half-strength houseplant fertilizer.	75° to 85° day; 65° to 70° night.
Red-margined dracaena (Dracaena marginata)	Foliage	General-purpose potting soil.	Can survive in low-light setting but will grow better with bright indirect or curtain-filtered sunlight.	Keep soil moist to the touch but do not let the pot stand in water. Feed every 6 months.	75° to 85° day; 65° to 70° night.
English ivy (Hedera helix)	Foliage	General-purpose potting soil or equal parts of loam, peat moss and sand.	Four or more hours a day of direct sunlight, but will grow fairly well in bright indirect light.	Keep soil barely moist at all times. Feed every 3 or 4 months. Pinch back frequently to promote bushiness.	68° to 72° day; 50° to 55° night, but will tolerate night temperatures as low as 35° without harm.
Grape ivy (Cissus rhombifolia)	Foliage	General-purpose potting soil.	Bright indirect or curtained sunlight or strong artificial light.	Let soil become moderately dry between thorough waterings. Feed every 4 months.	68° to 72° day; 50° to 55° night. Pinch off stem tips to encourage compact, bushy growth.
Coleus (Coleus blumei)	Foliage	General-purpose potting soil or equal parts of loam, peat moss and sand.	Four or more hours a day of direct sunlight, but will grow fairly well in bright indirect light.	Keep soil barely moist at all times. Feed every 3 months with half-strength houseplant fertilizer. Pinch off stem tips to encourage dense growth.	75° to 85° day; 65° to 70° night.
Jade plant (Crassula argentea)	Succulent	General-purpose potting soil or equal parts of loam, peat moss and sand.	Four or more hours a day of direct sunlight, but will grow fairly well in bright indirect light.	Let soil become nearly dry between thorough waterings. Feed every 3 or 4 months.	68° to 72° day; 50° to 55° night, but can tolerate range from 40° to 100°.

Plastics

Plastics have almost unlimited use in craft work. Those listed below are generic types that can be modified with additives to fit special applications. Terms used in plastics work are defined in the glossary that follows.

Acrylics: Glasslike thermoplastics available in clear, colored, or opaque form, as rods, tubes, fibers, blocks, or sheets, or in liquid or aerosol form as sealers, coatings, or water-soluble paints. Solids can be heated and re-formed. Rigid sheets can be cut and assembled to make boxes, tabletops, room dividers, and molds into which plastic resins can be poured. All transmit light, even around corners. Acrylics are sometimes mixed with polyester to make a superior casting resin.

Polyesters: Plastics that, in liquid thermosetting form, solidify with the addition of a hardener or catalyst and cannot be re-formed once they have cured. These are available as clear syrupy liquids, in rolls of cellophane film, or as thickened pastes. Pastes are used to patch and fill holes and cracks in pottery, household objects, cars, and boats. Films (such as Mylar) are used to line molds into which polyester or epoxy casting resins are poured. Liquids are used for casting, embedding, laminating, or surface coating, and to bind glass-fiber cloth in building or repairing boats and cars. Polyesters transmit light and can be thickened, thinned, colored, or made fracture-resistant or more flexible with additives. They shrink more than epoxies but are less subject to sunlight discoloration.

Epoxies: Clear liquid thermosetting plastics that solidify with the addition of a hardener or catalyst to form a strong adhesive bond, even between dissimilar materials. They cannot be re-formed after they solidify. Epoxies are also used for casting, embedding, enameling, waterproofing, and as a bond for glass-fiber cloth. They are more resistant to chemicals and temperature extremes than polyesters but less resistant to discoloration by sunlight. Shrinkage is negligible. Epoxies can be thinned or colored with various additives and can be made fire-retardant or less sensitive to sunlight as well.

Foams: Expanded (foamed) polystyrenes and polyurethanes are most frequently used in craft work. Foamed polystyrenes come in rigid sheets which can be carved, glued, and decorated to make centerpieces and other displays. They can also be laminated into larger blocks to fill areas needing insulation or to

Versatility of plastics is shown by flower and abalone shell embedments at left, yellow flower of dyed cast plastic, roll of clear vinyl and pieces of flexible and rigid plastic foams (rear right). Small pieces of clear plastic in foreground (some covered by protective paper), and rods and decorative shapes in plastic cylinders at right are all acrylic. Silver, red, and gold rolls are Mylar, a polyester film. White molds in foreground are polyethylene. Container in rear holds casting resin, those in left foreground hold dyes and other additives. Tube at left holds RTV silicone adhesive sealant, behind it is a calibrated syringe for injecting plastic working materials in measured amounts.

provide flotation in boats without adding significant weight. Small beads are available for stuffing pillows and chairs or to protect packaged materials.

Foamed polyurethanes come in sheets or blocks or as two components that, when mixed together, expand to fill the space where they are put. The latter can be poured over objects or into molds to make reproductions or dispensed from pressurized units to provide insulation and buoyancy. When hard, polyurethanes can be sawed, carved, rasped, or painted. (Polyurethanes in liquid form are applied to give durable, glossy finishes to tabletops and other furniture.)

RTV flexible mold materials: These synthetic rubbers are made of any of a number of plastics, including polyurethanes, polysulphides, and silicones. With a curing agent added, they harden chemically (without heat) into flexible

molds for casting objects with wax, plaster, plastics, cement, or low-melting-point metals. Unlike latex rubber, which must be built up with thin layers, thick layers of RTV compounds can be poured. Polysulphide and polyurethane compounds require a mold release agent to free the casting from the mold; silicone type may not.

Polyvinyls: Polymerized thermoplastic vinyl compounds that include polyvinyl chloride (PVC), polyvinyl alcohol (PVA) and polyvinyl acetate. Resistant to abrasion, solvents, and weathering, the polyvinyls are widely used as coatings and fabric finishes, or as liquids, pellets, or strands for low-cost casting or molding. In semirigid pipe form, PVC is used for plumbing and furniture, in film or roll form for making dress patterns, and in vacuum forming. PVA compounds are used as emulsifiers, adhesives, and mold-release agents. Polyvinyl acetates are used for low-temperature casting and molding.

Polyethylenes, Polypropylenes: Somewhat similar plastics used for making pipes, tubing, containers, kitchen wraps, and rigid molds for casting polyesters and epoxies. As mold materials, they leave castings with a smooth shiny surface.

Safety first

Face shield: Transparent protective shield used when sawing or cutting hard plastics and glass-fiber material.

Gloves: Plastic or rubber gloves always worn when working with plastics.

Respirator: A breathing apparatus to prevent inhalation of hazardous plastic and lacquer fumes.

Safety goggles: Devices to protect eyes during grinding, polishing, and carving plastics.

Materials, tools, and processes for plastics work

Accelerator: An additive that speeds hardening or curing.

Acetone: A solvent for cleaning remnants of epoxies, polyesters, and urethane foams from work surfaces and brushes.

Additive: Anything mixed with a plastic to change its characteristics.

Adhesive: A material that bonds plastics to plastic or other materials.

Agar-agar: A colorless vegetable gelatin used for life molds because it does not harm hair or skin.

Base pour: The first plastic poured into the mold, usually the top of the casting, without inclusions or embedments.

Blushing: Cloudiness caused by exposing plastic to moisture before it has fully cured.

Body putty: A plastic paste for repairing holes, dents, and cracks in wood, metal, or plastic objects.

Bond: The adhesion of two surfaces.

Bubble retarder or eliminator: An additive that minimizes air voids in castings.

Buffing or polishing compounds: Materials, such as jeweler's rouge, used for bringing plastic surfaces to a glasslike finish.

Carving: Using drills, burrs, and other cutting tools to shape or cut designs into solid plastics.

Cast: To create a shape by pouring liquid plastic into a mold and letting it harden without pressure.

Casting resins: Materials like polyester or epoxy resins that are poured into molds to make cast reproductons of an object, or to embed objects.

Catalyst: A chemical hardening agent that starts the curing process to turn liquid plastic into a solid.

Click hard: The stage in hardening when plastic is no longer tacky and will click when tapped with a stirring stick.

Colorants: Powder, paste, or liquid pigments or dyes added to plastics to color them.

Crack retarder: An additive used to minimize fractures in plastic casts and embedments.

Crazing: Cracks in a cast object caused by using too much catalyst (in polyesters), by heat-forming at too low a temperature (with acrylics), or by cleaning the casting with a solvent.

Curing: The process of transforming plastic from a liquid to a solid.

Dipping plastic: A liquid resin into which shaped wire forms are dipped to make decorative objects as the plastic forms a bridge between the wires.

Edge lighting: Applying light to one edge of acrylic or polyester to make other edges, carved surfaces, or inclusions glow.

Embedment: An object embedded in plastic for preservation or display.

Exothermic reaction: The generation of internal heat as part of the chemical reaction that changes a liquid plastic into a solid.

Fillers: Various powders, pastes, or liquid pigments or dyes added to plastic to strengthen, thicken, or lighten it or add bulk or opacity.

Foaming: Adding a foaming agent to liquid plastic to make it expand.

Gel point: The stage during hardening when liquid plastic thickens to a viscous consistency, much like jelly.

Hardener: In general, a catalyst; more specifically, the particular additive that increases the hardness of the surface of a plastic casting.

Hot carving knife: A tool with a razorlike blade fitted to a soldering-iron type of handle, heated for carving or cutting through plastics.

Inclusion: Material embedded in plastic that becomes a permanent part of the finished piece.

Flexible additive: Plasticizer added to resin to keep the casting flexible.

Laminating and coating resins: Epoxy or polyester resins made primarily for brush or spray applications or thin pours.

Latex: Water-soluble white liquid from rubber trees used for molds that will make a limited number of castings.

Melting pot: Controlled-temperature unit for melting waxes and vinyls and warming resins.

Metallic pigment: A powder additive that imparts an opaque metallic appearance to plastic.

Model: The original form from which a mold and then a cast is made.

Mold: A negative reproduction of a model; when it is filled with casting material, a positive reproduction results.

Mold-release agent: Material such as polyvinyl alcohol, silicone, or petroleum jelly applied to the surface of the mold or model so casting or molding materials do not stick; also called a parting agent.

Pearlescent pigment: An opaque additive that imparts a pearly sheen to plastics.

Plastic: Any flexible material or any of a group of compounds that can be formed or re-formed by heat, pressure, or chemical action.

Polymerization: Changing a liquid to a solid with the addition of a catalyst.

Pot life: The length of time a plastic, mixed with its catalyst, remains workable.

Pour: The layer of plastic created by a single pouring of liquid plastic; usually a number of pours are needed to complete a casting.

Promoter: Another name for the accelerator additive that speeds up hardening or curing.

Reinforcement materials: Mats, strands, and cloths made of material like glass fibers used to strengthen plastic.

Reproduction: A cast object that duplicates the model.

Shelf life: The length of time that unmixed plastic, kept in a sealed container, remains usable.

Solvent: Any material such as acetone used for dissolving plastics.

Stirring sticks: Wood sticks, like tongue depressors, used for stirring catalysts into plastic or as small ramps down which liquid plastic can be poured to minimize bubble formation.

Thermoplastic: Any plastic such as acrylic that can be heated and reshaped.

Thermosetting plastic: Any plastic such as polyester or epoxy that cannot be reshaped by reheating once it has been cured to the solid state.

Thickening and thinning agents: Additives that thicken or thin casting resins.

UV stabilizer: An additive that minimizes discoloration or deterioration of plastic from exposure to ultraviolet light.

Vacuum forming: Using a vacuum to draw thin sheet plastic into the contours of a mold.

Wood

Softwoods

Softwoods are used in general construction; hardwoods for furniture, cabinets, flooring, and those craft projects where durability and appearance are important. There are three classes of softwood lumber: yard lumber for appearance and light construction; structural lumber which is more than 2 inches in nominal thickness and width to take heavy working stresses, as in framing; and factory or shop lumber for commercial construction. Softwood yard lumber, used for most craft projects, comes in the quality grades and sizes listed at right.

Common softwoods	Common hardwoods
Cedar	Ash
Cypress	Beech
Fir	Birch
Juniper	Hickory
Hemlock	Holly
Pine	Maple
Redwood	Oak
Spruce	Walnut

Hardwoods

Hardwood lumber is sold in random widths and standard lengths, ranging in 1-foot increments from 4 to 16 feet. Standard thicknesses for rough-cut boards and dressed boards (surfaced on two sides and called S2S) are in inches as follows:

STANDARD THICKNESS

Rough	Surfaced (S2S)
3/8	3/16
1/2	5/16
5/8	7/16
3/4	9/16
1	15/16
1-1/4	1-1/16
1-1/2	1-5/16
1-3/4	1-1/2
2	1-3/4
2-1/2	2-1/4
3	2-3/4
3-1/2	3-1/4
4	3-3/4

SOFTWOOD QUALITY GRADES

Select (for good finishing qualities)	Description	Uses
1 and 2 Clear (or A and B)	Almost blemish free. A or 1 has fewer blemishes than B or 2.	Finest cabinet work. Can take natural finishes
C	Limited number of small blemishes finish will cover	Cabinets, good interior trim
D	More small knots, checks, and blemishes paint will cover	Painted interior trim and cabinets
Common (for general construction)		
1	Knots tight, sound, and not large or numerous. Rated watertight	Knotty paneling, exterior trim
2	Larger knots and coarser blemishes	Some knotty paneling, exterior trim
3	Still larger, coarser, more numerous knots, pitch, checking, and some knotholes	Shelving, some exterior siding
4	More big, loose knots, holes, pitch, and other coarse defects	Out-of-sight construction such as subflooring and sheathing
5	Large, numerous holes, splits and other major defects	Rarely used by craftsmen

SOFTWOOD LUMBER SIZES

Nominal size (inches)	Actual size (inches)*	Designation
1 by 2	3/4 by 1-1/2	Strips
1 by 3	3/4 by 2-1/2	
1 by 4	3/4 by 3-1/2	
1 by 5	3/4 by 4-1/2	
1 by 6	3/4 by 5-1/2	
1 by 8	3/4 by 7-1/4	Boards
1 by 10	3/4 by 9-1/4	
1 by 12	3/4 by 11-1/4	
2 by 2	1-1/2 by 1-1/2	Dimensioned lumber
2 by 3	1-1/2 by 2-1/2	
2 by 4	1-1/2 by 3-1/2	
2 by 6	1-1/2 by 5-1/2	
2 by 8	1-1/2 by 7-1/4	
2 by 10	1-1/2 by 9-1/4	Planks
2 by 12	1-1/2 by 11-1/4	
3 by 4	2-1/2 by 3-1/2	
3 by 6	2-1/2 by 5-1/2	
4 by 4	3-1/2 by 3-1/2	
4 by 6	3-1/2 by 5-1/2	
6 by 6	5-1/2 by 5-1/2	Timbers
8 by 8	7-1/4 by 7-1/4	

*Lumber smaller than 1-by-2-inch nominal size is sold as molding by exact measure. Rough lumber, when available, has somewhat larger dimensions but a rougher surface.

Lumber is sold by the board foot based on nominal sizes in inches. The formula for calculating board feet is:

$$\frac{length \times thickness \times width}{12} = board\ feet$$

HARDWOOD GRADES

Grades and Designation	Description and uses
Firsts and seconds*	Minor blemishes and stains but no splits or knots over most of board. Good for natural finishes.
Selects	Most of front surface free of knots or splits; most of back surface can have knots, stains or other small blemishes but must be free of rot. Can often be given natural finish.
No. 1 Common	Larger area of front and back may show blemishes but takes paint well.
No. 2 Common	Similar to No. 1 Common except flaws can extend over larger area of board.
Sound wormy	Equal to No. 1 Common except natural characteristics of worm holes, bird pecks, stain and knots not over 3/4 inch in diameter are permitted.
No. 3A Common	One third of better face must equal No. 2 Common in quality.
No. 3B Common	One quarter of board must be free of rot, lengthwise separations, soft core spots, bark or missing areas on edges, but knots and holes that do not affect strength allowed in this area. Not recommended for craft projects.

*Firsts and seconds are combined in one grade with an allowable percentage of firsts in the grade ranging from 20 to 40 percent, depending on the type of wood.

PLYWOOD APPEARANCE GRADES

Label designation	Description and uses
N-N, N-A, N-B INT	Almost blemish free. Use N-N or N-A where both sides show. For natural finish furniture, cabinet doors, built-ins. Special-order items.
N-D INT	For natural finish interior paneling. Special-order item.
A-A INT or EXT	Use where both sides show. INT-type for indoor built-ins, cabinets, furniture, partitions: EXT-type for fences, signs, other permanent outdoor structures. Smooth faces suitable for painting or natural finish if appearance is not critical.
A-B EXT	For outside use where appearance of one side is more important but both sides must be smooth and paintable.
A-C EXT	For outside use where appearance of only one side counts (sidings, soffits).
B-B EXT	Utility panel with solid faces that may have circular repair plugs and tight knots not over 1 inch across the grain, plus some minor splits. For exterior use.
B-C EXT	Utility panel for outdoor use in work sheds, farm buildings, and as a base for exterior walls, roofs.
HDO EXT	Has abrasion-resistant, high-density resin fiber overlay. For concrete forms, cabinets, countertops, signs.
MDO EXT	Has smooth, opaque medium-density resin fiber overlay on one or both faces as a base for paint on outdoor structures.
303 SIDING EXT	Panels for exterior siding, fencing, etc., that have special surface treatment such as V or channel grooves, striations, or brushed on rough-sawn surfaces.
T 1-11	303 panel with 1/4-inch-deep 3/8-inch-wide grooves spaced 4 or 8 inches on center, and shiplapped edges. Available unsanded, textured and with medium-density resin finish.
PLYRON EXT	Tempered hardboard (composition or particle board) faces on both sides; available with smooth or screened surface.
MARINE EXT	Made of Douglas fir or western larch. For boat hulls with special solid-jointed core construction.

Dimensions of hardwood lumber 1 inch or thicker may be given in quarter inches as 4/4 (1 inch), 5/4 (1¼ inches), 6/4 (1½ inches) and so on. In calculating board feet, all hardwood lumber less than 1 inch thick is counted as 1 inch thick, and all surfaced boards are counted as equivalent to rough sizes before surfacing.

Plywood

Plywood comes in panels of thin veneer glued to the face and back of inner wood plies. It is graded according to the type and quality of the veneer facings, and the panel's suitability for indoor or outdoor use. Two major classes of veneer facings are **Construction and Industrial** with softwood facings, and **Hardwood and Decorative,** usually with hardwood facings. Each class has its own grading system. Plywood panels commonly come in 4-foot widths and 7-, 8-, 10- and 12-foot lengths, with thicknesses ranging from ⅛ to ¾ inches. Other sizes may be special-ordered.

Construction and Industrial Plywood carries an APA label (for American Plywood Association). Veneer facings available include Douglas fir, cedar, cypress, hemlock, spruce, pine, and other domestic softwoods, as well as such imported woods as apitong, keruing, and red meranti. This plywood is available in the appearance grades shown at left and will be stamped with a label similar to one of those shown below.

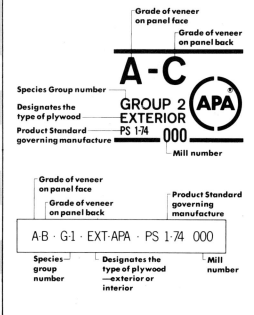

Nails

Diameters of common, casing, and finishing nails generally increase with nail length. Flat-head nails are measured from under the head to the tip of the point; oval or round head nails from larger diameter of head to tip; flat countersunk or cement-coated nails from top of head to tip.

Wood Screws

Screws are used to give maximum strength or to permit the work to be disassembled later. Wood screws are made of steel (for strength) or brass or aluminum alloy (for lighter work) with plain, plated, galvanized, or black finishes.

COMMON TYPES OF WOOD SCREWS

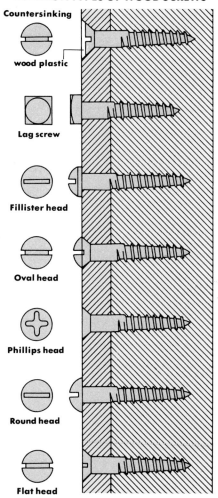

Countersinking
wood plastic
Lag screw
Fillister head
Oval head
Phillips head
Round head
Flat head

NAILS MOST USED

Name	Uses and sizes
Common	For general carpentry where wide, flat heads need not be hidden.
Box	Thin nails for rough construction where common nails might split the wood.
Casing	For fine carpentry where heads can be countersunk and concealed.
Finishing	Thin nails for fine carpentry where small, rounded heads can be countersunk and concealed.

For rustproof applications galvanized or copper nails are used (or brass or bronze if copper is too soft). Aluminum or alloy nails are used to fasten aluminum sheet. Brads are small, thin nails with heads shaped like those of finishing nails. They are available in 3/8- to 6-inch lengths.

NAIL SIZES AND WEIGHTS

Penny(d) size	Length (inches)	Approximate number per pound		
		Common	Casing	Finishing
2d	1	847	1090	1473
3d	1-1/4	543	654	880
4d	1-1/2	294	489	630
5d	1-3/4	254	414	535
6d	2	167	244	288
7d	2-1/4	150	215	254
8d	2-1/2	101	147	190
9d	2-3/4	92	133	178
10d	3	66	96	124
12d	3-1/4	61	88	113
16d	3-1/2	47	74	93
20d	4	30		65
30d	4-1/2	23		
40d	5	17		
50d	5-3/8	14		

WOOD SCREW DIMENSIONS

Screw No.	Range of available lengths	Shank (body) diameter	Pilot or thread hole drill diameter		Shank hole diameter	
			Softwood	Hardwood	Softwood	Hardwood
0	1/4	1/16	not needed	1/32	not needed	not needed
1	1/4	5/64	not needed	3/64	not needed	not needed
2	1/4–1/2	3/32	not needed	1/16	not needed	3/32
3	1/4–5/8	7/64	not needed	1/16	not needed	7/64
4	3/8–3/4	1/8	not needed	5/64	not needed	1/8
5	3/8–3/4	1/8	not needed	5/64	not needed	1/8
6	3/8–1-1/2	9/64	1/16	5/64	not needed	5/32
7	3/8–1-1/2	5/32	1/16	3/32	3/32	5/32
8	1/2–2	11/64	5/64	3/32	3/32	3/16
9	5/8–2-1/4	3/16	3/32	7/64	5/32	3/16
10	5/8–2-1/4	3/16	3/32	7/64	5/32	3/16
12	7/8–2-1/2	7/32	7/64	1/8	5/32	7/32
14	1–2-3/4	1/4	7/64	9/64	7/32	1/4
16	1-1/4–3	9/32	9/64	5/32	7/32	9/32
18	1-1/2–4	5/16	9/64	3/16	7/32	5/16
20	1-3/4–4	21/64	11/64	13/64	7/32	21/64
24	3-1/2–4	3/8	3/16	7/32	1/4	3/8

Patterns

More than 100 patterns that can be used in executing a great variety of crafts projects appear in this section. The motifs include abstractions, animal designs, costumes, family scenes, floral designs, music, mythology, nature scenes, sports, and transportation. The instructions that preceed the patterns will enable you to enlarge any pattern to any size desired.

Enlarging designs with grids

Enlarging designs with grids

The design patterns in this volume are printed on a grid, but unlike the patterns in other volumes of **The Family Creative Workshop**, which represent specific projects, these are not accompanied by directions for enlargement to a particular size. Following the steps given below, however, which utilize the pattern (Figure A) as an example, you can enlarge all the patterns in this volume to any size you require for any given project. Using the same principles, you can also adapt any pattern elsewhere in the series to the size you want for other projects.

Figure B: Determine the size you want the design to be. On a plain piece of paper, draw a rectangle large enough to contain the full-sized design. Here the pattern is being enlarged to 7 by 9 inches. Count the number of grid squares across the widest part of the reduced pattern. Measure and mark with dots the same number of squares across the top and bottom width of the rectangle you have drawn. (To determine how far apart you should space the dots, divide the width of the enlarged rectangle by the number of squares needed. The resulting figure is the space to allow between dots.) The example pattern is 7 squares across its widest point; to enlarge it to 7 inches wide, you would mark 6 dots on the rectangle's top and bottom—the first, 1 inch from the side of the rectangle and each of the others, 1 inch from the last. Join the dots with straight parallel lines, as shown.

Figure C: Using the same measure (in this case 1 inch), mark dots along the left and right sides of the rectangle. Join the dots with straight parallel lines. You now have an enlarged grid containing the same number of squares as the original grid.

Figure D: To enlarge the design, copy the pattern lines, one square at a time, from the smaller grid to the larger grid. It helps to use a ruler to reproduce straight lines, and a compass or a French curve to reproduce curved lines.

Figure E: When you have copied all the lines, the enlarged pattern will be reproduced with the same proportions as the original, and ready for use.

A

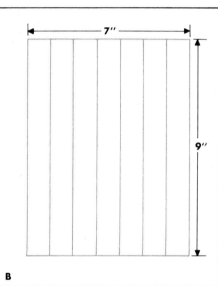

B

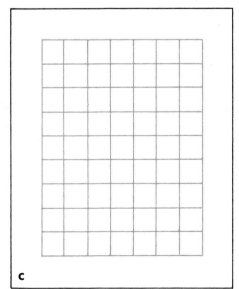

C

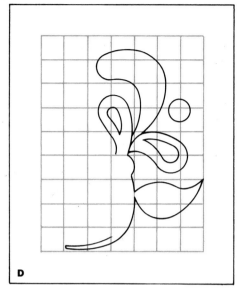

D

E

Enlarging designs without grids

You can also enlarge designs that are not printed on grids. For example, you might want to embroider a pillow design using a motif from your wallpaper; or you might need to enlarge a small original sketch that you like. To do this, simply trace the design on tracing paper, and draw your own grid over it. Depending upon the complexity of the design, your grid might range in size from 1/8- to 1-inch squares. (The more complex the design, the smaller the grid.) You can achieve the same results by purchasing transparent graph paper and tracing the design onto that. In either case, follow the procedure described at far left for enlarging the design.

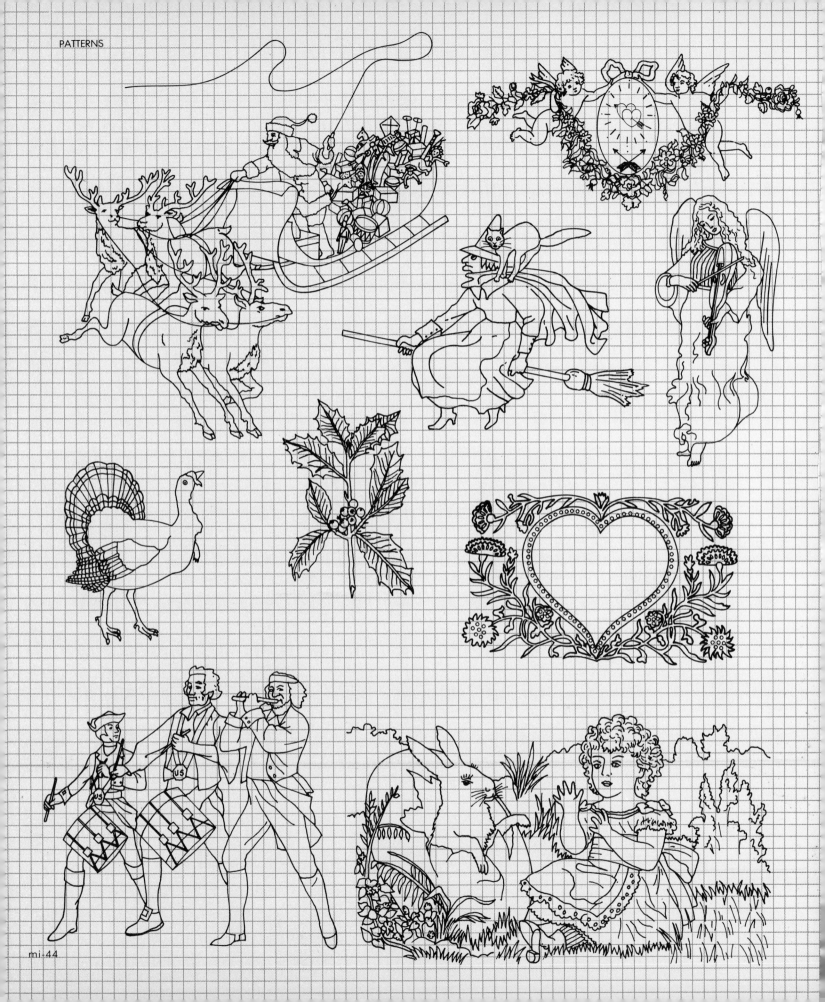

mi-47

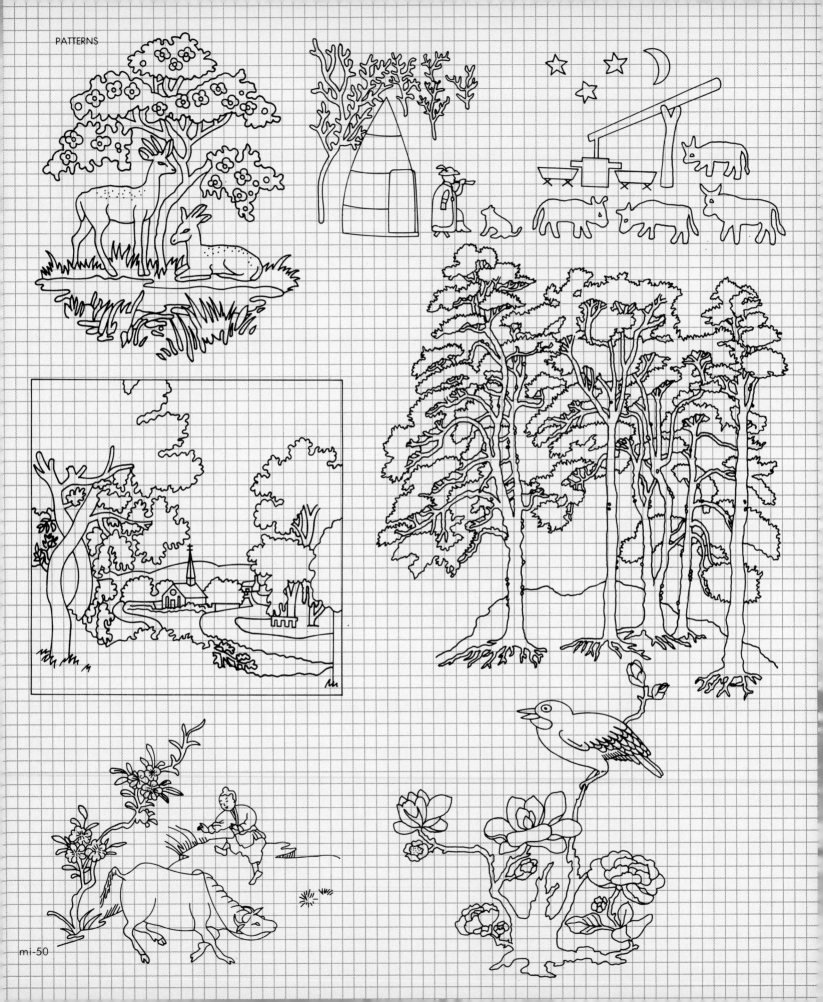

mi-53

Mythology

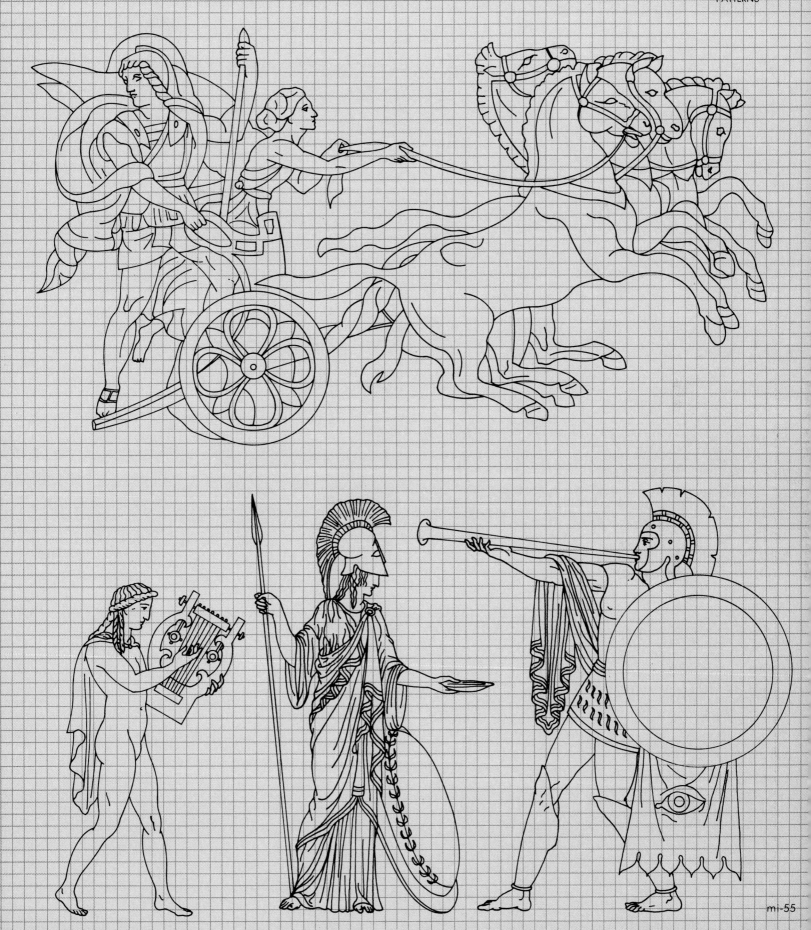

mi-55

Costumes

mi-57

Workers

Music and dance

mi-63

mi-67

Transportation

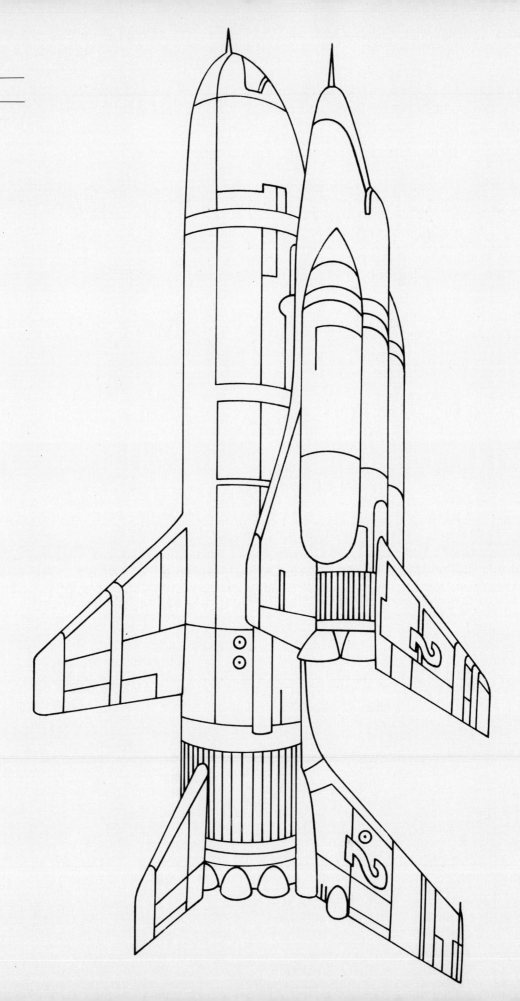

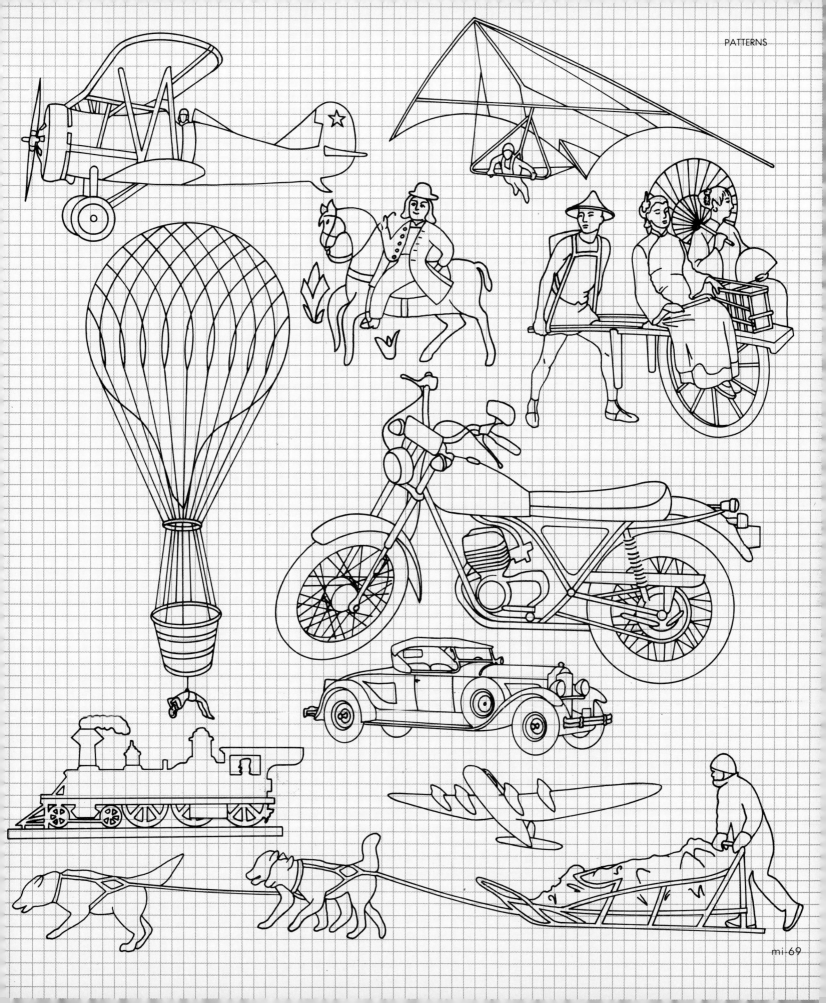

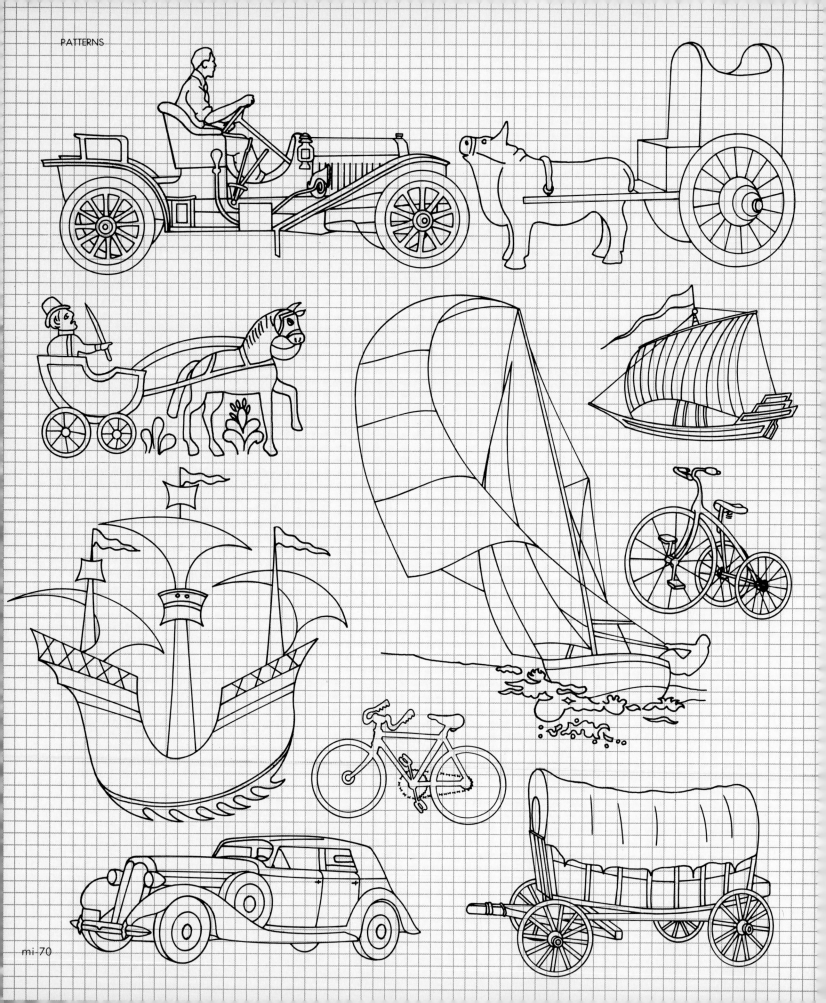

mi-71

Master index and project-evaluation lists

The master index for **The Family Creative Workshop** and three special project-evaluation lists appear in the section that follows. The lists are designed to help you find a project in a desired craft that meets your requirements in terms of three factors: cost, time, and the level of skill required. How to use the master index is explained at the beginning of that index.

Master index

This master index is designed to help you locate—at a glance—**The Family Creative Workshop** projects that interest you the most. Boldface type highlights general craft categories (such as **Needlecrafts**) or groups of individual projects that are related to one another (such as **folk art**). Both are listed alphabetically, but craft-category headings are capitalized, while related-project headings are not. The individual projects are listed alphabetically under both kinds of headings. In the page citation, page numbers are set in lightface type, while the volume number preceding the relevant page numbers is set in medium-bold type.

A

acrylics, **1**: 10-23
    automobile decoration, **1**: 21-23
    conics in box, **18**: 2271, 2280-81
    cubes, kaleidoscopic, **8**: 960-61
    kaleidoscope, Hue View, **8**: 962-63
    paperweight, shell, **2**: 141
    poured acrylics, **1**: 15-20
    room divider, **1**: 11-14
    serving tray, **14**: 1772
    teleidoscope, **8**: 963-65
    See also **casting; mineralogy; mobiles; molding methods; sculpture; stained glass; supergraphics**
afghan stitch, **1**: 24-29
    afghan, popcorn and leaf, **1**: 29
    basic stitch, **1**: 31
    pillow, tic-tac-toe, **1**: 28
    skirt, child's, **1**: 24-28
    vest, **1**: 24-28
    See also **appliqué; crochet; granny squares; knitting to fit; patchwork; quilts and quilting; traditional knitting motifs**
African rope mask, **10**: 1192-95
airplanes
    paper airplanes, **1**: 32-41
        Barnaby, **1**: 35
        Dartmouth Dart, **1**: 33-34
        Falcon, **1**: 38-39
        Flying Tiger, **1**: 36-37
        Pegasus, **1**: 40-41
    soft sculpture airplane, **17**: 2107-9
    See also **kites and kite making; origami**
alabaster sculpture, **16**: 1935-37
alligators
    pod and cone, **13**: 1585, 1589
    stuffed doll, **1**: 62-63
American Indian crafts, **1**: 42-53
    basket, coil, **1**: 115

belt, cowboy, **2**: 168, 170-71
breechcloth, **2**: 151
chain, beaded daisy, **1**: 45
costumes, paper, **5**: 528-29
doll, pieces, **5**: 608
loom beading, **1**: 47
makeup, face, **17**: 2070-71
medallion, **1**: 46
moccasins, Apache, **1**: 49-53
ring, beaded, **1**: 44
sand painting and layering, **15**: 1889-91
tepees, **16**: 2020-23
totem-mask wall plaque, **20**: 2541-42
totem poles
    full-sized, **20**: 2546-47
    miniature, **20**: 2543
See also **basketry; beadwork; belts and buckles; canoeing; carryalls; clambakes; Colonial crafts; flowers, artificial; jewelry; leathercrafts, leather working; mineralogy; mittens and mukluks; pottery; repoussé and chased metal; sandal making; shelters and tents; silversmithing; supergraphics; totem poles; vegetable dyes; woven tapestries**
Anagrams, **19**: 2373-74
anemometer, weather forecasting, **22**: 2741-42
animals, live. See **ant farms; beachcombing; birds and birdhouses; insects; pet habitats; preschool activities; tropical fish; vivariums**
animals, representations of
    doll animals, stuffed, **1**: 54-63
        alligator, **1**: 62-63
        elephant, **1**: 56-59
        lion, **1**: 60-62
    painted stone animals, **18**: 2256-57
    soft sculpture animals, **17**: 2120-21
    utility pole animals, **23**: 2904-5
    See also **dollhouses and furniture; dolls and doll clothes; marionettes; papier-mâché; pod and cone art; puppets and puppetry; rag dolls; sewing without pattern; tying flies;** names of animals
announcement cards, birth, **7**: 845
    fraktur traufscheine, **6**: 708
ant farms, **1**: 64-69
    ant farm, **1**: 66-69
    Mason-jar ant house, **1**: 65-66
antiquing furniture, **1**: 70-81
    distressing, **1**: 74-77
    gilding, **1**: 81
    glazes, **1**: 70-73, 78
    hardware, **1**: 80
    marbleizing, **1**: 79
    spattering, striping, wiping, **1**: 78
    See also **boxes; caning and rushing; decoupage; folk art; frames and framing; gold leafing; marquetry;**

refinishing furniture; rosemaling; stenciling; tables; upholstery
appliqué, **1**: 82-91
    doll, cloth, **5**: 612-13
    flower, embroidered, **6**: 652
    by hand, **1**: 82-85
    by machine, **1**: 87-89
    pillows
        people, **1**: 90
        suede, **9**: 1070-71
    quilts
        Dresden-plate, **14**: 1702-5
        rainbow-cloud, **14**: 1707-9
    tablecloth, **1**: 91
    T-shirt, **14**: 1772-73
        lion, **21**: 2587-88
    vest and skirt, quilted, **14**: 1706-7
    wall hanging, **9**: 1109-11
    See also **afghan stitch; crewel; dolls and doll clothes; embroidery; Florentine stitch; granny squares; machine stitchery; needlepoint; patchwork; quilting; reverse appliqué; ribboncraft; samplers; sewing without pattern; tambour; trapunto**
apron-shawl, bias-cut, **16**: 1974-76
aquariums, **21**: 2626-39
    assembly, **21**: 2628-34
    filters, **21**: 2629-30
    freshwater fish, **21**: 2634-37
    heaters, **21**: 2629-30
    maintenance, **21**: 2635
    oxygen supply, **21**: 2629-30
    plants, aquatic, **21**: 2632-33
    marine, **21**: 2638-39
        seawater, synthetic, **21**: 2639
    tank construction, **2**: 138
    water pH, **21**: 2631
armatures. See **papier-mâché; topiary**
assemblages. See **boxes; collages and assemblages; stone painting; wood assemblages**
association football, **18**: 2265
astringent, homemade, **5**: 523
astronomy, **1**: 92-105
    constellations, locating, **1**: 94-100
    planets, locating, **1**: 98-99
    sky charts, **1**: 94-95
    stars, locating, **1**: 94-100
    telescope, **1**: 101-5
    time telling
        noon light show, **20**: 2490-93
        star dial, **20**: 2497-99
    zodiac, locating, **1**: 100
    See also **maps and pathfinding; photographic printing; sundials; time telling**
automobiles
    antique automobiles
        decorating, pin stripe, **13**: 1542, 1551
        restoring, pin stripe, **13**: 1542, 1551
    customized automobiles
        painting, **1**: 21-23
        pin striping, **13**: 1548-50
    soapbox and skate vehicles, **17**: 2086-97
    toy, spool racing, **17**: 2157

B

baby foods, 1: 106-11
   breakfast cookies, 1: 110-11
   preparing baby foods, 1: 107-9
   **See also ice cream, sherbet, and ices;
     marmalades and preserves;
     pickled and canned foods; seed
     sprouting; syrups**
back pack, canvas, 4: 395
   stenciling on, 18: 2247
bags
   clutch purse, beaded, 5: 553
   decoration for, Florentine stitch,
     6: 681-82
   duffle bag, leather, 4: 399
   evening bag, ribbon, 14: 1771
   handbags
     Swedish huck work, 19: 2341-42
     trapunto batik, 21: 2586
   handle, bag, inkle-woven, 8: 932
   purse, pine-straw, 14: 1723
   rag doll bag, 14: 1730-31
   shoulder bags
     granny squares, 7: 814-15
     knit, traditional motif, 21: 2570
     quilted, 14: 1694-96
     raffia, 14: 1718
     tablet-woven, 19: 2399-2401
   tote bags
     granny squares, 7: 814-15
     leather, 4: 396-99
     patchwork, 12: 1451-52
   reverse appliqué, 14: 1759-60
   sprang, 17: 2167
   trapunto, 9: 1113-14
   vinyl, 4: 392-94
   weft-faced, 22: 2770-71
baking
   breads, 3: 280-89
   bread sculptures, 3: 290-91
   cakes, birthday, 2: 202-5
   for children, 2: 206-7
   gingerbread, 6: 762-68
balance toys, spool, 17: 2160-61
balsa wood mobile, 10: 1224-25
bands, inkle-woven
   for hat, with matching bag handle,
     8: 932
   watchband, 8: 933
banners, felt
   club, 6: 670-71
   decorative, as wall hanging, 6: 668,
     674-75
banquette, plywood and foam, 13: 1579-83
barometer, bottle, 22: 2742-43
baseball, running bases game, 18: 2264
basketry, 1: 112-19
   hanging basket, 1: 116-17
   Indian coil basket, 1: 115
   pencil holder, 1: 114
   shopping basket, 1: 118-19
   sisal basket, 23: 2884-86
   wire basket, 23: 2832-33
   See also American Indian crafts;

**bottle cutting; caning and rush-
   ing; carryalls; raffia and straw;
   vegetable dyes; wire sculpture;
   wrapped and coiled work**
bath oils, 17: 2103
batik, 1: 120-28
   floor pillow, 1: 128
   handbag, trapunto, 21: 2586
   table mat, 1: 127
   wall hangings, 1: 126
   **See also egg decoration; flags and
     banners; stenciling; tie dyeing;
     vegetable dyes; woven tapestries**
beachcombing, 2: 134-43
   aquarium tank, 2: 138
   beach glass mosaic, 2: 139
   driftwood constructions, 2: 142-43
   lobster-man and shell paperweight, 2:
     140-41
   mosaic light sculpture, 10: 1274-75
   **See also ant farms; bonsai; bottle
     cutting; canoeing; clambakes;
     gold panning; insects; lamps and
     lampshades; mosaics; sand
     characters and castles; seashells;
     stone painting; tropical fish; tying
     flies**
beads
   glass beads, 7: 786
   kitchen clay beads, 13: 1629
   lead glass beads, 7: 776-77
   seashells and, jewelry, 16: 1945
beadwork, 2: 144-57
   bag, beaded, 5: 553
   belt, beaded, 2: 172-73
   breechcloth, 2: 151
   chain, beaded daisy, 1: 45
   earrings, pearl, 2: 156-57
   fruit, beaded, 2: 152-53
   loom beading, 1: 47
   making beads, 2: 145-47
   medallion, 1: 46
   necklace, safety-pin, 2: 154
   ring, bead, 2: 154-55
   ring, beaded, 1: 44
   stringing beads, 2: 148-50
   **See also American Indian crafts;
     Colonial crafts; embroidery;
     flowers, artificial; jewelry**
bean-bags, 2: 158-67
   furniture, bean-bag, 2: 164-66
   games, bean-bag, 2: 162-63
   paperweights, felt, 2: 161
   toy, toss, 2: 160
   wall hanging, bean-bag, 2: 167
   **See also birthday celebrations;
     sewing without pattern; soft
     sculpture; spool toys; table games;
     yard toys; yo-yos**
beaters, metal, music making, 11: 1287,
   1292
bedroom, model for redecorating, 10:
   1235-40

beds
   loft beds, 18: 2284, 2288-93
   sculptural foam bed, queen-size, 13:
     1572
bedspreads. See quilts and quilting
beef with broccoli, 23: 2839-41
beer, ginger, brewing, 3: 298-301
belts and buckles, 2: 168-77
   adjustable, macramé, 9: 1120-21
   beaded, 2: 172-73
   buckle assembly techniques, 2: 176-77
   cowboy, 2: 168, 170-71
   elastic, 2: 174-75
   forged, 23: 2828-29
   leather, magic braided, 9: 1072-73
   pick-up pattern, inkle-woven, 8: 935
   raffia, crocheted, 14: 1716
   signature, needlepoint, 11: 1324
   sprang, 17: 2168
   tablet-woven, 19: 2398
   tin buckle, cast, 4: 430-33
   **See also American Indian crafts;
     casting; Leathercrafts, leather
     working; sandal making;
     silversmithing**
benches
   banquette, plywood and foam, 13:
     1597-83
   cushioned, 21: 2654-57
   modular, 19: 2384-87
   platform, 13: 1576-78
   toy-chest, 3: 262-269
   utility, Shaker, 16: 2006-8
   See also upholstery
beverage cases
   curio cabinet from, 3: 266
   milk-crate desk and seat, 3: 262-65
**beverages. See brewing; syrups; tea;
   wine making**
bicycles and bicycling, 2: 178-89
   choosing bicycle, 2: 181-82
   clubs, bicycle, 2: 188-89
   flats, fixing, 2: 185
   maintenance, 2: 183-84
   repairs, 2: 183-84
   safety rules, 2: 187-88
   tires, 2: 185
   touring, 2: 186-87
   types, bicycle, 2: 181-82
   **See also canoeing; gold panning;
     kayaks; maps and pathfinding;
     shelters and tents; soapbox and
     skate vehicles**
birds and birdhouses, 2: 190-99
   birdbath, concrete, 2: 198-99
   birdcage, five-story, 12: 1472-75
   bluebird house, 2: 192
   feeder, bird, 2: 194-95
   feeding stations, bird, 14: 1790
   purple martin house, 2: 196-97
   wren house, 2: 193
   **See also ant farms; pet habitats;
     sundials; tropical fish; vivariums**
birth announcement card, 7: 845
birthday celebrations, 2: 200-9
   baking for children, 2: 206-7

birthday celebrations, continued
cakes, **2:** 202-5
party games, **2:** 208-9
samurai hat, **11:** 1381
sugar place card, **18:** 2304
See also **bean-bags; bread sculpture; card tricks; Christmas celebrations; confections and comfits; flags and banners; greeting cards; ice cream, sherbet, and ices; magic; marionettes; piñatas; puppets and puppetry; square dancing; street games; sugar shapes; table games; yard toys; yo-yos**
black work embroidery
owl, **6:** 656-57
tissue covers, **6:** 654-55
blender, baby foods preparation, **1:** 108-9
blocking. See **Needlecrafts**
block printing, 2: 210-19
eraser prints, **2:** 214-15
linoleum prints, **2:** 216-19
on scarf, **9:** 1096-98
vegetable prints, **2:** 210-13
See also **carving; folk art; greeting cards; heraldry; linoleum and woodcuts; lithography; monoprinting; papermaking; serigraphy; silhouettes; tie dyeing**
blueprints, reading, **7:** 823
boats and boating
child's rocking boat, **14:** 1777-78
helm, pin stripe decoration for, **13:** 1547
pennant for, nylon, **6:** 672-73
sailboat piñata, **12:** 1535
toy stern-wheel boat, **20:** 2554-55
See also **canoeing; kayaks; piloting small boats; sail making and repair; ship models**
boards
bread board, rosemaling, **15:** 1805-7
busy board, skill improvement, **13:** 1625-27
chessboard, marquetry, **10:** 1179
chopping board, treen, **21:** 2609
bobbin lace
collar, **8:** 1019-21
cuffs, **8:** 1019-21
sash, **8:** 1017-18
body painting, 17: 2066, 2074-75
bones, engraving on, **15:** 1917-20
bonsai, 2: 220-29
cascade bonsai, **2:** 227
driftwood bonsai, **2:** 223-25
miniature bonsai, **2:** 229
rock-grown bonsai, **2:** 228
tropical bonsai, **2:** 226
See also **beachcombing; bottle gardens; dioramas; greenhouse construction; ikebana; terrariums; topiary; trellises**
bookbinding, 2: 230-43
denim bookcover, **2:** 233-35

leather-bound diary, **2:** 236-42
See also **gold leafing; papermaking**
bookcovers
block-printed, **2:** 210-13
denim, **2:** 233-35
book ends, mineral, **10:** 1207
bookmarks
card as, ribbon, **7:** 837
hardanger embroidered, **7:** 858
bookshelves
garden on, lighted indoor, **9:** 1086
plastic pipe, **13:** 1567-69
bottle cutting, 2: 244-51
basic cutting, **2:** 244-48
decorating bottles, **2:** 249-51
See also **basketry; beachcombing; lamps and lampshades; mosaics; terrariums**
bottle gardens, 2: 252-56
lab-bottle garden, **2:** 256
water-cooler bottle garden, **2:** 252-56
See also **bonsai; greenhouse construction; lighted indoor gardens; terrariums; vivariums**
bottles
lampblown glass, **7:** 774, 780-85
lamp from, potichomania, **9:** 1036-37
papier-mâché people on, **11:** 1401, 1403-4
ship model in, **16:** 2038-41
swizzle sticks from fragments of, **7:** 778-79
wheel-thrown pottery, **13:** 1620
yarn painting, bottle, **23:** 2917
bottling, wine, **22:** 2802
bouquet, dried-spice, **5:** 622-23
bowls
clay, **4:** 440
coiled, **4:** 441-43
copper, **17:** 2063-65
pewter, handwrought, **12:** 1480-83
stoneware, **13:** 1610-11
tin, **20:** 2508-9
treen, **21:** 2612-13
wheel-thrown, **18:** 2267
boxball, 18: 2267
boxes, 3: 262-71
assemblage, cigar box, **4:** 484-85
candle boxes
dovetailed Shaker, **16:** 2009-11
leaded glass, **9:** 1057, 1064-65
conics in, **18:** 2271, 2280-81
curio cabinet, beverage-case, **3:** 266
decorating boxes
cigar boxes, **3:** 270-71
marquetry, **10:** 1179
split-straw mosaics, **14:** 1712-13
stamp decoupage, **18:** 2237-39
desk and seat, milk-crate, **3:** 262-65
drawer organizer, kitchen-matchbox, **3:** 267
jewelry box, rosemaled, **15:** 1810-13
kaleidoscopic cubes, **8:** 960-61
mantel box, decoupage, **5:** 573
pewter, fabricated, **12:** 1484-87

plant box, leaded glass, **9:** 1057, 1064-65
restoring old boxes, **23:** 2898-99
shadow boxes
gilt-edged, **7:** 790-91
pod and cone art in, **13:** 1592
stoneware, **13:** 1609-10
Telemark, rosemaling, **15:** 1810-13
tin, antique stenciled, **20:** 2523-27
tops, ornamenting, **14:** 1746-48
toy-chest bench, **3:** 262, 269
valentine gift, **21:** 2674-75
wall sculpture, **3:** 268
box-illusion wall plaque, **23:** 2846-49
yard box toys, **23:** 2902-3
See also **antiquing furniture; cardboard; collages and assemblages; decoupage; dioramas; refinishing furniture; stamp decoupage; supergraphics**
bracelets
forged, **23:** 2828-29
fork, **8:** 955
hardware, **8:** 954
leather, painted, **9:** 1069-70
wrapped wire, **8:** 957
Braiding. See **Weaving, Braiding, and Knotting**
branch weaving, 19: 2402
brass
antiquing hardware, **1:** 80
rubbings, **15:** 1818-19
bread board, rosemaling, **15:** 1805-7
breads, 3: 280-89
sourdough bread, **3:** 284-89
trail breads, **3:** 282-83
See also **bread sculpture; cheeses and churning; Colonial crafts; gingerbread; marmalades and preserves; seed sprouting; soups**
bread sculpture, 3: 290-91
baker's clay, **3:** 291
bird, **3:** 291
dough recipe, **3:** 291
half-moon, **3:** 291
mirror, **3:** 291
sun and star, **3:** 291
See also **breads; gingerbread**
bread tray, raffia, **23:** 2886-87
breakfast, baby cookies for, **1:** 110-11
breechcloth, beaded, **2:** 151
brewing, 3: 292-301
ginger beer, **3:** 298-301
root beer and sarsaparilla, **3:** 294-97
See also **cheeses and churning; wine making**
briefcase, leather envelope, **9:** 1077-79
brittles, 4: 510-11
bronze tray, freehand painted, **20:** 2520-22
buckles. See **belts and buckles**
bull roarer, 20: 2550
buoys, 12: 1516
markings, **12:** 1514
burlap, Senufo wall hanging, **6:** 714-15
busy board, 13: 1625-27
butter, churning, **4:** 453

butterflies, collecting, **8:** 936, 938, 941, 943-44, 947
butter knife, silver, **17:** 2056-57
buttons, 3: 302-11
    cuff links, button, **3:** 305
    clay buttons, **3:** 308-9
    hand-painted buttons, **3:** 310-11
    mosaics, **10:** 1270-71
    seashell buttons, **3:** 306-7
    See also **casting; ceramics; embroidery; jewelry; seashells; sewing without pattern**

C

cabbage, spicy, **23:** 2839
cabinets
    kitchen cabinet, marquetry, **10:** 1179
    wooden cabinet, decoupage, **5:** 577
cable-spool, yard toys from, **23:** 2906-7
cabochons, gemstone, **9:** 1048-51
cactus terrarium, 20: 2460-61
caftans
    block-dyed, **20:** 2489
    costume, **5:** 534
    sewn without pattern, **16:** 1977 1978-80
cakes, birthday, **2:** 202-5
calligraphy, 3: 312-21
    chancery cursive, **3:** 316-18
    illumination, hand, **3:** 312, 319-21
    quill pen, making, **14:** 1686-89
    See also **cartooning; folk art; gold leafing; greeting cards; papermaking; quill pens; serigraphy; watercolors**
cameras, 3: 322-29
    camera obscura, **3:** 322-26
        cartooning, **4:** 413
    pinhole camera, **3:** 327-29
    See also **photographic printing**
camping
    bicycle touring and, **2:** 186-87
    breads, trail, **3:** 280-83
    canoeing and, **3:** 363
    shelters and tents, **16:** 2012-23
candies
    hard, **4:** 509
    quick, **4:** 508
candle boxes
    dovetailed, Shaker, **16:** 2009-11
    leaded glass, **9:** 1064-65
candle clock, 20: 2494-95
candle holders
    papier-mâché, **11:** 1401
    pod and cone, **13:** 1590-91
candlemaking, 3: 330-41
    confectionary candles, **3:** 336-37
    dried-flower candles, **3:** 341
    hand-dipped candles, **3:** 330-33
    honeycomb candles, **3:** 334-35
    molded candles, **3:** 338-40
    pop-art candle, **10:** 1253-55
    sand-casted candle, **15:** 1875-77
    See also **casting; carving;**
        decoupage; dried flowers; molding methods; sand casting; sculpture; stenciling; time telling
candle sconce and snuffer, 20: 2504-7
cane, spiral-design, **22:** 2718-19
caning and rushing, 3: 342-53
    chair, recaning, **3:** 348-50
    chair seats
        rush, **3:** 351-53
        splint, **3:** 344-47
    See also **antiquing furniture; basketry; macramé; refinishing furniture; upholstery**
canister, tin painted, **20:** 2518-19
canning
    fruit recipes, **12:** 1511
    tomato recipes, **12:** 1507-8
    vegetable recipes, **12:** 1509-10
    vinegars, **22:** 2701
    See also **marmalades and preserves**
canoeing, 3: 354-65
    aluminum canoe repair, **3:** 365
    camping, canoe, **3:** 363
    capsizing, **3:** 356
    fiberglass canoe repair, **3:** 364
    paddle, selecting, **3:** 358
    paddling, **3:** 357-59
    parts, canoe, **3:** 357
    portaging, **3:** 359-61
    repairing canoes, **3:** 364-65
    white water canoeing
        canoeing, **3:** 361-63
        paddling, **3:** 362-63
    See also **American Indian crafts; beachcombing; bicycles and bicycling; carryalls; clambakes; kayaks; maps and pathfinding; piloting small boats; sail making and repair; shelters and tents; soapbox and skate vehicles; weather forecasting**
caps
    scarf and cap set, granny squares, **7:** 812
    tassel cap, knit to fit, **8:** 1006-7
    visor, crocheted raffia, **14:** 1718-19
cape, hooded, **16:** 1980-81
cardboard, 3: 366-75
    cabaña, cat, **12:** 1468-69
    doll piñata, **12:** 1534
    furniture, cardboard, **3:** 372-74
    headboard, **3:** 367, 375
    sailboat piñata, **12:** 1535-36
    snail mobile, **10:** 1223
    train, toy, **3:** 366, 368
    weathervane, whirligig, **3:** 369-71
    wishing-well piñata, **12:** 1530-34
    See also **boxes; collages and assemblages; models and mock-ups; puppets and puppetry; wycinanki**
cards. See **greeting cards;** names of printing methods
card tricks, 3: 376-84

    burglar's meeting, **3:** 381
    conjuring card, **3:** 382-83
    easy-up trick, **3:** 382
    fans, card, **3:** 384
    flourish, card, **3:** 384
    glossary of terms, **3:** 378
    locator card, using, **3:** 381
    magic pencil trick, **3:** 381
    mathematical tricks, **3:** 378-81
    mind reading, **3:** 378-79
    mini mind reading, **3:** 380
    prearranged deck, **3:** 382
    self-working tricks, **3:** 380-81
    sleight-of-hand, **3:** 382-83
    See also **birthday celebrations; magic; table games**
carnival festivals, 12: 1419-20
carrick bend chain, 14: 1788
carryalls, 4: 390-401
    back pack, canvas, **4:** 395
    rag doll bag, **14:** 1730-31
    tote bags
        leather, **4:** 396-99
        patchwork, **12:** 1451-52
        pet, two-in-one, **12:** 1470-72
        reverse appliqué, **14:** 1759-60
        sprang, **17:** 2167
        vinyl, **4:** 392-94
        weft-faced, **22:** 2770-71
    See also **American Indian crafts; basketry; canoeing; hammocks and slings; Leathercrafts, leather working**
cart, crate, **17:** 2089-90
cartooning, 4: 402-13
    comic strips, **4:** 410-11
    figures and hands, **4:** 406-7
    heads, faces, expressions, **4:** 404-5
    self-starter cartoons, **4:** 412-13
    single-panel cartoons, **4:** 408-9
    See also **calligraphy; cameras; greeting cards; photographic printing; sand characters and castles; silhouettes; stone painting; valentines; zoetrope toys**
carving, 4: 417-21
    soap fish, carved, **4:** 415-16
    vegetables and fruits, carving, **4:** 418-21
    wax reliefs, carving, **4:** 417
    See also **block printing; candlemaking; dioramas; foam forms; masks; pipe making; puppets and puppetry; scrimshaw; sculpture; soapbox and skate vehicles; totem poles; walking sticks; whistles and flutes; winter sculpture**
Carving and Molding
    candlemaking, 3: 330-41
        confectionary candles, **3:** 336-37
        dried-flower candles, **3:** 341
        hand-dipped candles, **3:** 330-33
        honeycomb candles, **3:** 334-35
        molded candles, **3:** 338-40
    casting, 4: 422-33
        buckle, tin belt, **4:** 430-33

casting, continued
head, plaster-cast, **4**: 424-29
dioramas, 5: 583-91
portable diorama, **5**: 583-91
foam forms, 6: 704-7
fish impression, **6**: 706-7
giraffe, synthetic stone, **6**: 704-5
folk art, 6: 716-17
reindeer weathervane, **6**: 716-17
molding methods, 10: 1246-55
hand mold and cast, **10**: 1248-49
latex molding, **10**: 1251-52
pop-art candle, **10**: 1253-55
pewtersmithing, 12: 1476-79
cast figurine, **12**: 1476, 1478-79
pieced molds and reinforcements, 10: 1255
pipe making, 13: 1552-61
briar pipe, **13**: 1556-60
corncob pipe, **13**: 1555-56
sand casting, 15: 1872-81
candle, sand-casted, **15**: 1875-77
sea animals, cast, **15**: 1874-75
weed pot, **15**: 1878-81
sand characters and castles, 15: 1882-87
scrimshaw, 15: 1912-20
color-engraved scrimshaw, **15**: 1919-20
hair piece, bone, **15**: 1917-18
sculpture, 16: 1930-37
alabaster sculpture, **16**: 1935-37
rosewood serving tray, **16**: 1930-33
sharpening chisels and gouges, 16: 1934
totem poles, 20: 2538-47
full-sized totem pole, **20**: 2546-47
miniature totem pole, **20**: 2543
wall plaque, totem-mask, **20**: 2541-42
treen ware, 21: 2602-13
kitchen utensils, **21**: 2604-9
party table accessories, **21**: 2610-13
walking sticks, 22: 2714-16, 2718-21
spiral-design cane, **22**: 2718-19
sculptured walking stick, **22**: 2720-21
winter sculpture, 22: 2812-16
ice sculptures, **22**: 2812-16
cases
briefcase, envelope, leather, **9**: 1077-79
display case, ship model, **16**: 2037
eyeglass case, Florentine stitched, **6**: 680-81
casseroles. See terrines and timbales
casting, 4: 422-33
belt buckle, tin, **4**: 430-33
figurine, cast, **12**: 1476, 1478-79
hand, cast and mold, **10**: 1248-49
head, plaster-cast, **4**: 424-29
slab-glass, **18**: 2223-24
See also **acrylics; belts and buckles; buttons; candlemaking; foam forms; jewelry; molding methods; papier-mâché; sand casting; sculpture; stained glass**
cats
cabaña for, **12**: 1468-69

woven rya, **15**: 1834-37
catchalls, wall-hanging, **16**: 1968-70
ceilings, stenciled, **18**: 2248-49
centerpieces, table
bird, quillwork, **14**: 1681-83
candle holder, pod and cone, **13**: 1590-91
flowers, artificial
fabric, **6**: 696-97
feather, **6**: 692-93
foil, **6**: 690-91
ice sculptures, **22**: 2812-15
Ceramics
ceramics, 4: 434-45
bowl, clay, **4**: 440
bowl, coiled, **4**: 441-43
buttons, clay, **3**: 308-9
coat hooks, **4**: 444-45
glazes, ceramic, **8**: 986-87
mural, tile, **10**: 1278-80
tiles, clay, **4**: 434-39
enameling metal, 6: 658-64
dish, copper, **6**: 664
pendant, copper, **6**: 661-63
kilns, 8: 976-87
raku kiln, **8**: 983-85
sawdust kiln, **8**: 980-82
pottery, 13: 1606-21
hand-built pottery, **13**: 1609-11
kick wheel, building, **13**: 1612-13
wheel-thrown pottery, **13**: 1614-21
sculpture, 16: 1926-29
clay figure, **16**: 1926-29
chains
beaded daisy, **1**: 45
carrick bend, **14**: 1788
chairs
bean-bag, **2**: 164-66
gilded, **7**: 792
plastic pipe, **13**: 1564-66
plywood and foam, **13**: 1572-75
ragdoll, **14**: 1731
recaning, **3**: 348-50
rocking, child's, **14**: 1776
seats
padded, **21**: 2658
rush, **3**: 351-53
splint, **3**: 344-47
stuffed, **21**: 2659-65
See also **benches**
chameleon lizards, 22: 2710-11
chancery cursive, 3: 316-18
charts. See astronomy; maps and path-finding; organic gardening; piloting small boats; weather forecasting
checkers, Lasca, **19**: 2374-75
cheeses and churning, 4: 446-53
cheeses, **4**: 450-52
churning, **4**: 453
yogurts and sour cream, **4**: 446-49
See also **breads; brewing; Colonial crafts; herbs; wine making**
chessboard, marquetry, **10**: 1179

chests
elephant toy chest, **20**: 2549, 2556-58
hope chest, **6**: 710-11
toy-chest bench, **3**: 262, 269
chicken
julienne, **17**: 2126
soup, **17**: 2127
Tai Chien, **23**: 2844
chimes, 11: 1287, 1292
Chinese meal, 23: 2845
chocolates, coated, **4**: 512
chopping board, treen, **21**: 2609
Christmas celebrations, 4: 454-67
cards, Christmas, **4**: 479
eggs, decorated, **14**: 1680-81
gift wrapping, **4**: 462
ornaments
edible, **4**: 460
handmade, **4**: 459
origami, **11**: 1385
paper, **4**: 461
patchwork, **4**: 459
quilted, **14**: 1675-77
trims, **4**: 460-61
potpourris, seasonal, **13**: 1599
recipes, Christmas, **4**: 466-67
trees, Christmas, **4**: 454-57
decorating, **4**: 454-55, 457-61, **7**: 787
wreaths
candy, **4**: 464
pod and cone, **13**: 1591
traditional, **4**: 465
wheat and flour, **4**: 463
See also **birthday celebrations; confections and comfits; dried flowers; egg decoration; foam forms; gingerbread; granny squares; greeting cards; papier-mâché; piñatas; pod and cone art; ribboncraft; spool toys; square dancing; sugar shapes**
churning. See cheeses and churning
chutney, 10: 1165
cider vinegars, 22: 2698
cigar boxes
assemblage, **4**: 484-85
decorative, **3**: 270-71
ciphers, devising and solving, **5**: 561-64
circus parade, 12: 1417
cityscape, oil painting, **11**: 1344-45
clambakes, 4: 468-77
clamming, **4**: 476-77
cleaning up, **4**: 475
cooking, **4**: 472-73
dessert, **4**: 475
materials, **4**: 470
pit, setting up, **4**: 470-72
portions, calculating, **4**: 470
serving, **4**: 474-75
small clambakes, **4**: 470
See also **American Indian crafts; beachcombing; canoeing; kayaks; sail making and repair; seashells; soups**
claves, 11: 1287, 1288, 1291

clays
  bowl, **4**: 440
  buttons, **3**: 308-9
  kitchen, **13**: 1628-29
  modeling, **4**: 424-29
  sculpture, **16**: 1926-29
  tiles, **4**: 434-39
cleansing creams, 17: 2104-5
climbing bars, plastic pipe, **13**: 1569
clocks
  mineral base for, decorative, **10**: 1207-8
  time telling
    candle clock, **20**: 2494-95
    noon light show, **20**: 2490-93
    sandglass, **20**: 2495-96
    star dial, **20**: 2497-99
clogs
  needlepoint, **15**: 1869-71
  ribbon, **15**: 1871
clothespin doll, 5: 608
clothing. See dolls and doll clothes; fur recycling; recycling clothes; names of articles of clothing and methods of making clothing
cloud forms, 22: 2738-39
clown faces
  marionette, **13**: 1645, 1648-51
  mask, **10**: 1184-85
  yarn, **23**: 2912-14
coasters, braided, **3**: 275
coat hooks, ceramic, **4**: 444-45
coats
  kimono, **16**: 1977-78
  shortening, **6**: 744-45
codes, cryptography
  making and breaking, **5**: 559-66
  Morse code, **5**: 564-65
  Semaphore, **5**: 564-65
cold creams, 5: 520-22
collages and assemblages, 4: 478-87
  animal collage, stamp decoupage, **18**: 2235-36
  cigar box assemblage, **4**: 484-85
  free-form assemblages, **4**: 486-87
  glass collage, laminated panel, **18**: 2217, 2222-23
  map collage, stamp decoupage, **18**: 2235
  pure-paper collage, **4**: 480-81
  scrap lumber collage, **4**: 482-83
  seashell collage, **16**: 1944
  See also **boxes; cardboard; decoupage; greeting cards; mosaics; preschool activities; seashells; stamp decoupage; valentines; wood assemblages**
collars
  bobbin lace, **8**: 1019-21
  fur, recycled, **6**: 746-48
  shell-cluster motif, **19**: 2424-25
collecting, insect, **8**: 942-47
cologne, 12: 1462-63
Colonial crafts, 4: 488-97
  apple-head doll, **5**: 609
  blacksmithing, **4**: 494
  broommaking, **4**: 493

candle dipping, **4**: 492
churning butter, **4**: 491
clothing, **4**: 489, 490-91
cornhusk doll, **5**: 610
daily life, **4**: 490-95
  building, **4**: 493
  diet, **4**: 491-92
  entertainment, **4**: 493
  farming, **4**: 491-93
  self-sufficiency of, **4**: 495
  woodcutting, **4**: 494-95
fall, **4**: 493
haying, **4**: 492
log splitting, **4**: 494
maple sugaring, **4**: 488
pewtermaking, **4**: 495
plowing, **4**: 491
rocking cradle, **14**: 1778-79
spinning, **4**: 490
spring, **4**: 491-92
summer, **4**: 492-93
tinsmithing, **4**: 495
traditional braided rug, **3**: 276-77
walnut and egg dolls, **5**: 606-7
weaving, **4**: 490
winter, **4**: 493-95
yarnmaking, **4**: 496-97
  dyeing yarn, **4**: 496-97
  preparing wool, **4**: 496
  sheep shearing, **4**: 496
  wool carding, **4**: 496-97
See also **American Indian crafts; beadwork; breads; cheeses and churning; folk art; genealogy; heraldry; herbs; pewtersmithing; pottery; quilting; rugs; silversmithing; spinning; square dancing; tin painting; tin and pierced work; treen ware**
Color. See Paint and Color
color psychology, 4: 498-505
  animal vision, **4**: 502
  appetite and color, **4**: 504-5
  association, color, **4**: 505
  blindness, color, **4**: 502
  clothes and color, **4**: 503-5
  conditioned response to color, **4**: 502-5
    blue, **4**: 503
    green, **4**: 503
    yellow, **4**: 503
  fashion and color, **4**: 505
  human vision, **4**: 501-2
    primary pairing, **4**: 501
  industrial applications, **4**: 505
  innate response to color, **4**: 502
  light and color, **4**: 500-1
  primary colors, **4**: 500
  taste and, **4**: 505
  See also **light; oil painting; stained glass; supergraphics; vegetable dyes; watercolors**
comic strips. See cartooning

communications, signal, **5**: 564-65
compass
  making, **9**: 1146-48
  using
    maps and pathfinding, **9**: 1146-48
    piloting small boats, **12**: 1520-21
confections and comfits, 4: 506-12
  brittles and fudges, **4**: 510-11
  coated chocolates, **4**: 512
  hard candies, **4**: 509
  quick candies, **4**: 508
  See also **birthday celebrations; Christmas celebrations; ice cream, sherbet, and ices; marmalades and preserves; sugar shapes; syrups**
conics in box, 18: 2271, 2280-81
constructions
  cup, **6**: 700-1
  driftwood, **2**: 142-43
  spool, **17**: 2155-56
  stage, **18**: 2202-3
containers, stamp decoupage, **18**: 2237-39
cookie cutters, 20: 2502-3
cookies
  breakfast, **1**: 110-11
  gingerbread, **6**: 767-68
cooking. See Kitchen Favorites and Celebrations
copper
  bowl, **17**: 2063-65
  box top ornamentation, **14**: 1746-48
  mobile, **10**: 1225-26
corking, wine bottle, **22**: 2802
corncobs, -husks
  doll, **5**: 610
  pipe, **11**: 1555-56
cosmetics, 5: 518-25
  astringent, **5**: 523
  cleansing creams and masks, **17**: 2104-5
  cold creams, **5**: 520-22
  powder and shadow, **5**: 524-25
  See also **costumes; perfumes; potpourri and pomanders; skin painting; soaps and bath products**
costumes, 5: 526-37
  basic dress pattern, **5**: 533
  body painting, **17**: 2066, 2074-75
  caftans, **5**: 534
  circular patterns, **5**: 531
  drapes and wraparounds, **5**: 530
  historic costumes, **5**: 527, 532
  makeup, **5**: 536-37
  paper costumes, **5**: 528-29
  parade and festival costumes, **12**: 1424
  period dress, **5**: 535
  See also **cosmetics; dollhouses and furniture; marionettes; masks; puppets and puppetry; sewing without pattern; skin painting; stagecraft**
coverlet, quilted, **16**: 1975, 1983-84
covers
  lampshade cover, **9**: 1039
  plastic box cover, Florentine stitch, **6**: 683-84

covers, continued
    vase cover, inkle-woven, **8:** 933
    See also **pillows; quilts and quilting**
creams
    cleansing, **17:** 2104-5
    cold, **5:** 520-22
    sour, **4:** 446-49
cradles
    doll, **14:** 1780-81
    infant, **14:** 1778-79
cranes, origami, **11:** 1375, 1383
crepe paper flowers, **6:** 694-96
crewel, 5: 538-49
    embroidery sampler, **5:** 538-41, 546-49
    See also **appliqué; dolls and doll
        clothes; embroidery; frames and
        framing; hardanger embroidery;
        lace; machine stitchery;
        needlepoint; samplers; smocking;
        Swedish huck work; tambour**
crochet, 5: 550-57
    afghans, patchwork crochet
        floral, **7:** 811
        popcorn stitch, **7:** 813
        traditional, **7:** 807-8
    bag, beaded, **5:** 553
    cap and scarf, **7:** 812
    dress, evening, **5:** 554-55
    mask, lion-hoop, **10:** 1186-87
    pincushion, **5:** 556
    place mat, **7:** 810
    shoulder bag, raffia, **14:** 1718
    sisal rug, **5:** 557
    stitches, **1:** 30-31, **10:** 1187, **14:** 1717
    tie, **5:** 552
    tote bag, **7:** 814-15
    See also **afghan stitch; granny
        squares; knitting to fit; lace;
        mittens and mukluks; spinning;
        tambour**
cryptography, 5: 558-65
    ciphers, **5:** 561-64, 565
    codes, **5:** 559-60
    signal communications, **5:** 564-65
cuffs and cuff links
    bobbin lace cuffs, **8:** 1019-21
    button cuff links, **3:** 305
    fur cuffs, **6:** 746-48
cups
    constructions, foam, **6:** 700-1
    decorations, foam, **6:** 702-3
    drinking, origami, **11:** 1378
curd, 10: 1163
curio cabinet, beverage-case, **3:** 266
cursive, chancery, **3:** 316-18
curtains
    café, sewn without pattern, **16:** 1984-85
    white-on-white, tambour, **19:** 2412
cushions, bean-bag, **2:** 164-66
cutters, cookie, **20:** 2502-3
Cutting and Folding. See **Paper Cutting
    and Folding**
cutouts
    decoupage techniques, **5:** 566-72
    wycinanki animal chain, **23:** 2890-91

D

dancing. See **square dancing**
darkrooms, 12: 1490
Dart, Dartmouth, **1:** 33-34
Decorations. See **Designs and
    Decorations**
decoupage, 5: 566-77
    box, switch, lamp, **5:** 573
    cabinet, wooden, **5:** 577
    surface preparation, decoupage, **5:** 569
    techniques, decoupage, **5:** 568-72
    thinning prints for decoupage, **5:** 569
    tin-can decoupage, **5:** 574
    tortoise-shell base, **5:** 575-76
    See also **antiquing furniture; boxes;
        candlemaking; collages and as-
        semblages; frames and framing;
        papier-mâché; refinishing furni-
        ture; stamp decoupage; valen-
        tines; wycinanki**
denim
    bookcover, **2:** 233-35
    patch, embroidered, **15:** 1858
    shoulder bag, raffia and straw, **14:** 1718
Designs and Decorations
    Christmas celebrations, 4: 454-61,
        464
        candy wreaths, **4:** 464
        Christmas-tree trims, **4:** 460-61
        handmade Christmas-tree ornaments,
        4: 459
        patchwork Christmas-tree ornaments,
        4: 458
    collages and assemblages, 4: 478-87
        cigar box assemblage, **4:** 484-85
        free-form assemblages, **4:** 486-87
        pure-paper collage, **4:** 480-81
        scrap lumber collage, **4:** 482-83
    decoupage, 5: 566-77
        box, switch, lamp, **5:** 573
        graphite transfer paper, **15:** 1802
        surface preparations, decoupage, **5:**
        569
        techniques, decoupage, **5:** 568-72
        thinning prints for decoupage, **5:**
        569
        tin-can decoupage, **5:** 574
        tortoise-shell base, **5:** 575-76
        wooden cabinet, **5:** 577
    herbs, 7: 884
        note cards, herb, **7:** 884
    models and mock-ups, 10: 1232-45
        bedroom redecorating model, **10:**
        1235-40
        drafting fundamentals, **10:** 1235
        garden structures, **10:** 1232, 1241-44
        mock-ups, **10:** 1245
    mosaics, 10: 1268-73, 1276-80
        button mosaics, **10:** 1270-71
        grouted mosaics, **10:** 1277-78

        mirror frame, mosaic, **10:** 1272-73
        tile mural, **10:** 1278-80
        tiles, **10:** 1276
    papier-mâché, 11: 1400-4, 1405,
        1407-8
        bottle people, **11:** 1401, 1403-4
        dinosaur, papier-mâché, **11:** 1407-8
        drying papier-mâché, **11:** 1405
        strings and pulp, papier-mâché, **11:**
        1402
    pin striping, 13: 1542-51
        boat helm, **13:** 1547
        customizing, car, **13:** 1548-50
        door panel, **13:** 1546
        restoring antique automobiles, **13:**
        1542, 1551
    pod and cone art, 13: 1584-95
        alligator, pad and cone, **13:** 1585,
        1589
        candle holder, **13:** 1590-91
        Christmas wreath, **13:** 1591
        lion, pine-cone, **13:** 1584, 1587-88
        llama, pine-cone, **13:** 1584, 1586
        ostrich, pine-cone, **13:** 1588
        shadow box, **13:** 1592
        tree, wired, **13:** 1593-95
        turkey, pine-cone, **13:** 1590
        wiring pods and cones, **13:** 1595
    preschool activities, 13: 1629-31,
        1634
        junk sculpture, **13:** 1630-31
        kitchen clay, **13:** 1628-29
        woodworking, **13:** 1634
    raffia and straw, 14: 1712-13
        mosaics, split-straw, **14:** 1712-13
    rosemaling, 15: 1798-1813
        antiquing, **15:** 1813
        bread board, **15:** 1805-7
        design transfers, **15:** 1802
        hand mirror, **15:** 1803-4
        Telemark box, **15:** 1810-13
        Telemark plate, **15:** 1808-10
    seashells, 16: 1938, 1944-49
        collage, seashell, **16:** 1944
        figurines, shell, **16:** 1948-49
        flowers, seashell, **16:** 1946-47
        jewelry, seashell, **16:** 1945
    ship models, 16: 2024-41
        display case, ship model, **16:** 2037
        Philadelphia ship model, **16:** 2025-37
        ship in bottle, **16:** 2038-41
    skin painting, 17: 2066-71, 2074-75
        body painting, **17:** 2066, 2074-75
        heavenly-nights face makeup, **17:**
        2068-69
        leopard face makeup, **17:** 2068-69
        primitive face makeup, **17:** 2070-71
    soft sculpture, 17: 2116-21
        gorilla, soft sculpture, **17:** 2114,
        2116-19
    spool toys, 17: 2154-56
        constructions, spool, **17:** 2155-56
    stamp decoupage, 18: 2232-39
        container decoupage, **18:** 2237-39
        pieced pictures, **18:** 2235-36
    stenciling, 18: 2240-51

personalized note paper, **18**: 2244-45
floors, stenciled, **18**: 2250-51
place mats, stenciled, **18**: 2246-47
walls and ceilings, stenciled, **18**: 2248-49
stone painting, 18: 2253-54, 2256-57
animals, stone, **18**: 2256-57
assemblages, painted stone, **18**: 2253-54
time telling, 20: 2490-95
candle clock, **20**: 2494-95
noon light show, **20**: 2490-93
wood assemblages, 23: 2846-55
heraldic standards, **23**: 2852-55
sculpture, wood, **23**: 2850-52
wall illusion, **23**: 2846-49
yarn painting, 23: 2910-17
bottle yarn painting, **23**: 2917
clown face, yarn, **23**: 2912-14
landscape with feathers, **23**: 2916-17
landscape, yarn, **23**: 2915
paper-plate mask, **23**: 2914-15
desks
cardboard, corrugated, **3**: 374
milk-crate, **3**: 362-65
desserts
clambake, **4**: 475
flavored ice creams, **8**: 915-16
ices, **8**: 917
sherbet, **8**: 917
syrups, **19**: 2362-63
vanilla ice cream, **8**: 914-15
dial, star, **20**: 2497-99
diary, leather-bound, **2**: 236-42
dinosaur, papier-mâché, **11**: 1407-8
dioramas, 5: 578-91
portable diorama, **5**: 583-91
shell figurines, **16**: 1948-49
train diorama, **5**: 579-82
See also **bonsai; boxes; carving; dried flowers; foam forms; insects; models and mock-ups; papier-mâché**
dishes
clay bowl, **4**: 440
copper, enameled, **6**: 664
glass, gilded, **7**: 793-95
plastic, decoration for, **16**: 1970
salad bowl set, treen, **21**: 2612-13
serving dish, handwrought pewter, **12**: 1480-83
See also **bowls; serving trays**
distillations. See **Fragrances**
distressing, 1: 74-77
dividers, room
acrylic, **1**: 11-14
macramé screen, **9**: 1116, 1124
plastic pipe, **13**: 1569
doghouse, barrel, **12**: 1464, 1466-67
dollhouses and furniture, 5: 592-603
cradle, doll's, **14**: 1780-81
four-room dollhouse, **5**: 594-95
furniture, making, **5**: 596-97
people, dollhouse, **5**: 598-99
playing cards, miniature, **5**: 596
rooms, making, **5**: 594-95

wing chair, **5**: 596-97
wooden dollhouse, **5**: 592, 600-3
See also **animals, doll; costumes; dolls and doll clothes; models and mock-ups; ship models**
dolls and doll clothes, 5: 604-13
apple-head doll, **5**: 609
cloth doll, **5**: 612-13
clothespin doll, **5**: 608
clothing, doll, **5**: 598-99
cornhusk doll, **5**: 610
egg dolls, **5**: 606-7
pieces doll, **5**: 608
piñata doll, **12**: 1534
rag dolls, **14**: 1726-31
walnut dolls, **5**: 606-7
See also **animals, doll; appliqué; crewel; dollhouses and furniture; pod and cone art; puppets and puppetry; rag dolls; spool toys**
doormat, knotted rope, **14**: 1789
door panel, pin stripe decoration for, **13**: 1546
double dutch, 18: 2269
drafting, fundamentals of, **10**: 1235
dragonfly, tambour, **19**: 2417-19
drapes and wraparounds, 5: 530
drawer organizer, kitchen-matchbox, **3**: 267
dresses and dressmaking
appliquéd dress, child's, **14**: 1741-42
basic pattern, costume, **5**: 533
cotton, smocked, **17**: 2085
evening, crocheted, **5**: 554-55
lengthening, **14**: 1742-43
peasant, macraméd, **9**: 1122-23
period costume, **5**: 535
silk, smocked, **17**: 2083-84
yoked trapunto, **21**: 2580, 2584-85
dried flowers, 5: 614-23
air drying, **5**: 620-21
arrangements, dried-flower, **5**: 618-19, 621
bouquet, dried-spice, **5**: 622-23
candles, dried-flower, **3**: 341
cards, pressed-flower, **7**: 838
glycerin preserving, **5**: 620-21
potpourris, **13**: 1596-98
pressing, **5**: 620-21
sand drying, **5**: 614-15
seasonal potpourris, **13**: 1599
shadow box, **13**: 1592
silica gel drying, **5**: 615
techniques, drying, **5**: 614-21
times, drying, **5**: 615
wheat-and-flower wreath, **4**: 463
See also **candlemaking; Christmas celebrations; dioramas; flowers, artificial; ikebana; pod and cone art**
driftwood
bonsai, **2**: 223-25
constructions, **2**: 142-43
drop spindle spinning, 17: 2143-45

drums, 11: 1287, 1289-90
duck, deep-fried, **23**: 2843
dulcimers, 5: 624-33
Appalachian dulcimer, **5**: 624, 626-33
fretboard dulcimer, **5**: 625-26
See also **music making; square dancing; whistles and flutes; wind harps**
dusters, feather, **6**: 692-93
dutch, double, **18**: 2269
dyes and dyeing
colonial crafts, **4**: 496-97
eggs, margutis and pysanka, **5**: 634-37
vegetable dyes
colorfast, **21**: 2678-83
wool yarn, **21**: 2684-88
See also **tie dyeing**

E

earrings
button, **3**: 305
coconut shell, **8**: 951
feather, **8**: 950
pearl, **2**: 156-57
raffia, **14**: 1719
seashell, **16**: 1945
easy chairs
plastic pipe with footrest, **13**: 1563, 1564-66
plywood and foam with ottoman, **13**: 1572, 1573-1575
stuffed, **21**: 2659-65
ecology. See **Environmental Projects**
edging, handkerchief, **19**: 2421, 2424
egg decoration, 5: 634-40
gemstone eggs, **9**: 1045-48
Imperial Easter eggs, **5**: 638-40
margutis and pysanka eggs, **5**: 634-37
quilling, **14**: 1680-81
See also **batik; Christmas celebrations**
egg timer, hourglass, **20**: 2496
elephants
stuffed doll, **1**: 56-59
toy chest, **20**: 2549, 2556-58
ellipse, raised, string art, **18**: 2278-79
embedments, poured acrylic, **1**: 15-20
embossing. See **repoussé and chased metal**
embroidery, 6: 646-57
black work
owl, **6**: 656-57
tissue cover, **6**: 654-55
circles, **6**: 653
flower appliqué, **6**: 652
folk art hanging, **9**: 1107-8
huck work
handbag, **19**: 2341-42
hand towel, **19**: 2340
pillow, **19**: 2342-43
materials and use, **6**: 650-51
preparations and techniques, **5**: 540-41
samplers, **5**: 538-41, 546-49; **15**: 1848-61

samplers, continued

hoop-framed, **15**: 1855 57
perforated-paper, **15**: 1860-61
stitches, **1**: 86, **5**: 542-45, **7**: 857, **14**: 1737, **21**: 2574
See also **appliqué; beadwork; buttons; crewel; crochet; flags and banners; Florentine stitch; frames and framing; hardanger embroidery; lace; machine stitchery; needlepoint; reverse appliqué; samplers; smocking; Swedish huck work; tambour**
enameling metal, 6: 658-67
dish, copper, **6**: 664
firing enamel safely, **6**: 660
pendant, copper, **6**: 661-63
tiles, steel, **6**: 665-67
See also **ceramics; kilns; pewtersmithing; pottery; sculpture; silversmithing; stenciling; tiles**
enlargements, photographic, making, **12**: 1496-99
Environmental Projects
ant farms, 1: 64-69
ant farm, **1**: 66-69
Mason-jar ant house, **1**: 65-66
astronomy, 1: 92-105
telescope, **1**: 101-5
beachcombing, 2: 134-43
aquarium tank, **2**: 138
driftwood constructions, **2**: 142-43
lobster-man and shell paperweight, **2**: 140-41
birds and birdhouses, 2: 190-99
bird feeder, **2**: 194-95
birdbath, concrete, **2**: 198-99
bluebird house, **2**: 192
purple-martin house, **2**: 196-97
wren house, **2**: 193
greenhouse construction, 7: 816-35
blueprints, **7**: 823
cold frame, **7**: 818, 819
fasteners, **7**: 823
fiberglass greenhouse, curved, **7**: 822-35
hotbed, **7**: 818-19
pit greenhouse, **7**: 820-1
insects, 8: 936-47
collections, insect, **8**: 942-47
trapping insects, **8**: 940-42
masks, 10: 1192-95
African rope mask, **10**: 1192-95
organic gardening, 11: 1360-73
papermaking, 11: 1386-99
blender-made paper, **11**: 1390-93
handmade rag paper, **11**: 1394-99
pet habitats, 12: 1464-75
birdcage, five-story, **12**: 1472-75
cat cabaña, **12**: 1468-69
doghouse, barrel, **12**: 1464, 1466-67
tote, two-pet, **12**: 1470-72
quill pens, 14: 1684-89
making quill pens, **14**: 1686-89
spinning, 17: 2132-53

drop spindle spinning, **17**: 2143-45
flax on wheel, spinning, **17**: 2151-53
wool on wheel, spinning, **17**: 2146-50
sundials, 19: 2310-21
Egyptian sundial, **19**: 2313 14
horizontal sundial, **19**: 2316-21
portable sundial, **19**: 2315
tropical fish, 21: 2626-39
vivariums, 22: 2704-13
chameleon lizards, **22**: 2710-11
English hooded rat, **22**: 2708
guinea pigs, **22**: 2706-7
rodent vivariums, **22**: 2709
snakes, **22**: 2711-13
walking sticks, 22: 2716-18
hiking stick, **22**: 2716-18
weather forecasting, 22: 2734-51
cloud forms and weather forecasting, **22**: 2738-39
making weather instruments, **22**: 2740-45
using weather instruments, **22**: 2746-51
wind harps, 22: 2784-93
Aeolian harp, **22**: 2791-93
simple wind harps, **22**: 2786-90
See also **Greenery and Growing Things; Outdoor Activities**
eraser prints, 2: 214-15
espalier, 20: 2536-37
evening bag, ribbon, **14**: 1771
expressions, cartooning, **4**: 404-5
eyeglass case, Florentine stitch, **6**: 680-81

fabrics. See names of fabrics; names of finished products; methods of working with fabrics
face makeup
heavenly nights, **17**: 2068-69
leopard, **17**: 2068-69
primitive, **17**: 2070-71
stage, **17**: 2072-73
See also **cosmetics; soaps and bath products**
faces, cartooning, **4**: 404-5
See also **masks; origami**
Falcon, paper airplane, **1**: 38-39
farms, ant, **1**: 66-69
fasteners, 7: 829
feathers
flowers, feather, **6**: 692-93
jewelry, feather, **8**: 948-51
quill pens, **14**: 1684-86
yarn landscape with feathers, **23**: 2916-17
feeder, bird, **2**: 194-95
fermentation, wine making and, **22**: 2800-1
sealing, **22**: 2801
fern terrarium, 20: 2457-99
Festival of Roses (Pasadena), **12**: 1421

festivals. See **parades and festivals**
figures and figurines
cartooning, **4**: 406-7
cast, **12**: 1476, 1478-79
clay, **16**: 1926-29
shell, **16**: 1948-49
wire, **23**: 2822, 2834-35
findings, jewelry
scrimshaw, **15**: 1916
seashells, **16**: 1945
fingerprint, stationery, **10**: 1258-59
finishes. See **Furniture and Finishes**
fish
filleting fish, **15**: 1903
foam fish impression, **6**: 706-7
soap fish, carved, **4**: 415-16
steamed fish, **23**: 2841-42
See also **aquariums; sashimi and sushi; tropical fish; tying flies**
flags and banners, 6: 668-75
boat pennant, nylon, **6**: 672-73
club banner, **6**: 670-71
felt banner, **6**: 668, 674-75
See also **batik; birthday celebrations; embroidery; genealogy; heraldry; parades and festivals; sewing without pattern; woven tapestries**
flats, gemstone, **9**: 1052-53
flax, spinning, on wheel, **17**: 2151-53
fling, fur, **6**: 749
flipbook, 23: 2942-44
floats, parade and festival, **12**: 1420-21, 1424-25
building floats, **12**: 1424-25
flower float, **12**: 1421
suppliers of floats and decorations, **12**: 1424
floors, stenciled, **18**: 2250-51
Florentine stitch, 6: 676-87
cards, needlepoint, **7**: 838-39
eyeglass case, **6**: 680-81
pillow, **6**: 684-87
plastic box cover, **6**: 683-84
tote bag pocket, **6**: 681-82
See also **appliqué; embroidery; granny squares; hardanger embroidery; needlepoint; patchwork; quilts and quilting; rya and flossa; sewing without pattern; Swedish huck work**
flossa. See **rya and flossa**
flower arrangements, ikebana, **8**: 918-27
avant-garde ikebana, **8**: 926-27
cascading nageire, **8**: 924-25
upright moribana, **8**: 922-23
See also **bonsai; topiary; trellises**
flowerpot holders. See **planters, plant holders, plant hangers**
flowers, artificial, **6**: 688-97
crepe paper flowers, **6**: 694-96
fabric flowers, **6**: 696-97
feather flowers, **6**: 692-93
foil flowers, **6**: 690-91
mineral flowers, **10**: 1208-9
pencil posy, **6**: 688
tissue paper flowers, **6**: 689

wire flowers, **23**: 2831-32

See also **American Indian crafts; beadwork; dried flowers; origami; papier-mâché; pod and cone art; seashells**

flutes. See whistles and flutes

fly fishing and flies. See tying flies

foam forms, 6: 698-707

cup constructions, **6**: 700-1
fish impression, **6**: 706-7
foam cup decorations, **6**: 702-3
packing pieces sculpture, **6**: 699
puppets, foam, **13**: 1643
synthetic stone giraffe, **6**: 704-5

See also **carving; casting; Christmas celebrations; dioramas; molding methods; sculpture**

fob, key-chain, **18**: 2255-56

Folding. See Paper Cutting and Folding

folk art, 6: 708-17

African rope mask, **10**: 1192-95
antique stenciled tin box, **20**: 2523-27
bread board, rosemaled, **15**: 1805-7
bread sculpture, **3**: 290-91
country tin painting, **20**: 2513-17
festivals, folk, **12**: 1416, 1418-20
fraktur traufscheine, **6**: 708-9
gongs and chimes, **11**: 1287, 1292
hand mirror, rosemaled, **15**: 1803-4
hanging, reverse appliqué, **14**: 1760-61
hooked rugs, **8**: 902-3
hope chest, **6**: 710-11
Japanese tea ceremony, **20**: 2447-51
marimbas, **11**: 1287, 1294-99
mirror frame, foil, **14**: 1748-50
mittens, **10**: 1210-15
mukluks, **10**: 1216-19
ornamented box tops, **14**: 1746-48
oval tray, raffia and straw, **14**: 1722
painted canister, **20**: 2518-19
percussion instruments, **11**: 1287-91
round tray, raffia and straw, **14**: 1720-22
samplers, **15**: 1848-53
scrimshaw, **15**: 1912-13
Senufo wall hanging, **6**: 714-15
Telemark box, rosemaled, **15**: 1810-13
Telemark plate, rosemaled, **15**: 1808-10
weathervane, reindeer, **6**: 716-17
wheat-and-flower wreath, **4**: 463

See also **antiquing furniture; block printing; calligraphy; Colonial crafts; frames and framing; genealogy; heraldry; pewtersmithing; quill pens; refinishing furniture; sculpture; Shaker furniture; square dancing; Swedish huck work; tin painting; traditional knitting motifs; treen ware; woven tapestries**

follow-the-leader, 18: 2268

foods. See Kitchen Favorites and Celebrations; names of foods and methods of preparation

football, association, **18**: 2265

football ornament, feather, **8**: 950-51

footrest, plastic pipe, **13**: 1564-66

footwear. See moccasins; mukluks; sandal making

forks

bracelet made from, **8**: 955
treen forks, **21**: 2607
salad fork and spoon, **21**: 2612

fort, tree, **21**: 2601

fossils, fish impression, **6**: 706-7

Fragrances

cosmetics, 5: 518-25
astringent, **5**: 523
cold creams, **5**: 520-22
powder and shadow, **5**: 524-25
perfumes, **12**: 1454-63
colognes, **12**: 1462-63
homemade perfumes, **12**: 1457
men's perfumes, **12**: 1463
recipes, perfume, **12**: 1458-60
potpourris and pomanders, 13: 1596-1605
pillow potpourri, **13**: 1600
pomander-ball pendant, **13**: 1605
pomander balls, **13**: 1602-4
pomander buds, **13**: 1601
potpourris, **13**: 1596-98
seasonal potpourri, **13**: 1599
soaps and bath products, 17: 2098-2105
cleansing creams and masks, **17**: 2104-5
quick soaps, **17**: 2098-2102
shaving soap and bath oils, **17**: 2103

frame looms. See looms

frames and framing, 6: 718-25

barn siding background frame, **6**: 723
box frame, **6**: 725
foil frames, high relief, **14**: 1748-50
gilding frames, **1**: 81
metal frame, **6**: 721
mirror frames
foil, **14**: 1748-50
needlepoint, **11**: 1328-29
sprang wall hanging, frame for, **17**: 2172
stick frame, **6**: 722-23
watercolors, framing, **22**: 2733
wood frame, **6**: 719-21

See also **antiquing furniture; crewel; decoupage; embroidery; folk art; gold leafing; refinishing furniture; rubbings; watercolors**

frogs

bean-bag leapfrog game, **2**: 162-63
origami jumping frog, **11**: 1384-85

fruits

beaded fruit, **2**: 152-53
canning and pickling recipes, **12**: 1511
carving fruits, **4**: 418-21
soups, fruit, **17**: 2128-29
wine fruits, **22**: 2804-5
crushing and pressing, **22**: 2798-99

See also **potpourris and pomanders**

fudges, 4: 510-11

Furniture and Finishes

antiquing furniture, 1: 70-81
distressing, **1**: 74-77
feathering, **1**: 78
gilding, **1**: 81
glaze antiquing, **1**: 70-73, 78
hardware, antiquing, **1**: 80
marbleizing, **1**: 79
boxes, 3: 262, 266, 269-71
curio cabinet, beverage-case, **3**: 266
decorative cigar boxes, **3**: 270-71
toy-chest bench, **3**: 262, 269
caning and rushing, 3: 342-53
chair, recaning, **3**: 348-50
chair seat, rush, **3**: 351-53
chair seat, splint, **3**: 344-47
cardboard, 3: 366-67, 372-75
furniture, cardboard, **3**: 372-74
headboard, **3**: 367, 375
folk art, 6: 710-11
hope chest, **6**: 710-11
framing, 6: 718-25
barn siding background frame, **6**: 723
box frame, **6**: 724-25
metal frame, **6**: 721
stick frame, **6**: 722-23
wood frame, **6**: 719-21
gold leafing, 7: 788-92
chair, gilded, **7**: 792
shadow box, gilt-edge, **7**: 790-91
marquetry, 10: 1166-79
chessboard, marquetry, **10**: 1179
geometric marquetry design, **10**: 1167-76
special marquetry effects, **10**: 1177-78
plywood and foam furnishings, 13: 1572-83
banquette and bench, **13**: 1579-83
chair and ottoman, **13**: 1572-75
seating platforms, **13**: 1576-78
refinishing furniture, 6: 710-11, 726-39
applying finish, **6**: 736-39
bleaching, **6**: 735
blemishes, repairing, **6**: 730-31
brushes, **6**: 736
cleaning surfaces, **6**: 726-28
milk-based paints, removing, **6**: 729
natural finishes, **6**: 723
old finish, removing, **6**: 728-29
old finish, restoring, **6**: 728
rubbing and polishing, **6**: 736
sanding, **6**: 723-33
spattering, **1**: 78
staining, **6**: 733-35
striping, **1**: 78
techniques, refinishing, **1**: 78
types of finish, **6**: 726-28, 733-35, 737-39
waxing, **6**: 736
wiping, **1**: 78
wood types, **6**: 733
rockers and cradles, 14: 1774-76, 1778-79
rocking chair, child's, **14**: 1776
rocking cradle, **14**: 1778-79

Furniture and Finishes, continued

Shaker furniture, 16: 1998-2011
candle sconce, **16:** 2000-3
dovetailed candle box, **16:** 2009-11
side table, **16:** 2003-5
utility bench, **16:** 2006-8
structural furnishings, 18: 2284-99
lofts, **18:** 2284, 2288-93
platforms, **18:** 2294-99
table wall hanging, **18:** 2286-87
tables and benches, 19: 2378-91
modular tables and benches, **19:** 2384-87
nesting tables, **19:** 2388-91
plant table, **19:** 2382-83
sawhorse stool, **19:** 2379-81
upholstery, 21: 2652-65
bench, cushioned, **21:** 2654-57
chair seat, padded, **21:** 2658
easy chair, stuffed, **21:** 2659-65
See also names of pieces of furniture; furniture construction materials
fur recycling, 6: 740-49
collar and cuffs, fur, **6:** 746-48
fling, fur, **6:** 749
pillows, fur, **6:** 742-43
shortening coat, **6:** 744-45
See also **mittens and mukluks; recycling clothes; sewing without pattern; tying flies**

G

Games. See **Toys and Games**
gazebo, 10: 1232, 1241-44
gardens. See **Greenery and Growing Things; greenhouse construction**
gears, bicycle, adjusting, **2:** 183-84
gemstones
cabochons, **9:** 1048-51
eggs, **9:** 1045-48
flats, **9:** 1052-53
tumbling, **9:** 1042-44
genealogy, 6: 750-61
bibliography, **6:** 755
black Americans and, **6:** 758-59
chart making, **6:** 760-61
family tree, tracing, **6:** 750-51
information sources, **6:** 752-57
library research, **6:** 754
overseas sources, **6:** 757
periodicals, **6:** 756
public records, **6:** 754, 756
publishing results, **6:** 761
record keeping, regional differences in, **6:** 757
See also **Colonial crafts; folk art; greeting cards; heraldry; rubbings; wood assemblages**
gifts
herb gift basket, **7:** 884
valentine gift box, **21:** 2674-75
wrapping gifts, **4:** 462
See also **birthday celebrations;**

Christmas celebrations; names of gift items
gilding, 1: 81
ginger beer, 3: 298-301
gingerbread, 6: 762-68
cookies, gingerbread, **6:** 767-68
house, gingerbread, **6:** 762-66
See also **breads; bread sculpture; Christmas celebrations; pasta; sugar shapes**
giraffes
straw, **14:** 1713-14
stuffed, **13:** 1622-24
synthetic stone, **6:** 704-5
Glass and Plastics
acrylics, 1: 10-20
poured acrylics, **1:** 15-20
room divider, **1:** 11-14
beachcombing, 2: 139
mosaic, beach glass, **2:** 139
bean-bags, 2: 167
wall hanging, **2:** 167
bottle cutting, 2: 244-51
basic cutting, **2:** 244-48
decorating bottles, **2:** 249-51
cutting glass, 9: 1060-61, **18:** 2220-21
foam forms, 6: 698-701
cup constructions, **6:** 700-1
packing pieces sculpture, **6:** 699
foiling, 9: 1062
glass working, 7: 744-87
beads, glass, **7:** 786
beads, lead glass, **7:** 776-77
cutting glass, **9:** 1060-61, **18:** 2220-21
lampblown glass bottle, **7:** 774, 780-85
ornament, hanging, **7:** 787
rods, glass, making, **7:** 783
rod sculpture, glass, **7:** 779
swizzle sticks, **7:** 778-79
gold leafing, 7: 793-95
gilding glass, **7:** 793-95
lamps and shades, 9: 1036-37
potichomania lamp, **9:** 1036-37
leaded glass, 9: 1056-67
candle box or planter, **9:** 1064-65
foiling and soldering, **9:** 1062, **18:** 2227
lampshade, **9:** 1066-67
lead came, **9:** 1062
window panel, **9:** 1063
mosaics, 10: 1274-75
light sculpture, mosaic, **10:** 1274-75
plastic pipe constructions, 13: 1562-71
bookshelves, **13:** 1567-69
easy chair and footrest, **13:** 1564-66
lamp, sculptural, **13:** 1570-71
soldering, 9: 1062, **18:** 2227
stained glass, 18: 2216-31
laminated panel, **18:** 2217, 2222-23
mosaic, glass, **18:** 2225-26
necklace, copper-foiled, **18:** 2226-29

panel, stained-glass, **18:** 2229-31
slab-glass casting, **18:** 2223-24
time telling, 20: 2495-96
sandglass, **20:** 2495-96
glasses, wine, **22:** 2802
glass working, 7: 774-87
beads, glass, **7:** 786
beads, lead glass, **7:** 776-77
lampblown glass bottle, **7:** 774, 780-85
ornament, hanging, **7:** 787
rod sculpture, glass, **7:** 779
rods, glass, making, **7:** 783
swizzle sticks, **7:** 778-79
See also **bottle cutting; stained glass**
glazes and glazing
antiquing glazes, **1:** 70-73, 78
ceramic glazes, **4:** 438-39, **8:** 986-87
pottery, glazing, **13:** 1621
watercolors, glazing, **22:** 2730-31
glides, pulley-and-cable, **19:** 2348-51
gold leafing, 7: 788-97
chair, gilded, **7:** 792
glass, gilding, **7:** 793-95
lettering signs in gold, **7:** 795-97
shadow box, gilt-edge, **7:** 790-91
See also **antiquing furniture; bookbinding; frames and framing; gold panning; marquetry; refinishing furniture; repoussé and chased metal; upholstery**
gold panning, 7: 798-805
dry panning, **7:** 803
information sources, **7:** 805
locating placer gold, **7:** 799-800
map of placer deposits, **7:** 799
sniping, **7:** 800-1
techniques, panning, **7:** 798, 801-3
underwater prospecting, **7:** 804-5
See also **canoeing; kayaks; maps and pathfinding; mineralogy; shelters and tents**
gongs, 11: 1287, 1292
hanging gongs, **11:** 1293
gorilla, soft sculpture, **17:** 2114, 2116-19
granny squares, 7: 806-15
blocking, **7:** 808
cap and scarf, **7:** 812
floral afghan, **7:** 811
joining, **7:** 809
place mat, **7:** 810
popcorn stitch afghan, **7:** 813
shoulder tote bag, **7:** 814-15
traditional afghan, **7:** 807-8
See also **afghan stitch; appliqué; Christmas celebrations; crochet; Florentine stitch; knitting to fit; patchwork; tatting; traditional knitting motifs**
Graphic Arts
batik, 1: 120-28
floor pillow, **1:** 128
table mat, **1:** 127
wall hangings, **1:** 126
block printing, 2: 210-19
eraser prints, **2:** 214-15
linoleum prints, **2:** 216-19

vegetable prints, **2**: 210-13
bookbinding, 2: 230-43
book care, **2**: 243
covers and pages, cleaning, **2**: 243
denim bookcover, **2**: 233-35
leather-bound diary, **2**: 236-42
torn pages, repairing, **2**: 243
calligraphy, 3: 312-21
chancery cursive, **3**: 316-18
hand illumination, **3**: 312, 319-21
cameras, 3: 322-29
camera obscura, **3**: 322-26
pinhole camera, **3**: 327-29
cartooning, 4: 402-13
comic strips, **4**: 410-11
figures and hands, **4**: 406-7
heads, faces, expressions, **4**: 404-5
self-starter cartoons, **4**: 412-13
single-panel cartoons, **4**: 408-9
enameling metals, 6: 658, 665-67
steel tiles, **6**: 665-67
flags and banners, 6: 668, 674-75
felt banner, **6**: 668, 674-75
gold leafing, 7: 795-97
lettering signs in gold, **7**: 795-97
greeting cards, 7: 840-45
birth announcements, **7**: 845
cardboard printing, **7**: 844-46
paste-ups, preparing, **7**: 842-43
printing, preparing materials for, **7**: 842-43
stained-glass-window card, **7**: 840-41
linoleum and woodcuts, 9: 1094-1103
greeting cards, **9**: 1099-1101
scarf, block-printed, **9**: 1096-98
tools, sharpening, **9**: 1097
wall hanging, two-color, **9**: 1102-3
monoprinting, 10: 1256-67
greeting cards, fingerprint, **10**: 1259-60
litho-monoprint, **10**: 1263-64
place mat, Janus, **10**: 1267
reverse silhouettes, **10**: 1261-63
stationery, fingerprint, **10**: 1258-59
T-shirt, calligraphic, **10**: 1265-66
music making, 11: 1287, 1292
gongs and chimes, **11**: 1287, 1292
photographic printing, 12: 1488-1501
contact prints, **12**: 1494-96
developing negatives, **12**: 1491-94
dodging and burning photographs, **12**: 1500
enlargements, making, **12**: 1496-99
mounting photographs, **12**: 1501
retouching photographs, **12**: 1501
rubbings, 15: 1814-23
brass rubbings, **15**: 1818-19
high reliefs, reproducing, **15**: 1823
inking raised designs, **15**: 1820-21
tombstone rubbings, **15**: 1815-17
serigraphy, 16: 1960-73
cleaning silk screens, **16**: 1973
fillers, silk screen, **16**: 1973
garden print, **16**: 1960, 1971-72
making silk screen, **16**: 1966-67
mixing inks, **16**: 1973

plastic, printing on, **16**: 1970-71
poster print, **16**: 1963-65
solvents, silk screen, **16**: 1973
wall-hanging catchalls, **16**: 1968-70
string art, 18: 2270-83
children's string designs, **18**: 2282-83
conics in box, **18**: 2271, 2280-81
curves, string art, **18**: 2275
helios, **18**: 2276-77
raised ellipse, **18**: 2278-79
three adjacent hexagons, **18**: 2272-73
triple stellate forms, **18**: 2274-76
See also **Designs and Decorations; Paint and Color**
Greenery and Growing Things
bonsai, 2: 220-29
cascade bonsai, **2**: 227
driftwood bonsai, **2**: 223-25
miniature bonsai, **2**: 229
rock-grown bonsai, **2**: 228
tropical bonsai, **2**: 226
bottle gardens, 2: 252-56
lab-bottle garden, **2**: 256
water-cooler bottle garden, **2**: 252-56
Christmas celebrations, 4: 463, 465
traditional wreath, **4**: 465
wheat-and-flower wreath, **4**: 463
dried flowers, 5: 614-23
bouquet, dried-spice, **5**: 622-23
greenhouse construction, 7: 816-35
herbs, 7: 876-84
hanging garden, **7**: 882
harvesting and drying, **7**: 882-83
gift basket, herb, **7**: 884
where to see herb gardens, **7**: 887
ikebana, 8: 918-27
avant-garde ikebana, **8**: 926-27
cascading nageire, **8**: 924-25
upright moribana, **8**: 922-23
lighted indoor gardens, 9: 1080-93
bookcase shelf garden, **9**: 1086
corner garden, **9**: 1087-88
environments, plant, **9**: 1093
nursery, indoor, **9**: 1085
skylight floor garden, **9**: 1090-91
wall garden, **9**: 1081, 1091-93
window garden, **9**: 1088-89
organic gardening, 11: 1360-63
plants and painted pots, 13: 1632-33
sand-layered planter, 15: 1891-94
seed sprouting, 16: 1952-59
growing sprouts, **16**: 1952-59
tea, 20: 2439-42, 2444-46
herb cultivation, **20**: 2439-42
kinds of tea, **20**: 2444-46
terrariums, 20: 2452-61
cactus terrarium, **20**: 2460-61
fern terrarium, **20**: 2457-59
plants, terrarium, **20**: 2456
temperatures, terrarium **20**: 2456
tropical terrarium, **20**: 2454-55
topiary, 20: 2528-37
geometric topiary, **20**: 2530-31

privet hedge, **20**: 2533-35
three-ball ivy topiary, **20**: 2532
trellises, 21: 2614-25
doorway trellis, **21**: 2614, 2622-25
fan trellises, **21**: 2616-18
freestanding trellis, **21**: 2619-21
greenhouse construction, 7: 816-35
cold frame, **7**: 818, 819
curved fiberglass greenhouse, **7**: 822-35
hotbed, **7**: 818-19
pit greenhouse, **7**: 820-21
See also **bonsai; bottle gardens; herbs; ikebana; lighted indoor gardens; organic gardening; seed sprouting; terrariums; trellises; vivariums; yard toys**
greeting cards, 7: 836-45
birth announcements, **7**: 845
cardboard printing, **7**: 844-45
embroidered cards, **15**: 1860-61
fingerprint cards, **10**: 1259-60
linoleum and woodcut cards, **9**: 1099-1101
needlepoint cards, **7**: 838-39
pressed flower cards, **7**: 838
ribbon bookmark card, **7**: 837
stained-glass-window card, **7**: 840-41
valentine cards
gift box, **21**: 2674-75
lovebird, **21**: 2674
playing card, **21**: 2673
two-heart, **21**: 2672-73
See also **birthday celebrations; block printing; calligraphy; cartooning; Christmas celebrations; collages and assemblages; genealogy; linoleum and woodcuts; origami; papermaking; rubbings; serigraphy; silhouettes; stained glass; stamp decoupage; stenciling; wycinanki**
guides, natural, pathfinding and, **9**: 1148-52
guinea pigs, 22: 2706-7
guiro, 11: 1291

hair piece, bone, **15**: 1917-18
halter, 14: 1740
hammer man toy, 20: 2559-60
hammocks and slings, 7: 846-53
log sling, canvas, **7**: 850-51
naval hammock, **7**: 851-53
sprang hammock, **17**: 2174-76
See also **carryalls; macrame; rope knotting; sail making and repair; shelters and tents; swings**
handbags. See **bags**
handball, Chinese, **18**: 2262
hand illumination, 3: 312, 319-21
handkerchiefs, edging, **19**: 2421, 2424
hand towel, huck work, **19**: 2340
hangings. See **planters; wall hangings; window hangings; woven tapestries**

H, continued

hardanger embroidery, 7: 854-65
  bookmark, **7:** 858
  cocktail mat, **7:** 859-60
  red place mat and napkin, **7:** 861-62
  white place mat and napkin, **7:** 863-65
  See also **crewel; embroidery; Floren-
    tine stitch; needlepoint; samplers;
    smocking; Swedish huck work**
hardware
  antiquing furniture hardware, **1:** 80
  bracelets made from, **8:** 954
  outdoor swings, hardware for, **19:** 2353
  See also **fasteners; findings**
harps. See **wind harps**
hat rack, pegboard sampler, **15:** 1854
hats and caps
  band for, inkle-woven, **8:** 932
  crocheted raffia cap, **14:** 1718-19
  samurai hat, origami, **11:** 1381
  scarf and cap set, granny squares, **7:** 812
  straw hat, **14:** 1714-16
  tassel cap, knit, **8:** 1006-7
headboard, cardboard, **3:** 367, 375
heads and hands
  cartooning, **4:** 404-7
  cast and mold, **10:** 1248-49
  plaster-cast, **4:** 424-29
  poured acrylic, **1:** 20
  puppet heads, papier-mâché, **11:** 1405-7
hedges, privet, **20:** 2533-35
helios, 18: 2276-77
heraldry, 7: 866-75
  abstract heraldic standards, wood,
    23: 2852-55
  in America, **7:** 873
  coat of arms
    designing, **7:** 874-75
    displaying, **7:** 875
    finding, **7:** 873
    parts of, **7:** 872
  design, heraldic, **7:** 868-71
  European heraldic agencies, **7:** 872
  glossary of terms, **7:** 870
  patterns, heraldic, **7:** 868-69
  tinctures, **7:** 871
  See also **block printing; flags and
    banners; folk art; genealogy;
    totem poles; woven tapestries**
herbs, 7: 876-89
  cooking with herbs, **7:** 885-86
  gift basket, herb, **7:** 884
  ginger beer, **3:** 298-301
  hanging garden, **7:** 882
  harvesting and drying, **7:** 882-83
  note cards, herb, **7:** 884
  soaps, herb, **17:** 2102
  teas, herbal, **20:** 2441-42, 2444-46
    cultivation, **20:** 2439-42
  vinegars, herb-flavored, **22:**
    2699-2703
  wines, herbal, **22:** 2804-5
  See also **cheeses and churning;
    Colonial crafts; greenhouse con-
    struction; ikebana; lighted indoor
    gardens; perfumes; potpourris**

and pomanders; soups; terrines
    and timbales; vegetable dyes
hibachi and hot-pot cookery, 7: 890-96
  hibachi cooking, **7:** 892-93
  hot-pot cooking, **7:** 894-96
  See also **sashimi and sushi; seed
    sprouting; wok cookery**
hiking stick, 22: 2716-18
hit-the-penny, 18: 2265
holidays. See **birthday celebrations;
    Christmas celebrations; Kitchen
    Favorites and Celebrations;
    parades and festivals; square
    dancing**
hooked rugs. See **rugs,** hooked
hooks, coat, ceramic, **4:** 444-45
hoop-framed samplers, 15: 1855-57
hoop masks
  clown, **10:** 1184-85
  lion, **10:** 1186-87
hoop weaving, 19: 2393, 2405
hopscotch, 18: 2266
hors-d'oeuvres, treen wheel for, **21:** 2612
hotbed greenhouse, 7: 818-19
hot-plate pad, knotted, **14:** 1789
hot-pot cooking, 7: 894-96
huck work. See **Swedish huck work**
hydrometers, wine, **22:** 2799

ice cream, sherbet, and ices, 8: 910-17
  flavored ice creams, **8:** 915-16
  ices, **8:** 917
  sherbet, **8:** 917
  vanilla ice cream, **8:** 914-15
  See also **baby foods; birthday
    celebrations; confections and com-
    fits; marmalades and preserves;
    sugar shapes; syrups; winter
    sculpture**
ice cubes, decorative, **22:** 2815
ices, 8: 917
ice sculptures, 22: 2812-16
ikebana, 8: 918-27
  avant-garde ikebana, **8:** 926-27
  cascading nageire, **8:** 924-25
  upright moribana, **8:** 922-23
  See also **bonsai; bottle gardens;
    dried flowers; greenhouse con-
    struction; herbs; lighted indoor
    gardens; terrariums**
illumination, hand, **3:** 312, 319-21
inkle weaving, 8: 928-35
  hat band and bag handle, **8:** 932
  pick-up pattern belt, **8:** 935
  wall hanging, inkle, **8:** 929, 934-35
  watchband and vase cover, **8:** 933
  See also **sprang; tablet and frame
    weaving; woven tapestries**
insects, 8: 936-47
  collections, insect, **8:** 942-47
  trapping insects, **8:** 940-42
    black-light trap, **8:** 941-42

See also **ant farms; beachcombing;
    birds and birdhouses; dioramas;
    pet habitats; tropical fish;
    vivariums**
instruments, musical
  Appalachian dulcimer, **5:** 624, 626-33
  fretboard dulcimer, **5:** 625-26
  gongs and chimes, **11:** 1287, 1292
  marimbas, **11:** 1287, 1294-99
  percussion instruments, **11:** 1287-91
  See also **square dancing; whistles
    and flutes; wind harps**
interior decorating. See **models and
    mock-ups; stenciling; structural
    furnishings; supergraphics;** names
    of decorative objects (e.g., pillows,
    place mats, wall hangings)
invitations, personally designed, **3:** 316

J

jackets, twill, **22:** 2768-69
jam, 10: 1160-62
Japanese crafts
  hibachi and hot-pot cookery, **7:** 891-96
  ikebana, **8:** 918-27
  sashimi and sushi, **15:** 1900-11
  tea ceremony, **20:** 2447-51
jelly, 10: 1164
jellyfish, plastic, for shadow theater, **16:**
    1989, 1992
jewelry, 8: 948-57
  braclets
    forged, **23:** 2828-29
    fork, **8:** 955
    hardware, **8:** 954
    leather, painted, **9:** 1069-70
    wrapped wire, **8:** 957
  cabochons, gemstone, **9:** 1048-51
  coconut shell jewelry, **8:** 951
  color-engraved scrimshaw, **15:** 1919-20
  cuff links, button, **3:** 305
  earrings
    button, **3:** 305
    coconut shell, **8:** 951
    feather, **8:** 950
    pearl, **2:** 156-57
    raffia, **14:** 1719
    seashell, **16:** 1945
  feather jewelry, **8:** 948-51
  findings, jewelry, **8:** 953, **15:** 1916
  hair piece, bone, **15:** 1917-18
  medallion, American Indian, **1:** 46
  necklaces
    beaded, **1:** 45
    copper-foiled, **18:** 2226-29
    forged, **23:** 2829-31
    looped-link, **23:** 2823-25
    metal, embossed, **14:** 1751-53
    ojo de dios, **11:** 1355
    safety-pin, **2:** 154
  pendants
    copper, **6:** 661-63
    pomander-ball, **13:** 1605
    stone, neck ring and, **8:** 956-57

rings
  aurora-borealis, **2**: 154-55
  beaded, **1**: 44
  spoon, **8**: 955
tools, **8**: 952
See also **casting; lace; lapidary; macramé; mineralogy; repoussé and chased metal; seashells; silversmithing; stained glass; wire sculpture**
jewelry box, 15: 1810-13
Jewelry, Lapidary, and Metalwork
  American Indian crafts, 1: 42-47
    chain, beaded daisy, **1**: 45
    loom beading, **1**: 47
    medallion, **1**: 46
    ring, beaded, **1**: 44
  annealing metal, 17: 2062
  beadwork, 2: 144-57
    breechcloth, **2**: 151
    earrings, pearl, **2**: 156-57
    fruit, beaded, **2**: 152-53
    handsewing beads, **2**: 151
    making beads, **2**: 145-46
    necklace, safety-pin, **2**: 154
    ring, bead, **2**: 154-55
    stringing beads, **2**: 148-50
  finishing metal, 17: 2059
  jewelry, 8: 948-57
    coconut shell jewelry, **8**: 951
    feather jewelry, **8**: 948-51
    findings, jewelry, **8**: 953, **15**: 1916
    hardware bracelets, **8**: 954
    spoon ring and fork bracelet, **8**: 955
    stone pendant and neck ring, **8**: 956-57
    tools, jewelry, **8**: 952
    wrapped wire bracelet, **8**: 957
  lamps and lampshades, 9: 1030-32, 1035
    canister lamp, **9**: 1035
    overhead fixture, wiring, **9**: 1033
    table lamp, wiring, **9**: 1034
    tin lantern, **9**: 1030-32
  lapidary, 9: 1040-55
    cabochons, gemstone, **9**: 1048-51
    eggs, gemstone, **9**: 1045-48
    flats, gemstone, **9**: 1052-53
    gemstones, hand forming, **9**: 1046
    tumbling gemstones, **9**: 1042-44
  mineralogy, 10: 1196-1209
    decorative mineral projects, **10**: 1206-9
  mobiles, 10: 1220, 1224-31
    balsa wood mobile, **10**: 1224-25
    copper shapes mobile, **10**: 1225-26
    steel fin mobile, **10**: 1227-31
  pewtersmithing, 12: 1476, 1479-87
    fabricated pewter box, **12**: 1484-87
    handwrought pewter bowl, **12**: 1480-83
  repoussé and chased metal, 14: 1744-53
    foil mirror frame, **14**: 1748-50
    metal necklace, **14**: 1751-53
    ornamented box tops, **14**: 1746-48

seashells, **16**: 1950-51
  lampshade, shell, **16**: 1950-51
sheet metal, sawing, **17**: 2058
silversmithing, 17: 2054-65
  annealing metal, **17**: 2062
  bowl, copper, **17**: 2063-65
  butter knife, silver, **17**: 2056-57
  finishing metal, **17**: 2059
  spoon, silver, **17**: 2059-61
stone painting, 18: 2255-56
  key-chain fob, **18**: 2255-56
techniques, metal-working, **23**: 2826-27
tin and pierced work, 20: 2500-9
  candle sconce and snuffer, **20**: 2504-7
  cookie cutters, **20**: 2502-3
  fruit bowl, **20**: 2508-9
wire sculpture, 23: 2822-35
  basket, wire, **23**: 2832-33
  belt and bracelet, forged, **23**: 2828-29
  characteristics of wire, **23**: 2827
  figures, wire, **23**: 2822, 2834-35
  flowers, wire, **23**: 2831-32
  necklace, forged, **23**: 2829-31
  necklace, looped-link, **23**: 2823-25
  wire working, **23**: 2826-27
jewelry stand, 10: 1248
jib sail, making, **15**: 1847
Johnny-on-the-pony, 18: 2258-59
jumping jack, 20: 2552-53
Jungle Game, 19: 2366-67, 2370-72

K

kaleidoscopes, 8: 958-67
  cubes, kaleidoscopic, **8**: 960-61
  Hue View kaleidoscope, **8**: 962-63
  kaleidoscope, **8**: 965-67
  teleidoscope, **8**: 963-65
See also **acrylics; zoetrope toys**
kayaks, 8: 968-75
  building kayak, **8**: 970-75
    canvas, covering, **8**: 974
    cockpit, making, **8**: 973-74
    deck braces, making, **8**: 973
    frame, assembling, **8**: 971-72
    frame, cutting, **8**: 970-71
    keel, **8**: 975
    materials for, **8**: 970
    side stringers, attaching, **8**: 972-73
    trimming and painting, **8**: 975
  Eskimo kayaks, **8**: 969
  modern kayaks, **8**: 968-69
  paddling, **8**: 975
See also **bicycles and bicycling; canoeing; gold panning; maps and pathfinding; piloting small boats; sail making and repair; soapbox and skate vehicles; shelters and tents; weather forecasting**
kick-the-can, 18: 2261
kickball, 18: 2234
kilns, 8: 976-87
  raku kiln, **8**: 983-85
  sawdust kiln, **8**: 980-82

See also **ceramics; enameling metal; pottery; sculpture**
kimono coat, 16: 1977-78
Kitchen Favorites and Celebrations
  baby foods, 1: 106-11
    breakfast cookies, **1**: 110-11
    preparing baby foods, **1**: 107-9
  birthday celebrations, 2: 200-7
    baking for children, **2**: 206-7
    cake, **2**: 202-5
  breads, 3: 280-89
    sourdough bread, **3**: 284-89
    trail breads, **3**: 282-83
  brewing, 3: 292-301
    ginger beer, **3**: 298-301
    root beer and sarsaparilla, **3**: 294-97
  carving, 4: 418-21
    vegetables and fruits, carving, **4**: 418-21
  cheeses and churning, 4: 446-53
    cheeses, **4**: 450-52
    churning, **4**: 453
    yogurts and sour cream, **4**: 446-49
  Christmas celebrations, 4: 466-67
    recipes, Christmas, **4**: 466-67
  confections and comfits, 4: 506-12
    brittles and fudges, **4**: 510-11
    coated chocolates, **4**: 512
    hard candies, **4**: 509
    quick candies, **4**: 508
  dyes, natural, **5**: 636
  egg decoration, 5: 634-40
    Imperial Easter eggs, **5**: 638-40
    margutis and pysanka eggs, **5**: 634-37
  filleting fish, 15: 1903
  flowers, artificial, 6: 692-93, 697
    fabric flowers, **6**: 696-97
    feather flowers, **6**: 692-93
  gingerbread, 6: 762-68
    cookies, gingerbread, **6**: 767-68
    house, gingerbread, **6**: 762-66
  herbs, 7: 885-86
    bibliography, herb, **7**: 887
    cooking with herbs, **7**: 885-86
    sources, herb, **7**: 887
  hibachi and hot-pot cookery, 7: 890-96
    hibachi cooking, **7**: 892-93
    hot-pot cooking, **7**: 894-96
  ice cream, sherbet, and ices, 8: 910-17
    flavored ice creams, **8**: 915-16
    ices, **8**: 917
    sherbet, **8**: 917
    vanilla ice cream, **8**: 914-15
  marmalades and preserves, 10: 1158-65
    chutney, **10**: 1165
    curd, **10**: 1163
    jam, **10**: 1160-62
    jelly, **10**: 1164
    marmalade, **10**: 1162-63
  pasta, 12: 1426-37
    homemade pasta, **12**: 1428-31
    macaroni recipes, **12**: 1436-37

pasta, continued
  stuffed pasta, **12:** 1432-35
pickled and canned foods, 12: 1502-11
  fruit recipes, **12:** 1511
  pickle recipes, **12:** 1506
  tomato recipes, **12:** 1507-8
  vegetable recipes, **12:** 1509-10
sashimi and sushi, 15: 1900-11
  chirashi sushi, **15:** 1911
  nigiri sushi, **15:** 1905-7
  norimaki sushi, **15:** 1908-10
  sashimi, **15:** 1903-5
soups, 17: 2122-31
  chicken julienne, **17:** 2126
  chicken soup, **17:** 2127
  cupboard soups, **17:** 2131
  fruit soups, **17:** 2128-29
  vichyssoise, **17:** 2130-31
sugar shapes, 18: 2300-4
  brown sugar shapes, **18:** 2304
  ladybugs, sugar, **18:** 2303
  place card, sugar, **18:** 2304
  schoolhouse, sugar, **18:** 2302-3
  wedding bells, sugar, **18:** 2303
  winter scene, sugar, **18:** 2300, 2302
syrups, 19: 2358-65
  beverages and desserts, **19:** 2358-63
  main dishes, syrup-flavored, **19:** 2364-65
tea, 20: 2442-43
  brewing tea, **20:** 2442-43
terrines and timbales, 20: 2462-69
  terrines, **20:** 2463-66
  timbales, **20:** 2467-69
vinegars, 22: 2694-2703
  cider vinegars, **22:** 2698
  flavored vinegars, **22:** 2699-2703
  wine vinegar, **22:** 2696-97
wine making, 22: 2794-2807
wok cookery, 23: 2386-45
  beef with broccoli, **23:** 2839-41
  cabbage, spicy, **23:** 2839
  chicken, Tai Chien, **23:** 2844
  Chinese meal, **23:** 2845
  duck, deep-fried, **23:** 2843
  fish, steamed, **23:** 2841-42
kites and kite making, 8: 988-99
  Greek kite, **8:** 992-95
  Indian fighter kite, **8:** 989, 998-99
  sled kite, **8:** 991
  Thai dragon kite, **8:** 996-97
  See also **airplanes, paper; origami; swings**
knitting to fit, 8: 1000-11
  hooded parka sweater, **8:** 1010-11
  measurements, taking, **8:** 1003
  stitches, knitting, **8:** 1004-5, **21:** 2568-69
  sweater and skirt, knit, **8:** 1007-9
  tassel cap, **8:** 1006-7
  See also **afghan stitch; crochet; granny squares; lace; spinning; traditional knitting motifs**
knives
  silver butter knife, **17:** 2056-57
  treen spreaders and cutters, **21:** 2609

Knotting. See **Weaving, Braiding, and Knotting**
kvass, brewing, **3:** 301

L

lace, 8: 1012-24
  collar and cuffs, bobbin lace, **8:** 1019-21
  necklace, lace, **8:** 1023-24
  sash, bobbin lace, **8:** 1017-18
  stitches, needle lace, **8:** 1022
  window hanging, needle lace, **8:** 1013, 1021-23
  See also **crewel; crochet; embroidery; jewelry; knitting to fit; macramé; quilling; sprang; tatting**
ladle, treen, **21:** 2605
lamps and lampshades, 9: 1030-39
  canister lamp, **9:** 1035
  cover, lampshade, **9:** 1039
  decoupage lamp, **5:** 573
  globe lamp, **6:** 700-1
  hanging lamps, **2:** 248
  leaded glass lampshade, **9:** 1066-67
  potichomania lamp, **9:** 1036-37
  sculptural lamp, **13:** 1570-71
  seashell lampshade, **16:** 1950-51
  suede lampshade, **9:** 1038-39
  table lamp, driftwood, **2:** 142-43
  tin lantern, **9:** 1030-32
  See also **beachcombing; bottle cutting; leaded glass; seashells; tin and pierced work**
landscapes, yarn, **23:** 2915
  with feathers, **23:** 2916-17
lantern, tin, **9:** 1030-32
lapidary, 9: 1040-55
  cabochons, gemstone, **9:** 1048-51
  eggs, gemstone, **9:** 1045-48
  flats, gemstone, **9:** 1052-53
  techniques, advanced lapidary, **9:** 1055
  tumbling gemstones, **9:** 1042-44
  See also **jewelry; mineralogy; mobiles; pewtersmithing; silversmithing**
Lasca, 19: 2374-75
latex molding, 10: 1251-52
leaded glass, 9: 1056-67
  candle box or planter, **9:** 1064-65
  lampshade, **9:** 1066-67
  stained-glass panel, **18:** 2229-31
  window panel, **9:** 1063
  See also **color psychology; lamps and lampshades; stained glass**
lean-tos, 16: 2018
Leathercrafts
  American Indian crafts, 1: 48-53
    moccasins, Apache, **1:** 49-53
  belts and buckles, 2: 168-77
    attaching buckles, **2:** 176-77
    beaded belt, **2:** 172-73
    cowboy belt, **2:** 168, 170-71
    elastic belts, **2:** 174-75

  bookbinding, 2: 236-42
    diary, leather-bound, **2:** 236-42
  carryalls, 4: 390, 396-401
    tote bag, leather, **4:** 396-99
  cutting leather, 4: 401
  dyeing leather, 9: 1076
  lacing, leather, **4:** 400-1
    needles for, **4:** 400
  lamps and lampshades, 9: 1038-39
    suede shade, **9:** 1038-39
  leather working, 9: 1068-71, 1074-79
    appliquéd pillow, **9:** 1070-71
    bracelet, painted, **9:** 1069-70
    envelope briefcase, **9:** 1077-79
    sculpture, leather, **9:** 1068, 1079
  machine sewing, leather, 9: 1074-75
  riveting techniques, 2: 177
  sandal making, 15: 1862-68
    Italia sandal, **15:** 1867
    Riviera sandal, **15:** 1867-68
    Seville sandal, **15:** 1864-66
    T-tie sandal, **15:** 1868
  seams, pounding, **4:** 400
  sewing leather, 4: 400-1, **10:** 1212
    with lacing, **4:** 401
    zippers, **4:** 401
  suppliers, leather, **1:** 52, **9:** 1077, **15:** 1867
  tools, leather working, **4:** 400, **9:** 1076, **15:** 1864
  types of leather, 1: 52, **9:** 1076
lenses. See **astronomy; cameras; color psychology; kaleidoscopes; photographic printing**
letter opener, silver, **17:** 2056-57
light
  mosaic light sculpture, **10:** 1274-75
  noon light show, **20:** 2490-93
  stage lighting, **18:** 2206-13
  See also **color psychology; kaleidoscopes; stained glass**
lighted indoor gardens, 9: 1080-93
  artificial light environment, **9:** 1093
  bookcase shelf garden, **9:** 1086
  corner garden, **9:** 1087-88
  nursery, indoor, **9:** 1085
  skylight floor garden, **9:** 1090-91
  wall garden, **9:** 1081, 1091-93
  window garden, **9:** 1088-89
  See also **bottle gardens; greenhouse construction; herbs; ikebana; organic gardening; seed sprouting; terrariums; topiary; trellises**
linoleum and woodcuts, 9: 1094-1103
  greeting cards, **9:** 1099-1101
  prints, linoleum, **2:** 216-19
  scarf, **9:** 1096-98
  wall hanging, two-color, **9:** 1102-3
  See also **block printing; greeting cards; monoprinting; papermaking; scrimshaw; serigraphy; stenciling; tie dyeing**
lithography, simulated, **10:** 1263-64
  See also **block printing**
lizards, chameleon, **22:** 2710-11
llama, pine-cone, **13:** 1584, 1586
lobster-man, 2: 140-41

lofts, 18: 2284, 2288-93
looms
  beading loom, **1:** 47
  branch weaving loom, **19:** 2402
  four-harness loom, **22:** 2574
  inkle weaving loom, **8:** 928-30
  simple frame loom, **23:** 2861-63
  sprang loom, **18:** 2169
  tapestry frame loom, **23:** 2864-65
lost-wax casting, 4: 430-33
lounge chairs, sculptural, plywood and
  foam, **13:** 1577

M

macaroni recipes, 12: 1436-37
machine stitchery, 9: 1104-15
  bag, trapunto, **9:** 1113-14
  folk art hanging, **9:** 1107-8
  pillow, ribbon, **9:** 1114
  pillowcase, embroidered, **9:** 1115
  place mat, personalized, **9:** 1111-12
  stitches, **9:** 1109
  wall hanging, appliqué, **9:** 1109-11
  work shirt, free embroidery, **9:** 1106-7
  See also **appliqué; crewel;**
    embroidery; patchwork; quilting;
    recycling clothes; ribboncraft;
    sewing without pattern; trapunto
macramé, 9: 1116-27
  belt, adjustable, **9:** 1120-21
  dress yoke and sash, **9:** 1122-23
  hanging, micromé, **9:** 1126-27
  knots, **9:** 1118-19
  room-divider screen, **9:** 1116, 1124
  willow tree sculpture, **9:** 1125-26
  See also **caning and rushing;**
    hammocks and slings; inkle
    weaving; jewelry; lace; rope
    knotting; sculpture; sprang;
    tablet and frame weaving; tatting
magic, 9: 1128-39
  balancing trick, **9:** 1131
  coin vanishing trick, **9:** 1136-37
  color changing wand trick, **9:** 1133
  cups and balls trick, **9:** 1134
  cut and restored rope trick, **9:** 1132
  handkerchief trick, **9:** 1137-38
  multiplying ball trick, **9:** 1134
  paper bag tricks, **9:** 1137-38
  presenting magic, **9:** 1129
  salt vanishing trick, **9:** 1135
  sleight of hand, **9:** 1134-35
  torn and restored napkin trick, **9:** 1130
  tricks, **9:** 1130-39
  water in hat trick, **9:** 1138-39
  See also **birthday celebrations; card**
    tricks; table games
main dishes
  Chinese meal, **23:** 2845
  syrup-flavored, **19:** 2364-65
  See also **hibachi and hot-pot cookery;**
    sashimi and sushi; wok cookery
makeup, 5: 536-37
  heavenly-nights face makeup, **17:**
    2068-69

  leopard face makeup, **17:** 2068-69
  primitive face makeup, **17:** 2070-71
  stage face makeup, **17:** 2072-73
  See also **cold creams; cosmetics;**
    perfumes
Mancala, 19: 2368
maple beer, brewing, **3:** 301
maps and pathfinding, 9: 1140-52
  bicycle touring and maps, **2:** 188-89
  compass, making and using, **9:** 1146-48
  maps, making and using, **9:** 1141-44
  natural guides, **9:** 1148-52
  organic gardening and weather maps,
    11: 1372-73
  See also **astronomy; bicycles and**
    bicycling; canoeing; gold
    panning; kayaks; piloting small
    boats; shelters and tents;
    sundials; time telling; weather
    forecasting
marimbas, 11: 1287, 1294-99
marbleizing, furniture, **1:** 79
marine aquariums. See aquariums
marionettes
  clown, **13:** 1645, 1648-51
  paper, **13:** 1646-47
  See also **animals, doll; birthday cele-**
    brations; costumes; puppets and
    puppetry
marmalades and preserves, 10: 1158-65
  chutney, **10:** 1165
  curd, **10:** 1163
  jam, **10:** 1160-62
  jelly, **10:** 1164
  marmalade, **10:** 1162-63
  See also **baby foods; breads;**
    confections and comfits; ice cream,
    sherbet, and ices; pickled and
    canned foods; sugar shapes;
    syrups
marquetry, 10: 1166-79
  chessboard, marquetry, **10:** 1179
  geometric marquetry design, **10:**
    1167-76
  special effects, marquetry, **10:** 1177-78
  See also **antiquing furniture; gold**
    leafing; refinishing furniture;
    rosemaling
masks, 10: 1180-95
  African rope mask, **10:** 1192-95
  clown hoop mask, **10:** 1184-85
  facial masks, **17:** 2105
  heavenly-nights face makeup, **17:**
    2068-69
  leopard face makeup, **17:** 2068-69
  lion hoop mask, **10:** 1186-87
  newspaper bird mask, **10:** 1188-91
  paper-plate masks, **10:** 1182-83, **23:**
    2914-15
  primitive face makeup, **17:** 2070-71
  stage face makeup, **17:** 2072-73
  See also **carving; costumes; papier-**
    mâché; parades and festivals;
    puppets and puppetry; skin

  painting; stagecraft; totem poles;
    yarn painting
Mason-jar ant house, 1: 65-66
mayonnaise, 4: 453
mead, 22: 2804
medallion, American Indian, **1:** 46
metals. See Jewelry, Lapidary, and
  Metalwork; names of metals
Midsummer's Eve festivals, 12: 1418
milk-crates, desk and seat from, **3:** 262-65
Mill, 19: 2369-70
mineralogy, 10: 1196-1209
  decorative mineral projects, **10:** 1206-9
  displaying minerals, **10:** 1204-6
    lighting for, **10:** 1206
  finding minerals, **10:** 1203-4
  gemstones
    cabochons, **9:** 1048-51
    eggs, **9:** 1045-48
    flats, **9:** 1052-53
    tumbling, **9:** 1042-44
  identifying minerals, **10:** 1198-1203
    crystals, **10:** 1200-1
    fluorescence, **10:** 1202
    fracture and cleavage, **10:** 1200
    hardness, **10:** 1198, 1199
    luster, **10:** 1198, 1199
    specific gravity, **10:** 1199
    streak color, **10:** 1199
  See also **acrylics; American Indian**
    crafts; gold panning; jewelry;
    lapidary; pewtersmithing;
    silversmithing
mirrors
  frames, mirror
    foil, **14:** 1748-50
    mosaic, **10:** 1272-73
    needlepoint, **11:** 1328-29
  hand mirror, rosemaling, **15:** 1803-4
  See also **astronomy; kaleidoscopes;**
mittens and mukluks, 10: 1210-19
  mittens, **10:** 1211, 1213-15
  mukluks, **10:** 1216-19
mobiles, 10: 1220-31
  balsa wood mobile, **10:** 1224-25
  cardboard snail mobile, **10:** 1223
  copper-foiled mobile, **18:** 2226
  copper shapes mobile, **10:** 1225-26
  crane origami mobile, **11:** 1383, 1385
  disk mobile, **23:** 2896-97
  felt auto-mobile, **10:** 1222
  steel fin mobile, **10:** 1227-31
  See also **acrylics; lapidary; ojo de**
    dios; origami; piñatas; quilling;
    sculpture; tin and pierced work;
    wycinanki
moccasins, Apache, **1:** 49-53
models and mock-ups, 10: 1232-45
  bedroom redecorating model, **10:**
    1235-40
  garden structure, **10:** 1232, 1241-44
  mock-ups, **10:** 1245
  See also **dioramas; dollhouses and**
    furniture; ship models; soapbox
    and skate vehicles; structural
    furnishings; supergraphics;
    tables; tree houses

M, continued

molas, reverse appliqué, **14:** 1754-57, 1760-61

molding methods, 10: 1246-55
hand mold and cast, **10:** 1248-49
latex molding; **10:** 1251-52
pop-art candle, **10:** 1253-55
See also **acrylics; candlemaking; casting; foam forms; papier-mâché; sand casting; sand characters and castles; sculpture; stained glass; winter sculpture**

mollusks, 16: 1943

monoprinting, 10: 1256-67
greeting cards, fingerprint, **10:** 1259-60
litho-monoprint, **10:** 1263-64
place mat, Janus, **10:** 1267
reverse silhouettes, **10:** 1261-63
stationery, fingerprint, **10:** 1258-59
T-shirt, calligraphic, **10:** 1265-66
See also **block printing; papermaking; rubbings; serigraphy; tie dyeing; watercolors**

moonwinder, 20: 2548

moribana, upright, **8:** 922-23

mosaics, 10: 1268-80
beach glass mosaic, **2:** 139
button mosaics, **10:** 1270-71
grouted mosaics, **10:** 1277-78
light sculpture, mosaic, **10:** 1274-75
mirror frame, mosaic, **10:** 1272-73
mural, tile, **10:** 1278-80
split-straw mosaic, **14:** 1712-13
stained glass mosaic, **18:** 2225-26
See also **beachcombing; ceramics; collages and assemblages; stained glass; stamp decoupage; tiles**

moving-picture wheels, 23: 2930-33

mukluks, 10: 1216-19

mulching, benefits of, **11:** 1365-66

mural, tile, **10:** 1278-80

music making, 11: 1286-99
gongs and chimes, **11:** 1287, 1292
marimbas, **11:** 1287, 1294-99
percussion, instruments, **11:** 1287-91
See also **dulcimers; parades and festivals; shadow theater; square dancing; stagecraft; whistles and flutes; wind harps**

N

nageire, cascading, **8:** 924-25

napkins and napkin folding, 11: 1300-7
artichoke fold, **11:** 1306
band fold, **11:** 1305
candle fold, **11:** 1303
fan fold, **11:** 1307
fleur-de-lis fold, **11:** 1307
hardanger embroidered napkins
red, **7:** 861-62
white, **7:** 863-65
holders, napkin
monogrammed, **9:** 1112
treen, **21:** 2610-11

lily fold, **11:** 1304
palm leaf fold, **11:** 1301-2
pocket fold, **11:** 1304
sailboat fold, **11:** 1302

natural guides, pathfinding and, **9:** 2248-52

Nature and Ecology. See **Environmental Projects; Greenery and Growing Things; Outdoor Activities;** names of nature activities; names of natural materials

navigation. See **canoeing; kayaks; piloting small boats; weather forecasting**

neckerchief, butterfly, **11:** 1315

necklaces
copper-foiled, **18:** 2226-29
daisy chain, beaded, **1:** 45
feather, fringed, **8:** 948-50
forged, **23:** 2829-31
lace, **8:** 1023-24
looped-link, **23:** 2823-25
medallion, American Indian, **1:** 46
metal, embossed, **14:** 1751-53
ojo de dios, **11:** 1355
painted stone, **18:** 2255
ring and stone pendant, neck, **8:** 957
safety-pin and bead, **2:** 154
seashell, **16:** 1945
stringing beads for, **2:** 148-50
wrapped, **23:** 2880-82

neckties, 11: 1308-17
butterfly neckerchief, **11:** 1315
crochet tie, **5:** 552
illustrating ties, **11:** 1312-13
recycled tie skirt, **11:** 1316-17
tree design tie, **11:** 1311-12
tying ties, **11:** 1317
See also **tie dyeing**

Needlecrafts
afghan stitch, 1: 24-31
afghan, **1:** 29
pillow, tic-tac-toe, **1:** 28
vest and child's skirt, **1:** 24-28
animal dolls, 1: 54-63
alligator, stuffed, **1:** 62-63
elephant, stuffed, **1:** 56-59
lion, stuffed, **1:** 60-62
appliqué, 1: 82-91, **14:** 1700
hand appliqué, **1:** 82-85
machine appliqué, **1:** 87-89
pillows, people, **1:** 90
tablecloth, **1:** 91
bean-bags, 2: 164-66
furniture, bean-bag, **2:** 164-66
blocking, 7: 808
crewel embroidery, blocking, **5:** 546-47
knitting, blocking and steaming, **8:** 1011
tambour work, blocking, **19:** 2411
buttons, 3: 302-11
clay buttons, **3:** 308-9
cuff links, button, **3:** 305
hand-painted buttons, **3:** 310-11

seashell buttons, **3:** 306-7

carryalls, 4: 390-95
back pack, canvas, **4:** 395
tote bag, vinyl, **4:** 392-94

costumes, 5: 530-35
basic dress pattern, **5:** 533
caftans, **5:** 534
circular patterns, **5:** 531
drapes and wraparounds, **5:** 530
historic costumes, **5:** 527, 532
period dress, **5:** 535

crewel, 5: 538-49
embroidery sampler, **5:** 538-41, 546-49

crochet, 5: 550-57
bag, beaded, **5:** 553
beads, crocheting, **5:** 593
double crochet, **14:** 1717
dress, evening, **5:** 554-55
pincushion, **5:** 556
rug, sisal, **5:** 557
stitches, crochet, **1:** 30-31, **14:** 1717
tie, **5:** 552

embroidery, 6: 646-57
circles, **6:** 653
flower appliqué, **6:** 652
materials, embroidery, **6:** 650-51
mounting embroidery, **5:** 548-49
owl, black work, **6:** 656-57
stitches, embroidery, **1:** 86, **5:** 542-45, **7:** 857, **21:** 2574
techniques, embroidery, **5:** 540, **6:** 650-51
tissue covers, black work, **6:** 654-55

flags and banners, 6: 669-73
boat pennant, nylon, **6:** 672-73
club banner, **6:** 670-71

Florentine stitch, 6: 676-87
eyeglass case, **6:** 680-81
pillow, **6:** 684-87
plastic box cover, **6:** 683-84
tote bag pocket, **6:** 681-82

fur recycling, 6: 740-49
care, fur, **6:** 748
collar and cuffs, fur, **6:** 746-48
fling, fur, **6:** 749
pillow, fur, **6:** 742-43
sewing fur, **6:** 743
shortening, coat, **6:** 744-45

granny squares, 7: 806-15
cap and scarf, **7:** 812
floral afghan, **7:** 811
joining squares, **7:** 809
place mat, **7:** 810
popcorn stitch afghan, **7:** 813
shoulder tote bag, **7:** 814-15
traditional afghan, **7:** 807-8

greeting cards, 7: 838-39
needlepoint cards, **7:** 838-39

hardanger embroidery, 7: 854-65
bookmark, **7:** 858
cocktail mat, **7:** 859-60
red place mat and napkin, **7:** 861-62
white place mat and napkin, **7:** 863-65

knitting to fit, 8: 1000-11
  finishing knitting, **8:** 1011
  hooded parka sweater, **8:** 1010-11
  sweater and skirt, knit, **8:** 1007-9
  stitches, knitting, **8:** 1004-5, **21:** 2568-69
  seams, knitting, **8:** 1011
  tassel cap, **8:** 1006-7
lace, 8: 1021-24
  necklace, lace, **8:** 1023-24
  stitches, needle lace, **8:** 1022
  window hanging, needle lace, **8:** 1013, 1021-23
lamps and lampshades, 9: 1039
  cover, shade, **9:** 1039
machine stitchery, 9: 1104-15
  bag, trapunto, **9:** 1113-14
  hanging, folk art, **9:** 1107-8
  measurements, taking, **8:** 1003
  pillow, ribbon, **9:** 1114
  pillowcase, embroidered, **9:** 1115
  place mat, personalized, **9:** 1111-12
  stitches, machine embroidery, **9:** 1109
  wall hanging, appliquéd, **9:** 1109-11
  work shirt, free-embroidery, **9:** 1106-7
mittens and mukluks, 10: 1210-19
  mittens, **10:** 1210-15
  mukluks, **10:** 1216-19
mobiles, 10: 1220-22
  felt auto-mobile, **10:** 1222
neckties, 11: 1314, 1316-17
  making neckties, **11:** 1314
  recycled tie skirt, **11:** 1316-17
needlepoint, 11: 1318-33
  basic stitch, **11:** 1325
  belt, signature, **11:** 1324
  mirror frame, needlepoint, **11:** 1328-29
  pencil holder, gingham, **11:** 1322-23
  pillow, needlepoint, **11:** 1330-31
  rug, needlepoint, **11:** 1332-33
patchwork, 12: 1438-53, **14:** 1700
  crib quilt, **12:** 1447-48
  pillow, patchwork, **12:** 1443-46
  templates, making patchwork, **12:** 1441
  tote bag, patchwork, **12:** 1451-52
  traditional quilt, **12:** 1439, 1452-53
  vest, reversible, **12:** 1449-50
patterns, enlarging, **1:** 57
quilting, 14: 1690-1709
  Dresden-plate quilt, **14:** 1702-5
  patterns, traditional quilting, **14:** 1699
  rainbow-cloud quilt, **14:** 1707-9
  shoulder bag, quilted, **14:** 1694-96
  vest and skirt, quilted, **14:** 1706-7
  wall hanging, quilted, **14:** 1690, 1697-98
raffia and straw, 14: 1716-19, 1723
  belt, crocheted raffia, **14:** 1716
  cap, crocheted raffia, **14:** 1718-19
  earrings, raffia, **14:** 1719
  purse, pine-straw, **14:** 1723
  shoulder bag, raffia, **14:** 1718
rag dolls, 14: 1724-31
  making rag dolls, **14:** 1726-31

recycling clothes, 14: 1732-43
  casual top, **14:** 1739
  child's dress, appliquéd, **14:** 1741-42
  halter, **14:** 1740
  knits, working with, **14:** 1736
  lengthening, dress, **14:** 1742-43
  raglan top, **14:** 1736-38
  skirt and knit top, denim, **14:** 1733-35
reverse appliqué, 14: 1754-61
  hanging, reverse appliqué, **14:** 1760-61
  pillow, reverse appliqué, **14:** 1758-59
  tote bag, **14:** 1759-60
ribboncraft, 14: 1762-73
  evening bag, ribbon, **14:** 1771
  pillow, parquet ribbon, **14:** 1766-67
  pillow, patchwork and ribbon, **14:** 1768-69
  pillow, woven ribbon, **14:** 1764-66
  serving tray, **14:** 1772
  tennis racket cover, **14:** 1769-70
  T-shirt, appliquéd, **14:** 1772-73
rya and flossa, 15: 1824-34
  designing ryas, **15:** 1832-34
  knotting, rya, **15:** 1831
  pillow, needlepoint and rya, **15:** 1824, 1829-30
  pillow, rya, **15:** 1824, 1828-29
  wall hanging, wool, **15:** 1826-28
samplers, 15: 1848-61
  cross-stitch denim patch, **15:** 1857-58
  designing samplers, **15:** 1858-59
  hoop-framed samplers, **15:** 1855-57
  pegboard sampler, **15:** 1854
  perforated-paper sampler, **15:** 1860-61
  stitches, sampler, **15:** 1855
sandal making, 15: 1869-71
  needlepoint clogs, **15:** 1869-71
  ribbon clogs, **15:** 1871
sewing without pattern, 16: 1974-85
  apron shawl, bias-cut, **16:** 1974-76
  caftan, **16:** 1977, 1978-80
  cape, hooded, **16:** 1980-81
  coverlet, quilted, **16:** 1975, 1983-84
  curtains with valance, café, **16:** 1984-85
  kimono coat, **16:** 1977-78
  pillow cover, ruffled, **16:** 1985
  skirt, wraparound, **16:** 1982
  tablecloth, round, **16:** 1985
sewing tips, 14: 1736-37
  fur, sewing, **6:** 743
  leather, sewing, **4:** 400-1 **10:** 1212
smocking, 17: 2076-85
  dress, cotton, **17:** 2085
  dress, silk, **17:** 2083-84
  pillow, smock, **17:** 2078-81
  shirt, man's, **17:** 2081-82
soft sculpture, 17: 2106-16
  abstraction, soft sculpture, **17:** 2110-11
  airplane, soft sculpture, **17:** 2107-9

  faces, soft sculpture, **14:** 1729
  palm tree, soft sculpture, **17:** 2114-16
  tennis shoes, soft sculpture, **17:** 2112-14
stitches
  chain stitch, **14:** 1717
  construction stitches, **14:** 1736-37
  crochet stitches, **1:** 30-31, **14:** 1717
  embroidery stitches, **1:** 86, **5:** 542-45, **7:** 857, **21:** 2574
  huck work embroidery stitches, **19:** 2338-39
  knitting stitches, **21:** 2568-69
  machine embroidery stitches, **9:** 1109
  needle lace stitches, **8:** 1022
  needlepoint stitches, **11:** 1325, 1326-27
  sampler stitches, **15:** 1855
  slip stitch, **14:** 1717
  tambour stitches, **19:** 2410-11
Swedish huck work, 19: 236-43
  embroidery stitches, huck work, **19:** 2338-39
  handbag, huck work, **19:** 2341-42
  hand towel, huck work, **19:** 2340
  pillow, huck work, **19:** 2342-43
tambour, 19: 2406-19
  curtain, white-on-white, **19:** 2412
  dragonfly, tambour, **19:** 2417-19
  materials, tambour, **19:** 2409
  pillow, tambour, **19:** 2416-17
  rug, wool, **19:** 2413-15
  stitch, tambour, **19:** 2410-11
  tools, tambour, **19:** 2409
  transferring tambour designs, **19:** 2411
  wall hanging, tambour, **19:** 2415-16
thread tension, 14: 1737
traditional knitting motifs, 21: 2566-79
  bias-knit scarf, **21:** 2578-79
  Irish-knit top, child's, **21:** 2571-74
  Norwegian-pattern sweater, **21:** 2574-77
  shoulder bag, **21:** 2570
trapunto, 21: 2580-91
  dress, yoked, **21:** 2580, 2584-85
  face pillow, trapunto, **21:** 2588-89
  handbag, batik, **21:** 2586
  sheet and pillowcases, trapunto, **21:** 2582-84
  T-shirt, lion, **21:** 2587-88
  wall hanging, trapunto, **21:** 2590-91
needlepoint, 11: 1318-33
  belt, signature, **11:** 1324
  mirror frame, needlepoint, **11:** 1328-29
  pencil holder, gingham, **11:** 1322-23
  pillow, needlepoint, **11:** 1330-31
  rug, needlepoint, **11:** 1332-33
  stitches
    basic stitch, **11:** 1325
    decorative stitches, **11:** 1326-27
See also appliqué; crewel; embroidery; Florentine stitch; hardanger embroidery; samplers; sandal making

N, continued
negatives, developing, 12: 1491-94
nephoscope, cloud-movement, 22: 2745
net, butterfly, 8: 941
newspaper bird mask, 10: 1188-91
    See also **paper-mâché**
noodles, 12: 1428-29
note cards and paper
    herb note card, 7: 884
    note paper, personalized, 18: 2244-45
nursery, indoor, 9: 1085
nutrition
    breakfast cookies, 1: 110-111
    preparing baby foods, 1: 107-9
    See also **Kitchen Favorites and Celebrations**

oil painting, 11: 1334-47
    cityscape, 11: 1344-45
    materials, oil painting, 11: 1338
    mixing paints, 11: 1339
    perspective, 11: 1341
    portraits, 11: 1346-47
    priming canvas, 11: 1339
    sketching, 11: 1340
    still life, 11: 1342-43
    stretching canvas, 11: 1338
    studio, artist's, 11: 1338-39
    thinning paint, 11: 1339
    vocabulary, painting, 11: 1336-37
    See also **acrylics; color psychology; monoprinting; rosemaling; stagecraft; supergraphics; tin painting; watercolors; yarn painting**
oils
    bath oils, 17: 2103
    essential oils
        perfumes, 12: 1459-60
        potpourris and pomanders, 13: 1604
ojo de dios, 11: 1348-59
    evening star ojo, 11: 1357-58
    flat ojo, 11: 1351-53
    galaxy ojo, 11: 1358-59
    necklace, ojo, 11: 1355
    snowflake, ojo, 11: 1356
    woven ojo, 11: 1354-55
    See also **mobiles; piñatas; yarn painting**
organic gardening, 11: 1360-73
    companion planting, 11: 1367-68
    composting, 11: 1363-65
    container gardening, 11: 1370-71
    insects and, 11: 1366
    mulching, 11: 1365-66
    pesticides, organic, 11: 1367
    planting, 11: 1369-70
    plants, soil pH needs, 11: 1362
    soil, pH factor, 11: 1361-63
    water, air, and sun, 11: 1371
    weather maps, 11: 1372-73
    See also **greenhouse construction;**

seed sprouting; tea; topiary; trellises; weather forecasting
origami, 11: 1374-85
    carrier pigeon, 11: 1382
    crane, 11: 1375, 1383
    drinking cup, 11: 1378
    dog face and cat face, 11: 1376-77
    house, 11: 1378
    jumping frog, 11: 1384-85
    penguin, 11: 1380
    pinwheel, 11: 1379
    samurai hat, 11: 1381
    uses of origami, 11: 1385
    See also **airplanes, paper; flowers, artificial; greeting cards; kites and kite making; mobiles; papermaking; quilling; silhouettes; valentines; wycinanki**
ornaments, hanging, 7: 787
    Christmas-tree ornaments
        foam cup decorations, 6: 702-3
        handmade, 4: 459
        patchwork, 4: 458
        quilled, 14: 1675-77
ostrich, pine-cone, 13: 1588
ottoman, plywood and foam, 13: 1572-75
Outdoor Activities
    bicycles and bicycling, 2: 178-89
    canoeing, 3: 354-65
    clambakes, 4: 468-77
    cryptography, 5: 560-64, 565
        ciphers; 5: 561-64, 565
    gold panning, 7: 798-805
    kayaks, 8: 968-75
    maps and pathfinding, 9: 1140-52
        compass, making and using, 9: 1146-48
        Earth's circles, 9: 1145
        maps, making and using, 9: 1141-44
        natural guides, 9: 1148-52
    piloting small boats, 12: 1512-23
    sand characters and castles, 15: 1882-87
    sail making and repair, 15: 1838-47
        maintaining sails, 15: 1843
        Marconi dinghy sail, 15: 1844-47
        sewing sails, 15: 1842-43
    shelters and tents, 16: 2012-23
        camping information, 16: 2019
        supply sources, tenting, 16: 2019
        tarp tents and lean-tos, 16: 2014-18
        tepees, 16: 2020-23
        waterproofing tents, 16: 2019
        windproofing tents, 16: 2019
    swings, 19: 2344-53
        hardware for outdoor swings, 19: 2353
        rope for outdoor swings, 19: 2353
        rope swing, 19: 2344, 2346
        monkey swing, 19: 2351-52
        pulley-and-cable glides, 19: 2348-51
        tire swings, 19: 2345-48
    time telling, 20: 2497-99
        star dial, 20: 2497-99

tree houses, 21: 2592-2601
    grove tree house, 21: 2594-96
    outdoor platform, 21: 2596-99
    traditional tree house, 21: 2593, 2600-1
    tying flies, 21: 2640-51
        Rat-Faced MacDougall fly, 21: 2648-49
        Royal Coachman fly, 21: 2650-51
        TW Special fly, 21: 2645-47
    weather forecasting, 22: 2734-51
    winter sculpture, 22: 2806-11
        snow sculptures, 22: 2806-11
    yard toys, 23: 2900-9
    See also **Environmental Projects; Greenery and Growing Things**
owl, black work, 6: 656-57

packages, gift wrapping, 4: 462
pageants and parades. See parades and festivals
Paint and Color
    acrylics, 1: 21-23
        Volkswagen, painting, 1: 21-23
    folk art, 6: 708-9, 714-15
        fraktur traufscheine, 6: 708-9
        Senufo wall hanging, 6: 714-15
    neckties, 11: 1308-15
        butterfly neckerchief, 11: 1315
        illustrating ties, 11: 1312-13
        tree design tie, 11: 1311-12
    oil painting, 11: 1334-47
        cityscape, 11: 1344-45
        portraits, 11: 1346-47
        still life, 11: 1342-43
    preschool activities, 13: 1632-33
        plants and painted pots, 13: 1632-33
    sand painting and layering, 15: 1888-99
        fishbowl sand painting, 15: 1894-96
        garden, layered-sand, 15: 1896-99
        Navaho sand painting, 15: 1890-91
        planter, sand-layered, 15: 1891-94
    supergraphics, 19: 2322-35
        child's bedroom supergraphic, 19: 2327
        dark background supergraphic, 19: 2328
        diagonal stripes supergraphic, 19: 2330-31
        fabric design supergraphic, 19: 2334-35
        flowers supergraphic, 19: 2330-31
        free-form supergraphic, 19: 2332
        furniture framing supergraphic, 19: 2327-28
        geometric supergraphic, 19: 2324-26
        Indian motif supergraphic, 19: 2333
        reversed colors supergraphic, 19: 2329
        sunrise supergraphic, 19: 2323, 2330
    tie dyeing, 20: 2470-89
        knots and folds, tie dyeing, 20: 2474-75

stitchery, tie-dye, **20:** 2479-81
table throw, velvet, **20:** 2482-84
T-shirts, tie-dyed, **20:** 2476-79
wall hanging, block-dyed, **20:** 2484-87
tin painting, 20: 2510-27
antique stenciled tin box, **20:** 2523-27
canister, painted, **20:** 2518-19
country tin painting, **20:** 2513-17
freehand bronze tray, **20:** 2520-22
preparing and finishing tin surfaces, **20:** 2512
vegetable dyes, 21: 2676-88
colorfast dyes, **21:** 2678-83
wool yarn, dyeing, **21:** 2684-88
watercolors, 22: 2722-33
See also **Designs and Decorations; Furniture and Finishes; Graphic Arts**
palm tree, soft sculpture, **17:** 2114-16
panels
door panel, pin stripe decoration for, **13:** 1546
stained-glass panels
laminated, **18:** 2217, 2222-23
leaded, **18:** 2229-31
slab-glass casting, **18:** 2223-24
window panel, leaded glass, **9:** 1063
paper
tie-dyed paper, **20:** 2488
watercolor paper, **22:** 2724
stretching, **22:** 2724-26
See also **papermaking; papier-mâché**
Papercrafts. See **Paper Folding and Cutting**
Paper Folding and Cutting
airplanes, paper, 1: 32-41
Barnaby, **1:** 35
Dartmouth Dart, **1:** 33-34
Falcon, **1:** 38-39
Flying Tiger, **1:** 36-37
Pegasus, **1:** 40-41
boxes, 3: 262-65, 267-68
desk and seat, milk-crate, **3:** 262-65
drawer organizer, kitchen-matchbox, **3:** 267
wall sculpture, **3:** 268
cardboard, 3: 369-71
weathervane, whirligig, **3:** 369-71
Christmas celebrations, 4: 461-62
gift wrapping, **4:** 462
trims, Christmas-tree, **4:** 461
costumes, 5: 528-29
paper costumes, **5:** 528-29
flowers, artificial, 6: 689-91 694-96
crepe paper flowers, **6:** 694-96
foil flowers, **6:** 690-91
tissue paper flowers, **6:** 689
foam forms
decorations, foam cup, **6:** 702-3
greeting cards, 7: 836-38
pressed flower cards, **7:** 838
ribbon bookmark card, **7:** 837
mobiles, 10: 1220, 1223

cardboard snail mobile, **10:** 1223
napkin folding, 11: 1300-7
artichoke fold, **11:** 1306
band fold, **11:** 1305
candle fold, **11:** 1303
fan fold, **11:** 1307
fleur-de-lis fold, **11:** 1307
lily fold, **11:** 1304
palm leaf fold, **11:** 1301-2
pocket fold, **11:** 1304
sailboat fold, **11:** 1302
origami, 11: 1374-85
carrier pigeon, **11:** 1382
crane, **11:** 1375, 1383
dog face and cat face, **11:** 1376-77
drinking cup, **11:** 1378
house, **11:** 1378
jumping frog, **11:** 1384-85
penguin, **11:** 1380
pinwheel, **11:** 1379
samurai hat, **11:** 1381
squares, making, **11:** 1374
symbols, origami, **11:** 1376
uses of origami, **11:** 1385
quilling, 14: 1670-83
basic quilling, **14:** 1674
bird, quillwork, **14:** 1681-83
butterflies, quillwork, **14:** 1678-79
eggs, decorating, **14:** 1680-81
ornaments, Christmas tree, **14:** 1675-77
silhouettes, 16: 2042-48
mounting silhouettes, **16:** 2047
pictures, silhouette, **16:** 2046-48
repairing silhouettes, **16:** 2047
silhouettes, **16:** 2044-46
valentines, 21: 2666-75
gift box, valentine, **21:** 2674-75
lovebird valentine, **21:** 2674
playing card valentine, **21:** 2673
two-heart valentine, **21:** 2672-73
wycinanki, 23: 2888-99
animal chain cutout, **23:** 2890-91
applied wycinanki, **23:** 2898-99
disk mobile, **23:** 2896-97
stars, paper, **23:** 2892-93
tree-of-life, **23:** 2894-95
zoetrope toys, 23: 2926-44
flipbook, **23:** 2942-44
moving-picture wheels, **23:** 2930-33
thaumatropes, **23:** 2926-29
zoetropes, **23:** 2934-41
papermaking, 11: 1386-99
blender-made paper, **11:** 1390-93
rag paper, handmade, **11:** 1394-99
See also **airplanes, paper; block printing; bookbinding; calligraphy; greeting cards; linoleum and woodcuts; monoprinting; origami; quill pens; serigraphy; valentines; wycinanki**
paper-plate masks, 10: 1182-83, **23:** 2914-15

paperweights
bean-bag felt paperweight, **2:** 161
poured acrylic seashell paperweight, **2:** 141
papier-mâché, 11: 1400-8
bottle people, **11:** 1401, 1403-4
dinosaur, papier-mâché, **11:** 1407-8
hand puppets, **13:** 1635
heads, puppet, **11:** 1405-7
pop-up, finger, and junk puppets, **13:** 1638-40
See also **casting; Christmas celebrations; decoupage; dioramas; flowers, artificial; masks; molding methods; piñatas; puppets and puppetry; sculpture**
parachute toy, spool, **17:** 2159
parades and festivals, 12: 1414-25
costumes, **12:** 1424
Festival of Roses (Pasadena), **12:** 1421
floats, **12:** 1420-21
building floats, **12:** 1424-25
decorations, **12:** 1424-25
military parades, **12:** 1414, 1417
Shooters' and Mummers' Parade (Philadelphia), **12:** 1415, 1421-23
suppliers of floats and decorations, **12:** 1424
types of parades, **12:** 1414-20
folk festivals, **12:** 1416, 1418-20
parade enticing, **12:** 1417
parades of power, **12:** 1417
See also **flags and banners; masks; music making**
parties. See **birthday celebrations; card tricks; Christmas celebrations; clambakes; Kitchen Favorites and Celebrations; magic; music making; parades and festivals; square dancing**
pasta, 12: 1426-37
homemade pasta, **12:** 1428-31
macaroni recipes, **12:** 1436-37
stuffed pasta, **12:** 1432-35
See also **breads; soups; terrines and timbales**
patchwork, 12: 1438-53
Christmas-tree ornaments, patchwork, **4:** 458
crib quilt, **12:** 1447-48
Dresden-plate quilt, **14:** 1702-5
pillow, patchwork, **12:** 1443-46
rainbow-cloud quilt, **14:** 1707-9
reversible vest, **12:** 1449-50
tote bag, patchwork, **12:** 1451-52
traditional quilt, **12:** 1439, 1452-53
See also **afghan stitch; appliqué; Florentine stitch; granny squares; quilts and quilting; ribboncraft**
pathfinding. See **maps and pathfinding**
pavement games. See **street games**
Pegasus, paper airplane, **1:** 40-41
pegboard sampler, 15: 1854
penguin, origami, **11:** 1380
pennant, boat, nylon, **6:** 672-73

P, continued
pens and pencils
pen holder, mineral, **10:** 1206-7
pencil holder, needlepoint gingham, **11:** 1322-23
pencil posy, **6:** 688
quill pen, making, **14:** 1686-89
Performing Arts
costumes, 5: 536-37
makeup, **5:** 536-37
dulcimers, 5: 624-33
Appalachian dulcimer, **5:** 624, 626-33
fretboard dulcimer, **5:** 625-26
playing dulcimers, **5:** 633
tuning dulcimers, **5:** 633
masks, 10: 1180-81, 1184-91
bird mask, newspaper, **10:** 1188-91
clown hoop mask, **10:** 1184-85
lion hoop mask, **10:** 1186-87
music making, 11: 1286-87, 1294-99
marimbas, **11:** 1287, 1294-99
puppetry, 13: 1636-53
clown marionette, **13:** 1645, 1648-51
felt puppets, **13:** 1640-42
foam puppets, **13:** 1643
manipulating marionettes, **13:** 1652-53
paper marionettes, **13:** 1646-47
pop-up, finger, and junk puppets, **13:** 1638-40
shadow theater, 16: 1986-97
assembling shadow puppets, **16:** 1994-95
boxes, shadow, **16:** 1990
color silhouettes, **16:** 1991
paper shadow puppets, **16:** 1996-97
plastic jellyfish, **16:** 1989, 1992
plastic puppets, **16:** 1992-93
shadow play, **16:** 1993
silhouette puppets, **16:** 1988-89
skin painting, 17: 2072-73
stage face makeup, **17:** 2072-73
square dancing, 18: 2182-93
stagecraft, 18: 2194-2215
design, set, **18:** 2196-2201
door construction, **18:** 2214-15
flat construction, **18:** 2214
lighting, face, **18:** 2212-13
lighting, stage, **18:** 2206-13
painting techniques, scene, **18:** 2203-5
window construction, **18:** 2215
tea, 20: 2447-51
Japanese tea ceremony, **20:** 2447-51
whistles and flutes, 22: 2778-83
flutes, **22:** 2778-79
shepherd's pipe, bamboo, **22:** 2780-83
perfumes, 12: 1454-63
cologne, **12:** 1462-63
homemade perfumes, **12:** 1457
recipes, perfume, **12:** 1458-60
See also **cosmetics; herbs; potpourris and pomanders**
pesticides, organic gardening, **11:** 1367
pet habitats, 12: 1464-75
barrel doghouse, **12:** 1464, 1466-67

cat cabaña, **12:** 1468-69
five-story birdcage, **12:** 1472-75
two-pet tote, **12:** 1270-72
See also **ant farms; birds and birdhouses; insects; tropical fish; vivariums**
pewtersmithing, 12: 1476-87
bowl, handwrought pewter, **12:** 1480-83
box, fabricated pewter, **12:** 1484-87
figurine, cast, **12:** 1476, 1478-79
See also **Colonial crafts; sculpture; silversmithing; tin and pierced work; wire sculpture**
photographic printing, 12: 1488-1501
contact prints, **12:** 1494-96
developing negatives, **12:** 1491-94
dodging and burning, **12:** 1500
enlargements, making, **12:** 1496-99
mounting, **12:** 1501
retouching, **12:** 1501
See also **astronomy; cameras; cartooning**
pickled and canned foods, 12: 1502-11
fruit recipes, **12:** 1511
pickle recipes, **12:** 1506
tomato recipes, **12:** 1507-8
vegetable recipes, **12:** 1509-10
See also **baby food; confections and comfits; marmalades and preserves; soups; vinegars**
pigeon, carrier, origami, **11:** 1382
pillowcases and covers
monoprinted pillow cover, **10:** 1262-63
ruffled pillow cover, **16:** 1985
trapunto pillowcases, **21:** 2582-84
pillows
afghan stitch, tic-tac-toe pillow, **1:** 28
appliquéd, people pillow, **1:** 90
embroidered pillow, machine stitched, **9:** 1115
face pillow, trapunto, **21:** 2588-89
Florentine stitch pillow, **6:** 684-87
floor pillow, batik, **1:** 128
fur pillows, **6:** 741-43
huck work pillow, **19:** 2342-43
needlepoint pillows, **11:** 1330-31
needlepoint and rya, **15:** 1824, 1829-30
patchwork pillows, **12:** 1443-46
patchwork and ribbon, **14:** 1768-69
potpourri pillow, **13:** 1600
reverse appliqué pillow, **14:** 1758-59
ribbon pillows
machine stitched, **9:** 1114
parquet ribbon, **14:** 1766-67
patchwork and ribbon, **14:** 1768-69
woven ribbon, **14:** 1764-66
rya pillow, **15:** 1824, 1828-29
smock pillow, **17:** 2078-81
suede pillow, appliquéd, **9:** 1070-71
tambour pillow, **19:** 2416-17
woven pillows
geometric, **23:** 2866-67
plaid, **22:** 2755-63
ribbon, **14:** 1764-66

rya, **15:** 1834-37
twill, **22:** 2767
piloting small boats, 12: 1512-23
buoys, **12:** 1516
compasses, using, **12:** 1520-21
course, plotting, **12:** 1516-17
nautical charts, **12:** 1512-16
navigation, **12:** 1512-19
buoy markings, **12:** 1514
night navigation, **12:** 1522-23
position, fixing, **12:** 1521
speed and distance calculations, **12:** 1518-19
tidal current charts, **12:** 1517-18
wind drift, **12:** 1517-18
See also **canoeing; clambakes; kayaks; maps and pathfinding; sail making and repair; weather forecasting**
piñatas, 12: 1524-36
doll piñata, **12:** 1534
rabbit-foot piñata, **12:** 1529
sailboat piñata, **12:** 1535-36
star piñata, **12:** 1524-28
wishing-well piñata, **12:** 1530-34
See also **birthday celebrations; Christmas celebrations; mobiles; ojo de dios; papier-mâché; table games**
pincushion, crochet, **5:** 556
pine-cone constructions. See **pod and cone art**
pin striping, 13: 1542-51
boat helm, **13:** 1547
customizing car, **13:** 1548-50
door panel, **13:** 1546
restoring antique automobiles, **13:** 1542, 1551
See also **acrylics; soapbox and skate vehicles**
pinwheel, origami, **11:** 1379
pipe, shepherd's, bamboo, **22:** 2780-83
pipe making, 13: 1552-61
briar pipe, **13:** 1556-60
care of pipes, **13:** 1561
corncob pipe, **13:** 1555-56
selecting pipes, **13:** 1561
place cards, sugar, **18:** 2304
place mats
braided place mats, **3:** 276-77
Janus place mat, monoprinted, **10:** 1267
personalized place mat, machine stitched, **9:** 1111-12
red place mat, hardanger embroidered, **7:** 861-62
rope place mat, **14:** 1789
stenciled place mat, **18:** 2246-47
sunflower place mat, **19:** 2427-28
white place mat, hardanger embroidered, **7:** 863-65
planters, plant holders, and plant hangers
baby swing as plant hanger, **19:** 2354-57
coiled work plant hanger, **23:** 2882-84
hanging basket plant holder, **1:** 116-17

knotted planter hanging, **14:** 1790-92
leaded glass planter, **9:** 1064-65
sand-layered planter, **15:** 1891-94
tatted flowerpot holder, **19:** 2429-30
See also **bottle gardens; terrariums**
plants
aquatic, **21:** 2632-33
for preschool activity, **13:** 1632-33
soil acidity needs, **11:** 1362
See also **Greenery and Growing
Things;** names of materials from
plants (e.g., **pod and cone art**);
names of products utilizing plants
(e.g., **vegetable dyes**)
plaster
cast head, **4:** 424-29
molded plaque, **10:** 1248
plastic pipe constructions, 13: 1562-71
bookshelves, **13:** 1567-69
easy chair and footrest, **13:** 1564-66
lamp, sculptural, **13:** 1570-71
See also **benches; plywood and
foam furnishings; structural
furnishings; tables; tree houses;
upholstery; yard toys**
plastics. See **Glass and Plastics**
plate, Telemark, **15:** 1808-10
platforms
indoor platforms
seating platforms, **13:** 1576-78
as structural furnishing, **18:** 2294-99
outdoor, for tree houses, **21:** 2596-99
play. See **preschool activities, shadow
theater, Toys and Games**
playhouse, cable-spool, **23:** 2906-7
plywood and foam furnishings, 13:
1572-83
banquette and bench, **13:** 1579-83
chair and ottoman, **13:** 1572-75
seating platforms, **13:** 1576-78
See also **benches; plastic pipe constructions; Shaker furniture;
tables; upholstery**
pod and cone art, 13: 1584-95
alligator, pod and cone, **13:** 1585, 1589
candle holder, **13:** 1590-91
Christmas wreath, **13:** 1591
lion, pine-cone, **13:** 1584, 1587-88
llama, pine-cone, **13:** 1584, 1586
ostrich, pine-cone, **13:** 1588
shadow box, **13:** 1592
turkey, pine-cone, **13:** 1590
wired tree, **13:** 1593-95
See also **Christmas celebrations;
dried flowers; dolls and doll
clothes; flowers, artificial; seashells; spool toys**
pomanders. See **potpourris and
pomanders**
portraits, oil painting, **11:** 1346-47
poster print, 16: 1963-65
potichomania lamp, 9: 1036-37
potpourris and pomanders, 13:
1596-1605
pillow potpourri, **13:** 1600
pomander-ball pendant, **13:** 1605

pomander balls, **13:** 1602-4
pomander buds, **13:** 1601
potpourris, **13:** 1596-98
seasonal potpourris, **13:** 1599
See also **cosmetics; herbs; makeup;
perfumes**
pottery, 13: 1606-21
hand-built pottery, **13:** 1609-11
weed pot, **15:** 1878-81
wheel-thrown pottery, **13:** 1614-21
See also **American Indian crafts;
ceramics; colonial crafts;
enameling metal; kilns; sand
casting; sand characters and
castles; sculpture**
powder, face, **5:** 524
precipitation, annual, map, **11:** 1373
preschool activities, 13: 1622-35
busy board, **13:** 1625-27
hand puppets, **13:** 1635
junk sculpture, **13:** 1630-31
kitchen clay, **13:** 1628-29
pets, **13:** 1633
plants and painted pots, **13:** 1632-33
sand casting, **15:** 1874-75
stuffed giraffe, **13:** 1622-24
woodworking, **13:** 1634
See also **airplanes, paper; collages
and assemblages; puppets and
puppetry; puzzles; rockers and
cradles; shadow theater; spool
toys; street games; swings;
watercolors; yard toys; yo-yos;
zoetrope toys**
preserving. See **pickled and canned
foods**
pressed flowers. See **candlemaking;
dried flowers**
printing. See **block printing;
calligraphy; greeting cards;
monoprinting; papermaking;
photographic printing;
serigraphy**
privet hedge, 20: 2533-35
psychrometer, weather forecasting, **22:**
2743-44
pulley-and-cable glides, 19: 2348-51
puppets and puppetry, 13: 1636-53
clown marionette, **13:** 1645, 1648-51
felt puppets, **13:** 1640-42
foam puppets, **13:** 1643
hand puppets, **13:** 1635, 1636-37, 1640
paper shadow puppets, **16:** 1996-97
paper marionettes, **13:** 1646-47
papier-mâché puppets, **11:** 1405-7
plastic puppets, **16:** 1692-93
pop-up, finger, and junk puppets, **13:**
1638-40
silhouette puppets, **16:** 1988-89, 1991
stages, puppet, **13:** 1643-44
woven puppets, **23:** 2874
See also **animals, doll; birthday
celebrations; cardboard; carving;
costumes; dolls and doll clothes;
masks; papier-mâché; preschool

activities; shadow theater; stagecraft; whistles and flutes**
purses. See **bags**
puzzles, 13: 1654-64
block puzzle, **13:** 1661-62
counter puzzle, **13:** 1658-59
crossword puzzles, **13:** 1655-57
jigsaw puzzle, **13:** 1663-64
tangrams, **13:** 1659-60
See also **bean-bags; card tricks;
magic; preschool activities; table
games**

Q

Quick Trip, table game, **19:** 2376-77
quilling, 14: 1670-83
bird, quillwork, **14:** 1681-83
butterflies, quillwork, **14:** 1678-79
Christmas tree ornaments, **14:** 1675-77
eggs, decorated, **14:** 1680-81
See also **lace, mobiles; origami;
quill pens**
quill pens, 14: 1684-89
making quill pen, **14:** 1686-89
See also **calligraphy; folk art;
papermaking; quilling**
quilts and quilting, 14: 1690-1709
bias strips, **14:** 1704
coverlet, quilted, **16:** 1975, 1983-84
crib quilt, patchwork, **12:** 1447-48
Dresden-plate quilt, **14:** 1702-5
rainbow-cloud quilt, **14:** 1707-9
shoulder bag, quilted, **14:** 1694-96
traditional quilt, patchwork, **12:**
1439, 1452-53
wall hanging, quilted, **14:** 1690,
1697-98
vest and skirt, quilted, **14:** 1706-7
See also **afghan stitch; appliqué;
Colonial crafts; Florentine stitch;
machine stitchery; patchwork;
ribboncraft; sewing without
pattern; trapunto**

R

racers and racing. See **soapbox and
skate vehicles**
raffia and straw, 14: 1710-23
belt, crocheted raffia, **14:** 1716
cap, crocheted raffia, **14:** 1718-19
earrings, raffia, **14:** 1719
giraffes, straw, **14:** 1713-14
hat, straw, **14:** 1714-16
mosaics, split-straw, **14:** 1712-13
oval tray, **14:** 1722
purse, pine-straw, **14:** 1723
shoulder bag, raffia, **14:** 1718
round tray, **14:** 1720-22
See also **basketry; rugs, braided;
vegetable dyes; wrapped and
coiled work**

R, continued

rag dolls, 14: 1724-31
    making rag dolls, **14:** 1726-31
    See also animals, doll; dolls and doll clothes; soft sculpture
rag paper, handmade, **11:** 1394-99
rag rugs. See rugs, braided
rain gauge, 22: 2744-45
raised designs. See rubbings
raku. See Ceramics; kilns
rat, English hooded, **22:** 2708
recipes. See Kitchen Favorites and Celebrations
recycling clothes, 14: 1732-43
    appliquéd child's dress, **14:** 1741-42
    casual top, **14:** 1739
    denim skirt and knit top, **14:** 1733-35
    halter, **14:** 1740
    lengthening dress, **14:** 1742-43
    raglan top, **14:** 1736-38
    See also fur recycling; sewing without pattern
refinishing furniture, 6: 710-11 726-39
    applying finish, **6:** 736-39
    bleaching, **6:** 735
    blemishes, repairing, **6:** 730-31
    brushes, **6:** 736
    cleaning surfaces, **6:** 726-28
    milk-based paints, removing, **6:** 729
    natural finishes, **6:** 733
    old finish, removing, **6:** 728-29
    old finish, restoring, **6:** 728
    rubbing and polishing, **6:** 736
    sanding, **6:** 732-33
    spattering, **1:** 78
    staining, **6:** 733-35
    striping, **1:** 78
    techniques, refinishing, **1:** 78
    types of finish, **6:** 726-28, 733-35, 737-39
    waxing, **6:** 736
    wiping, **1:** 78
    wood types, **6:** 733
    See also antiquing furniture; gold leafing; marquetry; rosemaling; upholstery
reliefs. See repoussé and chased metal; rubbings
repoussé and chased metal, 14: 1744-53
    box tops, ornamented, **14:** 1746-48
    mirror frame, foil, **14:** 1748-50
    necklace, metal, **14:** 1751-53
    See also American Indian crafts; jewelry; pewtersmithing; silversmithing; tin and pierced work; wire sculpture
reverse appliqué, 14: 1754-61
    hanging, reverse appliqué, **14:** 1760-61
    pillow, reverse appliqué, **14:** 1758-59
    tote bag, **14:** 1759-60
    See also appliqué; embroidery
ribboncraft, 14: 1762-73
    Christmas wrappings, **4:** 462, 465
    clogs, ribbon, **15:** 1871
    evening bag, ribbon, **14:** 1771

    pillows
        parquet ribbon pillow, **14:** 1766-67
        patchwork and ribbon pillow, **14:** 1768-69
        woven ribbon pillow, **14:** 1764-66
    T-shirt, appliquéd, **14:** 1772-73
    serving tray, **14:** 1772
    tennis racket cover, **14:** 1769-70
    See also appliqué; Christmas celebrations; machine stitchery; patchwork; quilts and quilting; tablet and frame weaving
rice, sushi, **15:** 1905
ring-a-levio, street game, **18:** 2268
rings
    bead rings, **1:** 44, **2:** 154-55
    neck ring, **8:** 957
    spoon ring, **8:** 955
ring-toss game, 17: 2160-61
roarer, bull, **20:** 2550
rockers and cradles, 14: 1774-81
    boat, rocker, **14:** 1777-78
    child's rocking chair, **14:** 1776
    doll's cradle, **14:** 1780-81
    rocking cradle, **14:** 1778-79
    See also benches; preschool activities; Shaker furniture; swings; tables; upholstery; yard toys
room dividers
    acrylic, **1:** 10-14
    macramé, **9:** 1116, 1124
    plastic pipe, **13:** 1569
root beer, 3: 294-95
rope knotting, 14: 1782-92
    carrick bend chain, **14:** 1788
    hammock, naval, **7:** 851-53
    hot-plate pad, **14:** 1789
    log sling, canvas, **7:** 850-51
    planter hanging, knotted, **14:** 1790-92
    See also hammocks and slings; macramé; sprang; swings; tree houses; tying flies; wrapped and coiled work
rosemaling, 15: 1798-1813
    bread board, **15:** 1805-7
    hand mirror, **15:** 1803-4
    Telemark box, **15:** 1810-13
    Telemark plate, **15:** 1808-10
    See also antiquing furniture; marquetry; oil painting; refinishing furniture; tin painting
rubbings, 15: 1814-23
    brass rubbings, **15:** 1818-19
    high reliefs, reproducing, **15:** 1823
    inking raised designs, **15:** 1820-21
    tombstone rubbings, **15:** 1815-17
    See also frames and framing; genealogy; greeting cards; heraldry; monoprinting
rugs
    braided rugs, **3:** 272-79
        coasters, braided, **3:** 275

        petal-design rug, **3:** 278-79
        place mats, braided, **3:** 276-77
        traditional braided rug, **3:** 276-77
    crocheted rug, sisal, **5:** 557
    hooked rugs, **8:** 902-9
        geometric rug, **8:** 904-5
        "love" rug, **8:** 907-9
        owl rug, **8:** 906
    needlepoint rug, **11:** 1332-33
    rya rug, **15:** 1832-34
    wool rug, tambour, **19:** 2413-15
    See also Colonial crafts; raffia and straw; rya and flossa; wall hangings; woven tapestries
running bases, 18: 2264
rushing. See caning and rushing
rya and flossa, 15: 1824-37
    cat, woven rya, **15:** 1834-37
    designing ryas, **15:** 1832-34
    pillow, needlepoint and rya, **15:** 1824, 1829-30
    pillow, rya, **15:** 1824, 1828-29
    wall hanging, wool, **15:** 1826-28
    See also Florentine stitch; rugs; soft sculpture; tablet and frame weaving; woven tapestries

S

safety-pin and bead necklace, 2: 154
safety rules, bicycles and, **2:** 187-88
sail making and repair, 15: 1838-47
    Marconi dinghy sail, **15:** 1844-47
    See also canoeing; clambakes; hammocks and slings; kayaks; piloting small boats; ship models; weather forecasting
salad bowl set, treen, **21:** 2612-13
salads. See seed sprouting; vegetables; vinegars
samplers, 15: 1848-61
    cross-stitch denim patch, **15:** 1857-58
    designing samplers, **15:** 1858-59
    embroidery sampler, **5:** 538-41 546-49
    hoop-framed samplers, **15:** 1855-57
    pegboard sampler, **15:** 1854
    perforated-paper sampler, **15:** 1860-61
    sprang sampler, **17:** 2163-66
    stitches, **15:** 1855
    See also appliqué; crewel; embroidery; hardanger embroidery; needlepoint; smocking; Swedish huck work
sandal making, 15: 1862-71
    Italia sandal, **15:** 1867
    needlepoint clogs, **15:** 1869-71
    ribbon clogs, **15:** 1871
    Riviera sandal, **15:** 1867-68
    Seville sandal, **15:** 1864-66
    T-tie sandal, **15:** 1868
    See also American Indian crafts; belts and buckles; Leathercrafts, leather working; mittens and mukluks; needlepoint

sand casting, 15: 1872-81
    castle, sand casted, **15:** 1875-77
    sea animals, cast, **15:** 1874-75
    weed pot, **15:** 1878-81
    See also beachcombing; casting; molding methods; pottery; sculpture
sand characters and castles, 15: 1882-87
    carving and molding sand, **15:** 1886-87
    composition, sand, **15:** 1883
    flat modeling, **15:** 1884, 1886
    round modeling, **15:** 1884, 1886
    mounds, **15:** 1882, 1886
    painting sand sculpture, **15:** 1887
    preparing sand, **15:** 1883
    tools, sand sculpting, **15:** 1883-85
    sketching design, **15:** 1883
    See also pottery; sculpture; winter sculpture
sandglass, 20: 2495-96
sand painting and layering, 15: 1888-99
    fishbowl sand painting, **15:** 1894-96
    garden, layered-sand, **15:** 1896-99
    Navaho sand painting, **15:** 1890-91
    planter, sand-layered, **15:** 1891-94
    See also stone painting; terrariums; vegetable dyes
sarsaparilla, 3: 294-97
sashes
    bobbin lace sash, **8:** 1017-18
    macramé dress sash, **9:** 1122-23
sashimi and sushi, 15: 1900-11
    chirashi sushi, **15:** 1911
    nigiri sushi, **15:** 1905-7
    norimaki sushi, **15:** 1908-10
    sashimi, **15:** 1903-5
    See also hibachi and hot-pot cookery; seed sprouting; tying flies; wok cookery
sauces, pasta, **12:** 1430, 1431
scarves
    bias-knit scarf, **21:** 2578-79
    block-printed scarf, **9:** 1096-98
    granny square scarf, **7:** 812
    leno-weave scarf, **22:** 2765-67
    sprang scarf, **17:** 2169
    tie-dyed scarf, **20:** 2479-81
scents. See Fragrances
schoolhouse, sugar, **18:** 2302-3
sconces, candle
    Shaker sconce, **16:** 2000-3
    tin sconce, **20:** 2504-7
scooter, skate, **17:** 2088-89
screens. See room dividers
scrimshaw, 15: 1912-20
    bone hair piece, **15:** 1917-18
    color-engraved scrimshaw, **15:** 1919-20
    findings, jewelry, **15:** 1916
    techniques, scrimshaw, **15:** 1915
    See also carving; linoleum and woodcuts; pipe making; sculpture; walking sticks
sculpture, 16: 1926-37
    alabaster sculpture, **16:** 1935-37
    balsa wood mobile, **10:** 1224-25
    box-illusion wall plaque, **23:** 2846-49

cast figurine, **12:** 1476, 1478-79
clay figure, **16:** 1926-29
copper shapes mobile, **10:** 1225-26
felt auto-mobile, **10:** 1222
fish impression, **6:** 706-7
free-form assemblages, **4:** 486-87
glass rod sculpture, **7:** 779
heraldic standards, abstract, **23:** 2852-55
ice sculpture, **22:** 2812-16
junk sculpture, **13:** 1630-31
lamp, sculptural, **13:** 1570-71
latex molding, **10:** 1251-52
leather sculpture, **9:** 1068, 1079
mosaic light sculpture, **10:** 1274-75
packing pieces sculpture, **6:** 699
plaster-cast head, **4:** 424-29
rag dolls, soft-sculpture, **14:** 1728-30
reindeer weathervane, **6:** 716-17
room divider as, **1:** 11-14
rosewood serving tray, **16:** 1930-33
shell figurines, **16:** 1948-49
snow sculptures, **22:** 2806-11
steel fin mobile, **10:** 1227-31
stick and flower sculpture, **8:** 926-27
stone animals, **18:** 2256-57
string sculptures
    conics in box, **18:** 2271, 2280-81
    raised ellipse, **18:** 2278-79
synthetic stone giraffe, **6:** 704-5
walking stick, sculptured, **22:** 2720-21
wall sculpture, **3:** 268
willow tree sculpture, **9:** 1125-26
wire figures, **23:** 2822, 2834-35
wood sculpture, **23:** 2850-52
woven tapestries, **23:** 2874-75
See also acrylics; candlemaking; carving; casting; ceramics; enameling metal; foam forms; folk art; kilns; macramé; mobiles; molding methods; papier-mâché; pewtersmithing; pottery; sand casting; sand characters and castles; scrimshaw; soft sculpture; topiary; totem poles; treen ware walking sticks; winter sculpture; wire sculpture; wood assemblages
seashells, 16: 1938-51
    buttons, seashell, **3:** 306-7
    cleaning shells, **16:** 1943
    collage, seashell, **16:** 1944
    collecting seashells, **16:** 1941-43
    figurines, shell, **16:** 1948-49
    flowers, seashell, **16:** 1946-47
    jewelry, seashell, **16:** 1945
    lampshade, shell, **16:** 1950-51
    lobster-man and shell paperweight, **2:** 140-41
    mollusks, **16:** 1943
    See also beachcombing; collages and assemblages; flowers, artificial;

jewelry; lamps and lampshades; pod and cone art; stained glass; stone painting**
seed sprouting, 16: 1952-59
    growing sprouts, **16:** 1952-59
    See also baby foods; breads; greenhouse construction; herbs; hibachi and hot-pot cookery; lighted indoor gardens; organic gardening; sashimi and sushi; wok cookery
serigraphy, 16: 1960-73
    garden print, **16:** 1960, 1971-72
    inks, fillers, and solvents, **16:** 1973
    poster print, **16:** 1963-65
    printing on plastic, **16:** 1970-71
    silk screen, **16:** 1966-67
    wall-hanging catchalls, **16:** 1968-70
    See also block printing; greeting cards; linoleum and woodcuts; monoprinting; oil painting; stenciling; watercolors
serving trays
    ribbon craft, **14:** 1772
    rosewood, **16:** 1930-33
    treen
        hors-d'oeuvre wheel, **21:** 2612
        snack server, **21:** 2611
set design, stage, 18: 2196-2201
sewing without pattern, 16: 1974-85
    apron-shawl, bias-cut, **16:** 1974-76
    caftan, **16:** 1977, 1978-80
    cape, hooded, **16:** 1980-81
    coverlet, quilted, **16:** 1975, 1983-84
    curtains with valance, café, **16:** 1984-85
    kimono, coat, **16:** 1977-78
    pillow cover, ruffled, **16:** 1985
    skirt, wraparound, **16:** 1982
    tablecloth, round, **16:** 1985
    See also animals, doll; appliqué; bean-bags; buttons; costumes; flags and banners; Florentine stitch; fur recycling; machine stitchery; recycling clothes; soft sculpture; trapunto
shades. See lamps and lampshades
shadow boxes
    gilt-edge shadow-box, **7:** 790-91
    pod and cone art shadow box, **13:** 1952
    See also collages and assemblages
shadow theater, 16: 1986-97
    color silhouettes, **16:** 1991
    paper shadow puppets, **16:** 1996-97
    plastic jellyfish, **16:** 1989, 1992
    plastic puppets, **16:** 1992-93
    shadow play, **16:** 1993
    silhouette puppets, **16:** 1988-89
    See also music making; preschool activities; puppets and puppetry; stagecraft; zoetrope toys
Shaker furniture, 16: 1998-2011
    candle sconce, **16:** 2000-3
    dovetailed candle box, **16:** 2009-11
    side table, **16:** 2003-5
    utility bench, **16:** 2006-8
    See also benches; rockers and cradles; tables; upholstery

S, continued

shawl, bias-cut apron, **16:** 1974-76
shearing sheep, 17: 2133
sheetmetal, sawing, **17:** 2058
sheets, trapunto, **21:** 2582-84
shells. See seashells
shelters and tents, 16: 2012-23
    tarp tents and lean-tos, **16:** 2014-18
    tepees, **16:** 2020-23
    See also **American Indian crafts;**
        astronomy; bicycles and bicycling;
        breads; canoeing; clam bakes;
        gold panning; hammocks and
        slings; kayaks; maps and path-
        finding; sail making and repair;
        tree houses; weather forecasting
sherbet, 8: 917
Shinto festivals, 12: 1418
ship models, 16: 2024-41
    bottle, ship in, **16:** 2038-41
    display case for models, **16:** 2037
    Philadelphia ship model, **16:** 2025-37
    See also **airplanes, paper; models**
        and mock-ups; piloting small
        boats; sail making and repair;
        soapbox and skate vehicles
shirts
    man's shirt, smocking, **17:** 2081-82
    recycled shirt, **14:** 1739
    workshirt, free embroidered, **9:** 1106-7
    See also **T-shirts**
Shooters' and Mummers' Parade
    (Philadelphia), **12:** 1415, 1421-23
shoulder bags. See bags
shuttles, tatting, **19:** 2424
    large, making, **19:** 2430
signal communications, 5: 564-65
signs, lettering in gold, **7:** 795-97
silhouettes, 16: 2042-48
    pictures, silhouette, **16:** 2046-48
    reverse silhouettes, **10:** 1261-63
    silhouettes, **16:** 2044-46
    tree-of-life, **23:** 2894-95
    See also **block printing; cartooning;**
        greeting cards; origami; shadow
        theater; valentines; wycinanki
silk screening. See serigraphy
silversmithing, 17: 2054-65
    bowl, copper, **17:** 2063-65
    butter knife, silver, **17:** 2056-57
    spoon, silver, **17:** 2059-61
    See also **American Indian crafts; belts**
        and buckles; Colonial crafts;
        enameling metal; jewelry;
        mineralogy; pewtersmithing;
        repoussé and chased metal; tin
        and pierced work; wire sculpture
sink, mosaic tiled, **10:** 1276
sisal
    basket, coiled, **23:** 2884-86
    rug, crocheted, **5:** 557
skate vehicles. See soapbox and skate
    vehicles
sketching
    oil painting, **11:** 1340
    sand characters, **15:** 1883

    watercolors, **22:** 2726-27
skin painting, 17: 2066-75
    body painting, **17:** 2066, 2074-75
    heavenly-nights face makeup, **17:**
      2068-69
    leopard face makeup, **17:** 2068-69
    primitive face makeup, **17:** 2070-71
    stage face makeup, **17:** 2072-73
    See also **cosmetics; costumes; masks;**
        stagecraft
skirts
    child's skirt, afghan stitch, **1:** 24-28
    denim skirt, recycled, **14:** 1733-35
    knit skirt, **8:** 1007-9
    quilted skirt, **14:** 1706-7
    tie-dyed skirt, **20:** 2479-81
    tie skirt, recycled, **11:** 1316-17
    wraparound skirt, **16:** 1982
skullies, 18: 2260
skylight floor garden, 9: 1090-91
slab-glass casting, 18: 2223-24
slings. See hammocks and slings
smocking, 17: 2076-85
    cotton dress, **17:** 2085
    silk dress, **17:** 2083-81
    pillow, smock, **17:** 2078-81
    shirt, man's, **17:** 2081-82
    See also **crewel; embroidery; har-**
        danger embroidery; samplers;
        Swedish huck work; tatting
snakes, 22: 2711-13
snowflakes, paper, **23:** 2893
snow sculptures, 22: 2806-11
snuffer, candle, **20:** 2504-7
soapbox and skate vehicles, 17: 2086-97
    cart, crate, **17:** 2089-90
    racer, lay-back, **17:** 2091-97
    scooter, skate, **17:** 2088-89
    See also **bicycles and bicycling;**
        canoeing; carving; kayaks;
        models and mock-ups; pin
        striping; rockers and cradles; ship
        models; swings; wood
        assemblages; yard toys; yo-yos
soaps and bath products, 17: 2098-2105
    cleansing creams and masks, **17:** 2104-5
    quick soaps, **17:** 2098-2102
    shaving soaps and bath oils, **17:** 2103
    See also **cosmetics; herbs; perfumes**
soft sculpture, 17: 2106-21
    abstraction, soft sculpture, **17:** 2110-11
    airplane, soft sculpture, **17:** 2107-9
    gorilla, soft sculpture, **17:** 2114, 2116-19
    palm tree, soft sculpture, **17:** 2114-16
    tennis shoes, soft sculpture, **17:** 2112-14
    See also **animals, doll; bean-bags;**
        mobiles; rag dolls; rya and flossa;
        sculpture; sewing without pattern
soups, 17: 2122-31
    chicken julienne, **17:** 2126
    chicken soup, **17:** 2127
    cupboard soups, **17:** 2131
    fruit soups, **17:** 2128-29
    vichyssoise, **17:** 2130-31

    See also **breads; clambakes; herbs;**
        pasta; pickled and canned foods;
        terrines and timbales
sour cream, 4: 446-49
sourdough bread, 3: 284-89
spinning, 17: 2132-53
    carding wool, **17:** 2138-41
    drop spindle spinning, **17:** 2143-45
    drying wool, **17:** 2137
    flax on wheel, spinning, **17:** 2151-53
    making yarn, **17:** 2133-41
    oiling wool, **17:** 2138
    picking wool, **17:** 2135
    scouring wool, **17:** 2136-37
    shearing, **17:** 2133
    sorting wool fibers, **17:** 2134
    spinning wheels, **17:** 2141-42
    wool on wheel, spinning, **17:** 2146-50
    See also **Colonial crafts; crochet;**
        knitting to fit; rya and flossa;
        traditional knitting motifs;
        vegetable dyes; woven tapestries;
        yarn painting
sponges, free-form assemblage, **4:** 487
spool toys, 17: 2154-61
    auto race, spool, **17:** 2157
    balance toys, **17:** 2160-61
    constructions, spool, **17:** 2155-56
    knitting, spool, **17:** 2158
    parachute toy, **17:** 2159
    pull-along toys, **17:** 2156
    ring-toss game, **17:** 2160-61
    rocking toys, **17:** 2157
    streamers, spool, **17:** 2160-61
    wind-up toys, **17:** 2159
    See also **bean-bags; Christmas**
        celebrations; dolls and doll
        clothes; pod and cone art;
        preschool activities; yo-yos
spoons
    ring made from, **8:** 955
    salad spoon and fork, treen, **21:** 2612
    silver spoon, **21:** 2612
sprang, 17: 2162-76
    belt, sprang, **17:** 2168
    hammock, sprang, **17:** 2174-76
    loom, **17:** 2169
    sampler, sprang, **17:** 2163-66
    scarf, sprang, **17:** 2169
    tote bag, sprang, **17:** 2167
    twists and closings, **17:** 2170-71
    wall hanging, sprang, **17:** 2172-73
    See also **inkle weaving; lace;**
        macramé; rope knotting; tablet and
        frame weaving
spreaders and cutters, treen, **21:** 2609
spring beer, 3: 300
sprouting. See organic gardening; seed
    sprouting
spruce beer, 3: 301
spun-sugar cookery. See sugar shapes
spurtles, treen, **21:** 2608
square dancing, 18: 2182-93
    callers, **18:** 2184
    formations, square dance, **18:** 2185-87
    hash call, **18:** 2191-93

lessons, **18**: 2184-85
publications, square dance, **18**: 2182
regional styles, **18**: 2182
singing call, **18**: 2188-91
See also **dulcimers; music making; whistles and flutes; wind harps**
stagecraft, 18: 2194-2215
lighting, stage, **18**: 2206-13
makeup, face, **17**: 2072-73
painting techniques, scene, **18**: 2205-7
set design, **18**: 2196-2201
theaters
designers, **18**: 2202
management, **18**: 2202
technical staff, **18**: 2202
types of theaters, **18**: 2202
See also **costumes; masks; music making; puppets and puppetry; shadow theater; skin painting; whistles and flutes**
stained glass, 18: 2216-31
mosaic, glass, **18**: 2225-26
necklace, copper-foiled, **18**: 2226-29
panel, laminated, **18**: 2217, 2222-23
panel, leaded stained-glass, **18**: 2229-31
slab-glass casting, **18**: 2223-24
See also **acrylics; bottle cutting; casting; glass working; greeting cards; jewelry; leaded glass; molding methods; mosaics; seashells**
staircase, yard toy, **23**: 2908-9
stamp decoupage, 18: 2232-39
container decoupage, **18**: 2237-39
pieced pictures, **18**: 2235-36
See also **boxes; collages and assemblages; decoupage; greeting cards; mosaics; wycinanki**
standards. See **flags and banners; genealogy; heraldry; wood assemblages**
stars
evening star ojo de dios, **11**: 1357-58
paper, star, **23**: 2892-93
as pathfinding guide, **9**: 1148-52
piñata, star, **12**: 1524-28
star dial, **20**: 2497-99
triple stellate forms, string art, **18**: 2274-76
stationery
fingerprint stationery, **10**: 1258-59
herb note cards, **7**: 884
monogrammed stationery, vegetable print, **2**: 213
personalized note paper, **18**: 2244-45
blender-made stationery paper, **11**: 1390-93
steel
antiquing hardware, **1**: 80
mobile, steel fin, **10**: 1227-31
stenciling, 18: 2240-51
floors, stenciled, **18**: 2250-51
note paper, personalized, **18**: 2244-45
place mats, stenciled, **18**: 2246-47
tin box, antique stenciled, **20**: 2523-27

walls and ceilings, stenciled, **18**: 2248-49
See also **antiquing furniture; batik; candlemaking; enameling metal; greeting cards; linoleum and woodcuts; serigraphy; supergraphics; tin painting; wycinanki**
sterilizing, wine container, **22**: 2798
stickball, street, **18**: 2263
sticks. See **walking sticks**
still life, oil painting, **11**: 1342-43
stitches. See **Needlecrafts**
stone painting, 18: 2252-57
animals, stone, **18**: 2256-57
assemblages, painted stone, **18**: 2253-54
key-chain fob, **18**: 2255-56
See also **beachcombing; sand painting and layering; seashells; sculpture; watercolors**
stoneware. See **ceramics; pottery**
stools
cardboard stool, **3**: 372-73
sawhorse stool, **19**: 2379-81
stoopball, 18: 2267
straw. See **raffia and straw**
streamers, spool, **17**: 2160-61
street games, 18: 2258-69
association football, **18**: 2265
boxball, **18**: 2267
Chinese handball, **18**: 2262
double dutch, **18**: 2269
follow-the-leader, **18**: 2268
hit-the-penny, **18**: 2265
hopscotch, **18**: 2266
Johnny-on-the-pony, **18**: 2258-59
kickball, **18**: 2264
kick-the-can, **18**: 2261
ring-a-levio, **18**: 2268
running bases, **18**: 2264
skullies, **18**: 2260
stickball, street, **18**: 2263
stoopball, **18**: 2267
See also **preschool activities; yard toys; yo-yos**
stretching
canvas, **11**: 1338
watercolor paper, **22**: 2724-26
string art, 18: 2270-83
children's string designs, **18**: 2282-83
conics in box, **18**: 2271, 2280-81
helios, **18**: 2276-77
raised ellipse, **18**: 2278-79
three adjacent hexagons, **18**: 2272-73
triple stellate forms, **18**: 2274-76
See also **wire sculpture**
structural furnishings, 18: 2284-99
lofts, **18**: 2284, 2288-93
platforms, **18**: 2294-99
table, wall-hanging, **18**: 2286-87
See also **benches; models and mock-ups; plastic pipe constructions; plywood and foam furnishings; supergraphics;**

tables; upholstery; yard toys
sugar shapes, 18: 2300-4
brown sugar shapes, **18**: 2304
ladybugs, sugar, **18**: 2303
place cards, sugar, **18**: 2304
schoolhouse, sugar, **18**: 2302-3
wedding bells, sugar, **18**: 2303
winter scene. sugar, **18**: 2300, 2302
See also **birthday celebrations; Christmas celebrations; confections and comfits; gingerbread; marmalades and preserves; syrups**
sun, as pathfinding guide, **9**: 1148-52
sundials, 19: 2310-21
Egyptian sundial, **19**: 2313-14
horizontal sundial, **19**: 2316-21
portable sundial, **19**: 2315
See also **astronomy; birds and birdhouses; maps and pathfinding; time telling; weather forecasting**
supergraphics, 19: 2322-35
child's bedroom supergraphic, **19**: 2327
dark backround supergraphic, **19**: 2328
diagonal stripes supergraphic, **19**: 2330-31
fabric design supergraphic, **19**: 2334-35
flowers supergraphic, **19**: 2330-31
free-form supergraphic, **19**: 2332
furniture framing supergraphic, **19**: 2327-28
geometric supergraphic, **19**: 2324-26
Indian motif supergraphic, **19**: 2333
reversed colors supergraphic, **19**: 2329
sunrise supergraphic, **19**: 2323, 2330
See also **acrylics; boxes; color psychology; models and mock-ups; oil painting; stenciling; structural furnishings; watercolors**
sushi
chirashi sushi, **15**: 1911
nigiri sushi, **15**: 1905-7
norimaki sushi, **15**: 1908-10
sweaters
hooded parka sweater, **8**: 1010-11
knit sweater, **8**: 1007-9
Norwegian-pattern sweater, **21**: 2574-77
Swedish huck work, 19: 2336-43
handbag, huck work, **19**: 2341-42
hand towel, huck work, **19**: 2340
pillow, huck work, **19**: 2342-43
See also **crewel; embroidery; hardanger embroidery; lace; needlepoint; smocking**
swings, 19: 2344-57
baby swing, **19**: 2354-57
hardware for, **19**: 2353
monkey swing, **19**: 2351-52
pulley-and-cable glides, **19**: 2348-51
rope swing, **19**: 2344, 2346
tire swings, **19**: 2345-48
See also **hammocks and slings; kites and kite making; preschool activities; soapbox and skate vehicles; tree houses; yard toys**

S, continued

Switchel, Yankee, **3**: 300
syrups, 19: 2358-65
  beverages and desserts, **19**: 2358-63
  main dishes, syrup-flavored, **19**: 2364-65
  See also **baby foods; confections and comfits; ice cream, sherbet, and ices; marmalades and preserves; sugar shapes**

T

tablecloths
  appliquéd, **1**: 82-85, 91
  openwork, **19**: 2431-32
  round, **16**: 1985
  velvet, **20**: 2482-84
  See also **napkins and napkin folding; place mats**
table games, 19: 2366-77
  Anagrams, **19**: 2373-74
  Jungle Games, **19**: 2366-67, 2370-72
  Lasca, **19**: 2374-75
  Mancala, **19**: 2368
  Mill, **19**: 2369-70
  Quick Trip, **19**: 2376-77
  See also **bean-bags; birthday celebrations; card tricks; magic; piñatas; preschool activities; puzzles**
tables, 19: 2378-91
  cardboard table, **3**: 372-73
  mineral table top, **10**: 1209
  modular tables, **19**: 2384-87
  nesting tables, **19**: 2388-91
  plant table, **19**: 2382-83
  sawhorse stool, **19**: 2379-81
  side table, **16**: 2003-5
  wall-hanging table, **18**: 2286-87
  See also **antiquing furniture; benches; models and mock-ups; plastic pipe constructions; plywood and foam furnishings; refinishing furniture; rockers and cradles; Shaker furniture; structural furnishings; upholstery**
tablet and frame weaving, 19: 2392-2405
  bag, tablet-woven, **19**: 2399-2401
  belt, tablet-woven, **19**: 2398
  branch weaving, **19**: 2402
  frame weaving, geometric, **19**: 2403-4
  hoop weaving, **19**: 2393, 2405
  landscape frame weaving, **19**: 2404-5
  See also **inkle weaving; ribboncraft; rya and flossa; sprang; woven tapestries**
tableware
  butter knife, silver, **17**: 2056-57
  party accessories, treen, **21**: 2610-13
  spoon, silver, **17**: 2059-61
  See also **bowls; dishes; trays**
tambour, 19: 2406-19
  curtain, white-on-white, **19**: 2412

dragonfly, tambour, **19**: 2417-19
  pillow, tambour, **19**: 2416-17
  rug, wool, **19**: 2413-15
  stitches, tambour, **19**: 2410-11
  wall hanging, tambour, **19**: 2415-16
  See also **appliqué; crewel; crochet; embroidery; rugs, hooked; Swedish huck work**
tangrams, 13: 1559-60
tank, aquarium. See **tropical fish**
tannin, 22: 2800
tapestries. See **batik; wall hangings; woven tapestries**
tatting, 19: 2420-32
  child's vest, **19**: 2426-27
  flowerpot holder, **19**: 2429-30
  handkerchief edging, **19**: 2421, 2424
  collar, shell-cluster, **19**: 2424-25
  place mat, sunflower, **19**: 2427-28
  shuttles, **19**: 2424, 2430
  tablecloth, openwork, **19**: 2431-32
  See also **granny squares; lace; macramé**
tea, 20: 2438-51
  brewing tea, **20**: 2442-43
  herb cultivation, **20**: 2439-42
  Japanese tea ceremony, **20**: 2447-51
  kinds of tea, **20**: 2444-46
  See also **herbs; organic gardening; seed sprouting**
teleidoscope, 8: 963-65
telescope, 1: 101-5
temperature, organic gardening and, maps, **11**: 1372-73
  See also **weather forecasting**
tennis racket, ribboncraft cover for, **14**: 1769-70
tennis shoes, soft sculpture, **17**: 2112-14
tents, tarp, **16**: 2014-17
tepees, 20: 2020-23
terrariums, 20: 2452-61
  cactus terrarium, **20**: 2460-61
  fern terrarium, **20**: 2457-59
  in kaleidoscopic cube, **8**: 960-61
  sand-layered planter, **15**: 1891-94
  sand painting and layering for, **15**: 1897
  tropical terrarium, **20**: 2454-55
  See also **bonsai; bottle cutting; bottle gardens; greenhouse construction; ikebana; lighted indoor gardens; tropical fish; vivariums**
terrines and timbales, 20: 2462-69
  terrines, **20**: 2463-66
  timbales, **20**: 2467-69
  See also **breads; herbs; pasta; soups**
thaumatropes, 23: 2926-29
theaters
  designers, **18**: 2202
  management, **18**: 2202
  technical staff, **18**: 2202
  types of theaters, **18**: 2202
  See also **stagecraft**

thermometer, weather forecasting, **22**: 2743-44
tie dyeing, 20: 2470-89
  knots and folds, **20**: 2474-75
  stitchery, tie-dye, **20**: 2479-81
  table throw, velvet, **20**: 2482-84
  T-shirts, tie-dyed, **20**: 2476-79
  wall hanging, block dyed, **20**: 2484-87
  See also **batik; block printing; linoleum and woodcuts; monoprinting; neckties; vegetable dyes**
ties. See **neckties**
tiles
  clay, **4**: 434-439
  mosaics, **10**: 1276-80
  mural, **10**: 1278-80
  steel, **6**: 665-67
timbales, 20: 2467-69
time telling, 20: 2490-99
  candle clock, **20**: 2494-95
  Egyptian sundial, **19**: 2313-14
  horizontal sundial, **19**: 2316-21
  noon light show, **20**: 2490-93
  portable sundial, **19**: 2315
  sandglass, **20**: 2495-96
  star dial, **20**: 2497-99
  See also **astronomy; candlemaking; maps and pathfinding; weather forecasting;**
tin painting, 20: 2513-27
  antique stenciled tin box, **20**: 2523-27
  canister, painted, **20**: 2518-19
  country tin painting, **20**: 2513-17
  freehand bronze tray, **20**: 2520-22
  See also **folk art; decoupage; rosemaling; stenciling**
tin and pierced work, 20: 2500-9
  candle sconce and snuffer, **20**: 2504-7
  cookie cutters, **20**: 2502-3
  fruit bowl, **20**: 2508-9
  See also **Colonial crafts; lamps and lamp shades; mobiles; pewtersmithing; repoussé and chased metal; silversmithing; wire sculpture**
tires
  bicycle tires, **2**: 183-85
  yard toys, tire, **23**: 2902-3
  staircase, spiral, **23**: 2908-9
  swings, **19**: 2345-48
  trampoline, inner-tube, **23**: 2900-1
tissue paper, flowers from, **6**: 689
tombstone rubbings, 15: 1815-17
tomato, pickling and canning recipes, **12**: 1507-8
tooling. See **American Indian crafts; belts and buckles; bookbinding; gold leafing; Leathercrafts; repoussé and chased metal**
topiary, 20: 2528-37
  geometric topiary, **20**: 2530-31
  privet hedge, **20**: 2533-35
  three-ball ivy topiary, **20**: 2532
  See also **bonsai; ikebana; organic gardening; trellises**

tops, clothing
  casual top, **14**: 1739
  child's Irish-knit top, **21**: 2571-74
  knit top, **14**: 1733-35
  raglan top, **14**: 1736-38
tops, spool, **17**: 2159
tortoise-shell base, decoupage, **5**: 575-76
toss toy, bean-bag, **2**: 160
tote bags
  granny square shoulder tote bag, **7**: 814-15
  leather tote bag, **4**: 396-99
  log sling, canvas, **7**: 850-51
  patchwork tote bag, **12**: 1451-52
  reverse appliqué tote bag, **14**: 1759-60
  sprang tote bag, **17**: 2167
  two-pet tote, **12**: 1270-72
  vinyl tote bag, **4**: 392-94
  weft-faced tote bag, **22**: 2770-71
  See also **bags; carryalls**
totem poles, 20: 2538-47
  full-sized totem pole, **20**: 2546-47
  miniature totem pole, **20**: 2543
  wall plaque, totem-mask, **20**: 2541-42
  See also **American Indian crafts; carving; folk art; genealogy; heraldry; masks; sculpture; treen ware; walking sticks; wood assemblages**
towel, hand, huck work, **19**: 2340
Toys and Games
  bean-bags, 2: 158-63
    games, bean-bag, **2**: 162-63
    paperweight, felt, **2**: 161
    toss toy, **2**: 160
  birthday celebrations, 2: 208-9
    party games, **2**: 208-9
  cardboard, 3: 366-68
    train, toy, **3**: 366, 368
  cryptography, 5: 558-60, 564-65
    codes, **5**: 559-60
    signal communications, **5**: 564-65
  dioramas, 5: 578-82
    train diorama, **5**: 579-82
  dolls and doll clothes, 5: 604-13
    apple-headed doll, **5**: 609
    cloth doll, **5**: 612-13
    clothespin doll, **5**: 608
    cornhusk doll, **5**: 610
    pieces doll, **5**: 608
    repairing dolls, **5**: 611
    replacement parts, doll, **5**: 611
    walnut and egg dolls, **5**: 606-7
  flowers, artificial, 6: 688
    pencil posy, **6**: 688
  kaleidoscopes, 8: 958-67
    cubes, kaleidoscopic, **8**: 960-61
    Hue View kaleidoscope, **8**: 962-63
    kaleidoscope, **8**: 965-67
    teleidoscope, **8**: 963-65
  kites, 8: 988-99
    bamboo kite poles, **8**: 995
    Greek kite, **8**: 992-95
    Indian fighter kite, **8**: 989, 998-99
    sled kite, **8**: 991
    Thai dragon kite, **8**: 996-97

music making, 11: 1286-91, 1293
  percussion instruments, **11**: 1287-91
  stands and mounts, **11**: 1293
papier-mâché, 11: 1405-7
  puppet heads, **11**: 1405-7
piñatas, 12: 1524-36
  doll piñata, **12**: 1534
  rabbit-foot piñata, **12**: 1529
  sailboat piñata, **12**: 1535-36
  star piñata, **12**: 1524-28
  wishing-well piñata, **12**: 1530-34
preschool activities, 13: 1662-27, 1635
  busy board, **13**: 1625-27
  hand puppets, **13**: 1635
  stuffed giraffe, **13**: 1622-24
puzzles, 13: 1654-64
  block puzzle, **13**: 1661-62
  counter puzzle, **13**: 1658-59
  crossword puzzles, **13**: 1655-57
  jigsaw puzzle, **13**: 1663-64
  tangrams, **13**: 1659-60
rockers and cradles, 14: 1774-81
  boat, rocker, **14**: 1777-78
  child's rocking chair, **14**: 1776
  doll's cradle, **14**: 1780-81
soapbox and skate vehicles, 17: 2086-97
  crate cart, **17**: 2089-90
  lay-back racer, **17**: 2091-97
  skate scooter, **17**: 2088-89
spool toys, 17: 2154-61
  auto race, spool, **17**: 2157
  balance toys, **17**: 2160-61
  knitting, spool, **17**: 2158
  parachute toy, **17**: 2159
  pull-along toys, **17**: 2156
  ring-toss game, **17**: 2160-61
  rocking toys, **17**: 2157
  streamers, spool, **17**: 2160-61
  wind-up toys, **17**: 2159
street games, 18: 2258-69
  association football, **18**: 2265
  boxball, **18**: 2267
  Chinese handball, **18**: 2262
  double dutch, **18**: 2269
  follow-the-leader, **18**: 2268
  hit-the-penny, **18**: 2265
  hopscotch, **18**: 2266
  Johnny-on-the-pony, **18**: 2258-59
  kickball, **18**: 2264
  kick-the-can, **18**: 2261
  ring-a-levio, **18**: 2268
  running bases, **18**: 2264
  skullies, **18**: 2260
  stickball, street, **18**: 2263
  stoopball, **18**: 2267
table games, 19: 2366-77
  Anagrams, **19**: 2373-74
  Jungle Game, **19**: 2366-67, 2370-72
  Lasca, **19**: 2374-75
  Mancala, **19**: 2368
  Mill, **19**: 2369-70

  Quick Trip, **19**: 2376-77
toys, 20: 2548-60
  bull roarer, **20**: 2550
  elephant toy chest, **20**: 2549, 2556-58
  gee-haw whimmy-diddle, **20**: 2550-51
  hammer man, **20**: 2559-60
  jumping jack, **20**: 2552-53
  moonwinder, **20**: 2548
  sports car, **20**: 2553
  stern-wheel boat, **20**: 2554-55
whistles and flutes, 22: 2774-78
  dowel whistle, **22**: 2776-77
  hardwood whistle, **22**: 2778
yard toys, 23: 2900-9
  playhouse, cable-spool, **23**: 2906-7
  staircase, spiral, **23**: 2908-9
  tire and box toys, **23**: 2902-3
  trampoline, **23**: 2900-1
  utility pole animals, **23**: 2904-5
yo-yos, 23: 2918-25
  drawer-pull yo-yo, **23**: 2918-20
  sink-strainer yo-yos, **23**: 2920
  stringing yo-yos, **23**: 2921
  tournament tricks, **23**: 2922-25
  See also **airplanes, paper; animals, doll; carving; chests; soft sculpture; zoetrope toys**
traditional knitting motifs, 21: 2566-79
  bias-knit scarf, **21**: 2578-79
  child's Irish-knit top, **21**: 2571-74
  Norwegian-pattern sweater, **21**: 2574-77
  shoulder bag, **21**: 2570
  See also **Colonial crafts; folk art; knitting to fit; spinning**
trail breads, 3: 282-83
trains
  cardboard toy train, **3**: 366, 368
  diorama, train, **5**: 578-82
trampoline, inner-tube, **23**: 2900-1
trapunto, 21: 2580-91
  bag, trapunto, **9**: 1113-14
  dress, yoked, **21**: 2580, 2584-85
  face pillow, trapunto, **21**: 2588-89
  handbag, batik, **21**: 2586
  sheet and pillowcases, trapunto, **21**: 2582-84
  T-shirt, lion, **21**: 2587-88
  wall hanging, trapunto, **21**: 2590-91
  See also **appliqué; quilts and quilting**
trays
  bread tray, raffia, **23**: 2886-87
  bronze tray, freehand painted, **20**: 2520-22
  oval tray, raffia, **14**: 1722
  painted tray, tin, **20**: 2513-17
  round tray, raffia, **14**: 1720-22
  serving trays
    ribboncraft, **14**: 1722
    rosewood, **16**: 1930-33
    treen, **21**: 2611, 2612
tree houses, 21: 2592-2601
  grove tree house, **21**: 2594-96
  outdoor platform, **21**: 2596-99
  traditional tree house, **21**: 2593, 2600-1

tree houses, continued

See also **models and mock-ups; plastic pipe constructions; rope knotting; shelters and tents; structural furnishings; swings; yard toys**

treen ware, 21: 2602-13
kitchen utensils, 21: 2604-9
party table accessories, 21: 2610-13
See also **folk art; sculpture; totem poles**

trees
soil acidity needs, 11: 1362
tree-of-life, 23: 2894-95
wired tree, 13: 1593-95

trellises, 21: 2614-25
doorway trellis, 21: 2614, 2622-25
fan trellises, 21: 2616-18
freestanding trellis, 21: 2619-21
See also **greenhouse construction; lighted indoor gardens; topiary**

trims. See ornaments

tropical fish, 21: 2626-39
aquariums, 21: 2626-39
aquatic plants, 21: 2632-33
assembly, 21: 2628-34
filters, 21: 2629-30
heaters, 21: 2629-30
maintenance, 21: 2635
oxygen supply, 21: 2629-30
tank construction, 2: 128
water pH, 21: 2631
feeding aquarium fish, 21: 2635
freshwater aquarium fish, 21: 2634-37
pH requirements, 21: 2636-37
marine aquarium fish, 21: 2639
marine aquariums, 21: 2638-39
synthetic seawater, 21: 2639
See also **ant farms; birds and birdhouses; insects; pet habitats; tying flies; vivariums**

T-shirts
appliquéd, 14: 1772-73
calligraphic, 10: 1265-66
lion, trapunto, 21: 2587-88
recycled, 14: 1736-37
tie-dyed, 20: 2476-79

turkey, pine cone, 13: 1590

tying flies, 21: 2640-51
Rat-Faced MacDougall fly, 21: 2648-49
Royal Coachman fly, 21: 2650-51
TW Special fly, 21: 2645-47
See also **beachcombing; fur recycling; rope knotting; sashimi and sushi; tropical fish**

U

underpainting, oil painting and, 11: 1346-47

upholstery, 21: 2652-65
bench, cushioned, 21: 2654-57
chair seat, padded, 21: 2658
easy chair, stuffed, 21: 2659-65

See also **antiquing furniture; benches; caning and rushing; gold leafing; plastic pipe constructions; plywood and foam furnishings; refinishing furniture; rockers and cradles; Shaker furniture; structural furnishings; tables**

utensils, kitchen treen ware, 21: 2604-9
rack for, 21: 2606-7

utility bench, Shaker, 16: 2006-8

V

valances
café curtains with valance, 16: 1984-85
woven tapestry used as, 23: 2874

valentines, 21: 2666-75
gift box, valentine, 21: 2674-75
lovebird valentine, 21: 2674
playing card valentine, 21: 2673
two-heart valentine, 21: 2672-73
See also **cartooning; collages and assemblages; decoupage; greeting cards; origami; papermaking; silhouettes; wycinanki**

vegetable dyes, 21: 2676-88
colorfast dyes, 21: 2678-83
wool yarn, dyeing, 21: 2684-88
See also **American Indian crafts; basketry; batik; Colonial crafts; color psychology; herbs; Leathercrafts, leather working; raffia and straw; sand painting and layering; spinning; tie dyeing**

vegetables
block printing with, 2: 210-13
carving, 4: 418-21
pickling and canning recipes, 12: 1509-10
seed sprouting, 16: 1952-59
soil acidity needs, 11: 1362
See also **organic gardening**

vests
afghan stitch, 1: 24-28
child's, tatting, 19: 2426-27
quilted, 14: 1706-7
reversible, patchwork, 12: 1449-50

vichyssoise, 17: 2130-31

vinegars, 22: 2694-2703
cider vinegar, 22: 2698
flavored vinegars, 22: 2699-2703
wine vinegar, 22: 2696-97
See also **herbs; pickled and canned foods; wine making**

vivariums, 22: 2704-13
chameleon lizards, 22: 2710-11
guinea pigs, 22: 2706-7
rat, English hooded, 22: 2708
rodent vivarium, 22: 2709
snakes, 22: 2711-13

See also **ant farms; birds and birdhouses; bottle gardens; greenhouse construction; insects; pet habitats; terrariums; tropical fish**

Volkswagen, paint decoration for, 1: 21-23

W

walking sticks, 22: 2714-21
hiking stick, 22: 2716-18
sculptured walking stick, 22: 2720-21
spiral-design cane, 22: 2718-19
See also **carving; sculpture; totem poles; treen ware; wood assemblages**

wall hangings and decorations
appliquéd wall hanging, 9: 1109-11
banner, club, 6: 670-71
banner, felt, 6: 668, 674-75
batik wall hanging, 1: 126
bean-bag wall hanging, 2: 167
black work owl wall hanging, 6: 656-57
block-dyed wall hanging, 20: 2484-87
block-printed wall hanging, 9: 1102
box-illusion wall plaque, 23: 2846-49
box wall sculpture, 3: 268
carrick bend chain wall plaque, 14: 1788
cartoon wall decorations, 4: 413
catchalls, wall-hanging, 16: 1968-70
embroidery circles wall hanging, 6: 647, 653
foam cup wall hanging, 6: 700-1
folk art wall hanging, 9: 1107-8
garden print wallpaper, 16: 1971-72
gongs and chimes, wall-hanging, 11: 1287, 1292
inkle weaving wall hanging, 8: 929, 934-35
knotted wall hangings, 14: 1783
linoleum print wallpaper 2: 216-19
masks, wall-hanging, 10: 1181, 1187
micromé wall hanging, 9: 1126-27
packing pieces wall assemblage, 6: 699
quilted wall hanging, 14: 1690, 1697-98
reverse appliqué wall hanging, 14: 1760-61
rubbings, wall-hanging, 15: 1819
rya wall hanging, 15: 1832-34
Senufo wall hanging, 6: 714-15
shadow box, wall-hanging, 13: 1592
sprang wall hanging, 17: 2172-73
sprang sampler, wall-hanging, 17: 2163-66
stenciled walls, 18: 2248-49
table, wall-hanging, 18: 2286-87
tambour wall hanging, 19: 2415-16
totem-mask wall plaque, 20: 2541-42
trapunto wall hanging, 21: 2590-91
wool wall hanging, 15: 1826-28
woven wall hanging, 22: 2772-73
See also **ojo de dios; string art; supergraphics; tablet and frame weaving; window hangings; woven tapestries**

watchband, inkle-woven, 8: 933

watercolors, 22: 2722-33
  brushstrokes, **22:** 2730-31
  framing, **22:** 2733
  glazing, **22:** 2730-31
  materials, watercolor, **22:** 2723-24
  outdoor painting, **22:** 2724
  paint, watercolor, **22:** 2724
  paper, watercolor, **22:** 2724
  sketching, **22:** 2726-27
  stretching watercolor paper, **22:** 2724-26
  washes, **22:** 2728-29, 2731
  See also **calligraphy; color psychology; frames and framing; oil painting; preschool activities; stone painting; supergraphics**
wax
  casting, candle, **10:** 1253-55
  reliefs, carving, **4:** 417
weather forecasting, 22: 2734-51
  making weather instruments, **22:** 2740-45
  maps, weather, **22:** 2751
    organic gardening and, **11:** 1372-73
  using weather instruments, **22:** 2746-51
  See also **astronomy; canoeing; kayaks; maps and pathfinding; piloting small boats; sail making and repair; shelters and tents; sundials; time telling**
weathervanes
  reindeer weathervane, **6:** 716-17
  whirligig weathervane, **3:** 369-71
Weaving, Braiding, and Knotting
  basketry, 1: 112-19
    coil basket, Indian, **1:** 115
    hanging basket, **1:** 116-17
    pencil holder, **1:** 114
    shopping basket, **1:** 118-19
  braided rugs, 3: 272-79
    coasters, braided, **3:** 275
    petal-design rug, **3:** 278-79
    place mats, braided, **3:** 276-77
    traditional braided rug, **3:** 276-77
  hammocks and slings, 7: 846-53
    eye splice, **7:** 849
    flat stitching, canvas hem, **7:** 848
    grommet, stitching, **7:** 848
    log sling, canvas, **7:** 850-51
    naval hammock, **7:** 851-53
    short splice, permanent, **7:** 849
  hooked rugs, 8: 902-9
    geometric rug, **8:** 904-5
    "love" hooked rug, **8:** 907
    owl rug, **8:** 906
  inkle weaving, 8: 928-35
    belt, pick-up pattern, **8:** 935
    hat band and bag handle, **8:** 932
    wall hanging, inkle, **8:** 929, 934-35
    watchband and vase cover, **8:** 933
  lace, 8: 1012-21
    collar and cuffs, bobbin lace, **8:** 1019-21
    grounds, bobbin lace, **8:** 1016-17
    sash, bobbin lace, **8:** 1017-18
  leather working, 9: 1072-73
    belt, magic braid, **9:** 1072-73

macramé, 9: 1116-27
  belt, adjustable, **9:** 1120-21
  dress yoke and sash, **9:** 1122-23
  hanging, micromé, **9:** 1126-27
  knots, macramé, **9:** 1118-19
  room-divider screen, **9:** 1116, 1124
  sculpture, willow tree, **9:** 1125-26
ojo de dios, 11: 1348-59
  construction, ojo, **11:** 1350
  evening star ojo, **11:** 1357-58
  flat ojo, **11:** 1351-53
  galaxy ojo, **11:** 1358-59
  necklace, ojo, **11:** 1355
  snowflake, ojo, **11:** 1356
  woven ojo, **11:** 1354-55
raffia and straw, 14: 1710-11, 1713-16, 1720-22
  giraffes, straw, **14:** 1713-14
  hat, straw, **14:** 1714-16
  oval tray, **14:** 1722
  round tray, **14:** 1720-22
rope knotting, 14: 1782-92
  carrick bend chain, **14:** 1788
  hot-plate pad, **14:** 1789
  planter hanging, knotted, **14:** 1790-92
rya and flossa, 15: 1824-25, 1834-37
  cat, woven rya, **15:** 1834-37
sprang, 17: 2162-76
  belt, sprang, **17:** 2168
  closings, sprang, **17:** 2171
  hammock, sprang, **17:** 2174-76
  loom making, **17:** 2169
  sampler, sprang, **17:** 2163-66
  scarf, sprang, **17:** 2169
  tote bag, sprang, **17:** 2167
  twists, sprang, **17:** 2170
  wall hanging, sprang, **17:** 2172-73
swings, 19: 2354-57
  baby swing, **19:** 2354-57
tablet and frame weaving, 19: 2392-2405
  bag, tablet-woven, **19:** 2399-2401
  belt, tablet-woven, **19:** 2398
  branch weaving, **19:** 2402
  frame weaving, **19:** 2401
  goemetric frame weaving, **19:** 2403-4
  hoop weaving, **19:** 2393, 2405
  landscape frame weaving, **19:** 2404-5
  setting up tablet weaving, **19:** 2394-95
  tablets, weaving on, **19:** 2396-97
tatting, 19: 2420-32
  collar, shell-cluster, **19:** 2424-25
  flowerpot holder, **19:** 2429-30
  handkerchief edging, **19:** 2421, 2424
  place mat, sunflower, **19:** 2427-28
  shuttle, large, making, **19:** 2430
  shuttles, **19:** 2424
  stitches, tatting, **19:** 2422-23
  tablecloth, openwork, **19:** 2431-32
  vest, child's, **19:** 2426-27

weaving, 22: 2752-73
  four-harness loom, **22:** 2754
  jackets, twill, **22:** 2768-69
  pattern drafts, **22:** 2764
  pillow, plaid, **22:** 2755-63
  pillow, twill, **22:** 2767
  scarf, leno-weave, **22:** 2765-67
  tote bag, weft faced, **22:** 2770-71
  wall hanging, woven, **22:** 2772-73
woven tapestries, 23: 2856-75
  apple-tree tapestry, **23:** 2870-71
  field-of-flowers tapestry, **23:** 2872-73
  frame loom, simple, **23:** 2861-63
  frame loom, tapestry, **23:** 2864-65
  geometric pillow, **23:** 2866-67
  techniques, tapestry weaving, **23:** 2868-69
wrapped and coiled work, 23: 2876-87
  basket, sisal, **23:** 2884-86
  bread tray, raffia, **23:** 2886-87
  coiling, **23:** 2878-79
  necklace, wrapped, **23:** 2880-82
  plant hanger, **23:** 2882-84
wedding bells, sugar, **18:** 2303
weed pot, sand cast, **15:** 1878-81
welding, steel fin mobile, **10:** 1227-31
whistles and flutes, 22: 2774-83
  dowel whistle, **22:** 2776-77
  flutes, **22:** 2778-79
  hardwood whistle, **22:** 2778
  shepherd's pipe, bamboo, **22:** 2780-83
  See also **carving; dulcimers; music making; puppets and puppetry; square dancing; stagecraft; wind harps**
wild flowers and weeds. See **candlemaking; dried flowers; herbs; organic gardening; pod and cone art**
wildlife. See **ant farms; birds and birdhouses; dioramas; insects; tropical fish; vivariums**
wind chime, gemstone, **9:** 1052-53
  See also **mobiles; music making**
wind drift, piloting small boats and, **12:** 1517-18
wind harps, 22: 2784-93
  Aeolian harp, **22:** 2791-93
  simple wind harp, **22:** 2786-90
  See also **dulcimers; music making; square dancing; weather forecasting; whistles and flutes**
window gardens. See **bottle gardens; greenhouse construction; lighted indoor gardens; terrariums; vivariums**
window hangings and decorations
  glass mosaic window hanging, **18:** 2225-26
  leaded stained-glass panel, **18:** 2229-31
  laminated stained-glass panel, **18:** 2217, 2222-23
  needle lace window hanging, **8:** 1013, 1021-23
  slab-glass casting, window-hanging, **18:** 2225-26

W, continued
wind-up toys, spool, **17**: 2159
wine making, 22: 2794-2807
  acidity, **22**: 2800
    adding tannin, **22**: 2800
    testing for, **22**: 2800
  aging wine, **22**: 2802
  bottling wine, **22**: 2802
    corking, **22**: 2802
  color, wine, **22**: 2799
  crushing and pressing fruit, **22**: 2798-99
  fermentation, **22**: 2800-1
    adding yeast, **22**: 2800
    sealing container, **22**: 2801
  folk recipes, **22**: 2804-5
  fruit wines, **22**: 2804-5
  glasses, wine, **22**: 2802
  herbal wines, **22**: 2804-5
  materials, **22**: 2796-97
  mead, **22**: 2804
  mulled wine, **4**: 466
  serving wine, **22**: 2802
  sterilizing containers, **22**: 2798
  storing wine, **22**: 2802
  sugar content, **22**: 2799
    hydrometers, **22**: 2799
  See also **brewing; cheeses and churn-
    ing; vinegars**
winter sculpture, 22: 2806-16
  ice sculptures, **22**: 2812-16
  snow sculptures, **22**: 2806-11
  sugar winter scene, **18**: 2300, 2302
  See also **carving; ice cream, sherbet,
    and ices; molding methods; sand
    characters and castles; sculpture**
wire sculpture, 23: 2822-35
  basket, wire, **23**: 2832-33
  belt and bracelet, forged, **23**: 2828-29
  characteristics of wire, **23**: 2827
  figures, wire, **23**: 2822, 2834-35
  flowers, wire, **23**: 2831-32
  metalworking techniques, **23**: 2826-27
  necklace, forged, **23**: 2829-31
  necklace, looped-link, **23**: 2823-25
  See also **jewelry; pewtersmithing;
    repoussé and chased metal; sculp-
    ture; silversmithing; string art;
    tin and pierced work**
wok cookery, 23: 2836-45
  beef with broccoli, **23**: 2839-41
  cabbage, spicy, **23**: 2839
  chicken, Tai Chien, **23**: 2844
  Chinese meal, **23**: 2845
  duck, deep-fried, **23**: 2843
  fish, steamed, **23**: 2841-42
  See also **hibachi and hot pot cookery;
    sashimi and sushi; seed sprouting;**
wood. See names of products made from or
    with wood; names of woods
wood assemblages, 23: 2846-55
  driftwood construction, **2**: 142-43
  heraldic standards, **23**: 2852-55
  sculpture, wood, **23**: 2850-52
  wall illusion, **23**: 2846-49
  See also **collages and assemblages;
    sculpture; yard toys**

woodcarving. See **pipe making; ship
    models; totem poles; treen ware;
    walking sticks; whistles and flutes**
woodcuts. See **block printing; linoleum
    and woodcuts**
woodworking. See **antiquing furniture;
    birds and birdhouses; caning and
    rushing; dioramas; dulcimers;
    plywood and foam furnishings;
    refinishing furniture; rockers and
    cradles; soapbox and skate
    vehicles**
wool. See **spinning;** names of products
    made from wool; names of processes
    using wool
word games, 19: 2373-74
woven tapestries, 23: 2856-75
  apple-tree tapestry, **23**: 2870-71
  field-of-flowers tapestry, **23**: 2872-73
  frame loom, simple, **23**: 2861-63
  frame loom, tapestry, **23**: 2864-65
  geometric pillow, **23**: 2866-67
  techniques, **23**: 2868-69
  wool rug, **19**: 2413-15
  See also **inkle weaving; rya and
    flossa; tablet and frame weaving**
wraparounds and drapes, 5: 530
wrapped and coiled work, 23: 2876-87
  basket, sisal, **23**: 2884-86
  bread tray, raffia, **23**: 2886-87
  coiling, **23**: 2878-79
  plant hanger, **23**: 2882-84
  necklace, wrapped, **23**: 2880-82
  See also **basketry; rope knotting**
wreaths, Christmas
  candy, **4**: 464
  pod and cone, **13**: 1591
  traditional, **4**: 465
  wheat-and-flower, **4**: 463
wycinanki, 23: 2888-99
  animal chain cutout, **23**: 2890-91
  applied wycinanki, **23**: 2898-99
  disk mobile, **23**: 2896-97
  paper stars, **23**: 2892-93
  tree-of-life, **23**: 2894-95
  See also **decoupage; greeting cards;
    mobiles; origami; papermaking;
    silhouettes; stenciling; valentines**

Y

yard environments. See **greenhouse con-
    struction; plastic pipe
    constructions; shelters and tents;
    sundials; swings; topiary; totem
    poles; tree houses; trellises**
yard toys, 23: 2900-9
  animals, utility pole, **23**: 2904-5
  playhouse, cable-spool, **23**: 2906-7
  staircase, spiral, **23**: 2908-9

  tire and box toys, **23**: 2902-3
  trampoline, inner-tube, **23**: 2900-1
  See also **bean-bags; birthday cele-
    brations; plastic pipe construc-
    tions; swings; tree houses; wood
    assemblages**
yarn. See **spinning; vegetable dyes;**
    names of products made from wool
    yarn
yarn painting, 23: 2910-17
  bottle yarn painting, **23**: 2917
  clown face, yarn, **23**: 2912-14
  landscape, **23**: 2915
  landscape with feathers, **23**: 2916-17
  mask, paper-plate, **23**: 2914-15
  See also **masks; ojo de dios**
yeast, wine making and, **22**: 2800
  See also **breads**
yogurts, 4: 446-49
yo-yos, 23: 2918-25
  drawer-pull yo-yo, **23**: 2918-20
  sink-strainer yo-yos, **23**: 2920
  tournament tricks, **23**: 2922-25

Z

zoetrope toys, 23: 2926-44
  flipbook, **23**: 2942-44
  moving-picture wheels, **23**: 2930-33
  thaumatropes, **23**: 2926-29
  zoetropes, **23**: 2934-41
  See also **cartooning; kaleidoscopes;
    shadow theater**

Note: The following activities described in
The Family Creative Workshop encyclopedia
are presented as general techniques and not
as individual projects, hence they do not appear in the project-evaluation lists that begin
on the next page:

bicycles and bicycling, 2: 178-89
canoeing, 3: 354-65
clambakes, 4: 468-77
Colonial crafts, 4: 488-97
color psychology, 4: 498-505
dried flowers, 5: 614-23
genealogy, 6: 750-61
gold panning, 7: 798-805
heraldry, 7: 866-75
kayaks, 8: 968-75
magic, 9: 1128-39
organic gardening, 11: 1360-73
parades and festivals, 12: 1414-25
piloting small boats, 12: 1512-23
refinishing furniture, 6: 726-39
sand characters and castles, 15:
  1282-87
square dancing, 18: 2182-93
tropical fish, 21: 2626-39
watercolors, 22: 2722-33
wine making, 22: 2794-2807

Project-evaluation lists

Approximate Cost

¢ The projects that follow are low in cost, under $5, or free when "found" natural materials are used.

Carving and Molding
candlemaking
confectionary candles, **3:** 336-37
dried-flower candles, **3:** 341
hand-dipped candles, **3:** 330-33
honeycomb candles, **3:** 334-35
molded candles, **3:** 338-40
carving
soap fish, **4:** 415-16
foam forms
fish impression, **6:** 706-7
giraffe, synthetic stone, **6:** 704-5
molding methods
hand mold and cast, **10:** 1248-49
latex molding, **10:** 1251-52
pop-art candle, **10:** 1253-55
pipe making
corncob pipe, **13:** 1555-56
sand casting
sea animals, cast, **15:** 1874-75
totem poles
full-sized totem pole, **20:** 2546-47
miniature totem pole, **20:** 2543
totem-mask wall plaque, **20:** 2541-42
treen ware
kitchen utensils, **21:** 2604-9
party table accessories, **21:** 2610-13
walking sticks
sculptured walking stick, **22:** 2720-21
winter sculpture
ice sculptures, **22:** 2812-16

Designs and Decorations
Christmas celebrations
candy wreaths, **4:** 464
ornaments, Christmas-tree, hand-made, **4:** 459
ornaments, Christmas-tree, patch-work, **4:** 458
collages and assemblages
pure-paper collage, **4:** 480-81
decoupage
box, switch, lamp, **5:** 573
techniques, decoupage, **5:** 568-72
tin-can decoupage, **5:** 574
herbs
note cards, herb, **7:** 884

models and mock-ups
bedroom redecorating model, **10:** 1235-40
mosaics
button mosaics, **10:** 1270-71
papier-mâché
bottle people, **11:** 1401, 1403-4
dinosaur, papier-mâché, **11:** 1407-8
pod and cone art
alligator, pod and cone, **13:** 1585, 1589
candle holder, **13:** 1590-91
Christmas wreath, **13:** 1591
lion, pine-cone, **13:** 1584, 1587-88
llama, pine-cone, **13:** 1584, 1586
ostrich, pine-cone, **13:** 1588
shadow box, **13:** 1592
turkey, pine-cone, **13:** 1590
preschool activities
junk sculpture, **13:** 1630-31
kitchen clay, **13:** 1628-29
woodworking, **13:** 1634
raffia and straw
mosaics, split-straw, **14:** 1712-13
rosemaling
bread board, **15:** 1805-7
hand mirror, **15:** 1803-4
Telemark plate, **15:** 1808-10
seashells
collage, seashell, **16:** 1944
figurines, shell, **16:** 1948-49
flowers, seashell, **16:** 1946-47
jewelry, seashell, **16:** 1945
skin painting
body painting, **17:** 2066, 2074-75
heavenly-nights face makeup, **17:** 2068-69
leopard face makeup, **17:** 2068-69
primitive face makeup, **17:** 2070-71
spool toys
constructions, spool, **17:** 2155-56
stamp decoupage
pieced pictures, **18:** 2235-36
stenciling
note paper, personalized, **18:** 2244-45
stone painting
animals, stone, **18:** 2256-67
assemblages, painted stone, **18:** 2253-54
time telling
candle clock, **20:** 2494-95
noon light show, **20:** 2490-93
wood assemblages
heraldic standards, **23:** 2852-55
sculpture, wood, **23:** 2850-52
wall illusion, **23:** 2846-49
yarn painting
bottle yarn painting, **23:** 2917
clown face, yarn, **23:** 2912-14
landscape with feathers, **23:** 2916-17
landscape, yarn, **23:** 2915
paper-plate mask, **23:** 2914-15

Environmental Projects
ant farms
ant farm, **1:** 66-69
ant house, Mason-jar, **1:** 65-66

beachcombing
lobsterman and shell paperweight, **2:** 140-41
birds and birdhouses
birdbath, concrete, **2:** 198-99
bluebird house, **2:** 192
wren house, **2:** 193
masks
African rope mask, **10:** 1192-95
papermaking
blender-made paper, **11:** 1390-93
pet habitats
cat cabaña, **12:** 1468-69
quill pens
making quill pens, **14:** 1686-89
spinning
drop spindle spinning, **17:** 2143-45
sundials
Egyptian sundial, **19:** 2313-14
horizontal sundial, **19:** 2316-21
portable sundial, **19:** 2315
walking sticks
hiking stick, **22:** 2716-18
weather forecasting
making weather instruments, **22:** 2740-45

Fragrances and Distillations
cosmetics
astringent, **5:** 523
cold creams, **5:** 520-22
powder and shadow, **5:** 524-25
potpourris and pomanders
pomander-ball pendant, **13:** 1605
pomander balls, **13:** 1602-4
pomander buds, **13:** 1601
potpourris, **13:** 1596-98
seasonal potpourris, **13:** 1599
soaps and bath products
cleansing creams and masks, **17:** 2104-5
quick soaps, **17:** 2098-2102
shaving soaps and bath oils, **17:** 2103
Furniture and Finishes
antiquing furniture
distressing, **1:** 74-77
gilding, **1:** 81
glaze antiquing, **1:** 70-73
hardware, antiquing, **1:** 80
boxes
curio cabinet, beverage-case, **3:** 266
caning and rushing
chair seat, rush, **3:** 251-53
framing
barn siding background frame, **6:** 723
rockers and cradles
rocking chair, child's, **14:** 1776
rocking cradle, **14:** 1778-79
tables and benches
sawhorse stool, **19:** 2379-81

¢

Glass and Plastics
acrylics
poured acrylics, 1: 15-20
beachcombing
mosaic, beach glass, 2: 139
bottle cutting
decorating bottles, 2: 249-51
foam forms
constructions, cup, 6: 700-1
sculpture, packing pieces, 6: 699
stained glass
mosaic, glass, 18: 2225-26
necklace, copper-foiled, 18: 2226-29
panel, laminated, 18: 2217, 2222-23
time telling
sandglass, 20: 2495-96

Graphic Arts
batik
table mat, 1: 127
wall hanging, 1: 126
block printing
eraser prints, 2: 214-15
vegetable prints, 2: 210-13
bookbinding
denim bookcover, 2: 233-35
calligraphy
chancery cursive, 3: 316-18
hand illumination, 3: 312, 319-21
cartooning
comic strips, 4: 410-11
figures and hands, 4: 406-7
heads, faces, expressions, 4: 404-5
self-starter cartoons, 4: 412-13
single-panel cartoons, 4: 408-9
greeting cards
cardboard printing, 7: 844-45
stained-glass-window card, 7: 840-41
linoleum and woodcuts
greeting cards, 9: 1099-1101
scarf, block-printed, 9: 1096-98
wall hanging, two-color, 9: 1102-3
monoprinting
greeting cards, fingerprint, 10: 1259-60
litho-monoprint, 10: 1263-64
place mat, Janus, 10: 1267
silhouettes, reverse, 10: 1261-63
stationery, fingerprint, 10: 1258-59
T-shirt, calligraphic, 10: 1265-66
rubbings
brass rubbings, 15: 1818-19
inking raised designs, 15: 1820-21
reproducing high reliefs, 15: 1823
tombstone rubbings, 15: 1815-17
string art
children's string designs, 18: 2282-83

Greenery and Growing Things
Christmas celebrations
wreath, traditional, 4: 465
dried flowers
bouquet, dried-spice, 5: 622-23
herbs
gift basket, herb, 7: 884
harvesting and drying herbs, 7: 882-83
ikebana
avant-garde ikebana, 8: 926-27
cascading nageire, 8: 924-25
moribana, 8: 922-23
seed sprouting
growing sprouts, 16: 1952-59
tea
herb cultivation, 20: 2439-42
terrariums
tropical terrarium, 20: 2454-55
topiary
geometric topiary, 20: 2530-31
three-ball ivy topiary, 20: 2532

Jewelry, Lapidary, and Metalwork
American Indian crafts
daisy chain, beaded, 1: 45
loom beading, 1: 47
medallion, 1: 46
ring, beaded, 1: 44
beadwork
breechcloth, 2: 151
earrings, pearl, 2: 156-57
fruit, beaded, 2: 152-53
making beads, 2: 145-47
necklace, safety-pin, 2: 154
ring, bead, 2: 154-55
stringing beads, 2: 148-50
jewelry
coconut shell jewelry, 8: 951
feather jewelry, 8: 948-52
hardware bracelets, 8: 954
spoon ring and fork bracelet, 8: 955
lamps and shades
canister lamp, 9: 1035
tin lantern, 9: 1030-32
mobiles
balsa wood mobile, 10: 1224-25
repoussé and chased metal
box tops, ornamented, 14: 1746-48
mirror frame, foiled, 14: 1748-50
silversmithing
bowl, copper, 17: 2063-65
stone painting
key-chain fob, 18: 2255-56
tin and pierced work
cookie cutters, 20: 2502-3
wire sculpture
basket, wire, 23: 2832-33
belt and bracelet, forged, 23: 2828-29
figures, wire, 23: 2822, 2834-35
flowers, wire, 23: 2831-32
necklace, forged, 23: 2829-31
necklace, loop-link, 23: 2823-25

Kitchen Favorites and Celebrations
baby foods
breakfast cookies, 1: 110-11
preparing baby foods, 1: 107-9
birthday celebrations
baking for children, 2: 206-7
cake, 2: 202-5
breads
sourdough bread, 3: 284-89
trail breads, 3: 282-83
brewing
ginger beer, 3: 298-301
root beer and sarsaparilla, 3: 294-97
carving
vegetables and fruits, carving, 4: 18-21
cheeses and churning
churning, 4: 453
yogurts and sour cream, 4: 446-49
confections and comfits
brittles and fudges, 4: 510-11
coated chocolates, 4: 512
hard candies, 4: 509
quick candies, 4: 508
egg decoration
Imperial Easter eggs, 5: 638-40
margutis and pysanka eggs, 5: 634-37
flowers, artificial
fabric flowers, 6: 696-97
feather flowers, 6: 692-93
gingerbread
cookies, gingerbread, 6: 767-68
house, gingerbread, 6: 762-66
herbs
cooking with herbs, 7: 885-86
ice cream, sherbet, and ices
flavored ice creams, 8: 915-16
ices, 8: 917
sherbet, 8: 917
vanilla ice cream, 8: 914-15
marmalades and preserves
chutney, 10: 1165
curd, 10: 1163
jam, 10: 1164
marmalade, 10: 1162-63
masks
paper-plate masks, 10: 1182-83
pickled and canned foods
fruit recipes, 12: 1511
pickle recipes, 12: 1506
tomato recipes, 12: 1507-8
vegetable recipes, 12: 1509-10
soups
chicken julienne, 17: 2126
cupboard soups, 17: 2131
fruit soups, 17: 2128-29
sugar shapes
brown-sugar shapes, 18: 2304
ladybugs, sugar, 18: 2303
place cards, sugar, 18: 2304
schoolhouse, sugar, 18: 2302-3
wedding bells, sugar, 18: 2303
winter scene, sugar, 18: 2300, 2302
syrups
beverages and desserts, 19: 2358-63
main dishes, syrup-flavored, 19: 2364-65

tea
  brewing tea, **20**: 2442-43
vinegars
  cider vinegar, **22**: 2698
  flavored vinegars, **22**: 2699-2703
wok cookery
  beef with broccoli, **23**: 2389-41
  cabbage, spicy, **23**: 2839
  chicken, Tai Chien, **23**: 2844
  duck, deep-fried, **23**: 2843
  fish, steamed, **23**: 2841-42

Leathercrafts
  American Indian crafts
    moccasins, Apache, **1**: 49-53
  belts and buckles
    beaded belt, **2**: 172-73
    elastic belts, **2**: 174-75
  lamps and shades
    suede shade, **9**: 1038-39
  leather working
    bracelet, painted, **9**: 1069-70

Needlecrafts
  afghan stitch
    pillow, tic-tac-toe, **1**: 28
    vest and child's skirt, **1**: 24-28
  animal dolls
    alligator stuffed, **1**: 62-63
    elephant, stuffed, **1**: 56-59
    lion, stuffed, **1**: 60-62
  applique
    hand appliqué, **1**: 82-85
    machine appliqué, **1**: 87-89
    pillow, people, **1**: 90
    tablecloth, **1**: 91
  buttons
    clay buttons, **3**: 308-9
    cuff links, button, **3**: 305
    hand-painted buttons, **3**: 310-11
    seashell buttons, **3**: 306-7
  costumes
    basic dress pattern, **5**: 533
    caftan, **5**: 534
    circular patterns, **5**: 531
    drapes and wraparounds, **5**: 530
    historic costumes, **5**: 527, 532
    period dress, **5**: 535
  crewel
    embroidery sampler, **5**: 538-41,
    546-49
  crochet
    pincushion, **5**: 556
    tie, **5**: 552
  embroidery
    flower appliqué, **6**: 652
    owl, black work, **6**: 656-57
    tissue covers, black work, **6**: 654-55
  Florentine stitch
    eyeglass case, **6**: 680-81
    plastic box cover, **6**: 683-84
    tote bag pocket, **6**: 681-82
  fur recycling
    collar and cuffs, fur, **6**: 746-48

  fling, fur, **6**: 749
  pillows, fur, **6**: 749
  shortening, coat, **6**: 744-45
granny squares
  place mat, **7**: 810
greeting cards
  needlepoint cards, **7**: 838-39
hardanger embroidery
  bookmark, **7**: 858
  cocktail mat, **7**: 859-60
knitting to fit
  tassel cap, **8**: 1006-7
lace
  necklace, lace, **8**: 1023-24
  window hanging, needle lace, **8**:
  1013, 1021-23
lamps and shades
  shade cover, **9**: 1039
machine stitchery
  bag, trapunto, **9**: 1113-14
  folk art hanging, **9**: 1107-8
  pillow, ribbon, **9**: 1114
  pillowcase, embroidered, **9**: 1115
  wall hanging, appliquéd, **9**: 1109-11
  work shirt, free embroidery, **9**: 1106-7
mobiles
  felt auto-mobile, **10**: 1222
quilting
  shoulder bag, quilted, **14**: 1694-96
raffia and straw
  belt, crocheted raffia, **14**: 1716
  earrings, raffia, **14**: 1719
recycling clothes
  casual top, **14**: 1739
  child's dress, appliquéd, **14**: 1741-42
  denim skirt and knit top, **14**: 1733-35
  halter, **14**: 1740
  lengthening, dress, **14**: 1742-43
  raglan top, **14**: 1736-38
reverse appliqué
  hanging, reverse appliqué, **14**:
  1760-61
  pillow, reverse appliqué, **14**: 1758-59
  tote bag, **14**: 1759-60
ribboncraft
  T-shirt, appliquéd, **14**: 1772-73
samplers
  cross-stitch denim patch, **15**: 1858
  designing samplers, **15**: 1858-59
  hoop-framed samplers, **15**: 1855-57
  pegboard sampler, **15**: 1854
  perforated-paper sampler, **15**:
  1860-61
sewing without pattern
  pillow cover, ruffled, **16**: 1985
  skirt, wraparound, **16**: 1982
  tablecloth, round, **16**: 1985
Swedish huck work
  hand towel, huck work, **19**: 2340
traditional knitting motifs
  Irish-knit top, child's, **21**: 2571-74
  shoulder bag, **21**: 2570
trapunto
  T-shirt, lion, **21**: 2587-88

  ciphers, **5**: 561-64, 565
maps and pathfinding
  compass, making and using, **9**:
  1146-48
  maps, making and using, **9**: 1141-44
  natural guides, **9**: 1148-52
time telling
  star dial, **20**: 2497-99
tree houses
  grove tree house, **21**: 2594-96
  traditional tree house, **21**: 2593,
  2600-1
winter sculpture
  snow sculptures, **22**: 2806-11

Paint and Color
  folk art
    fraktur traufscheine, **6**: 708-9
  neckties
    butterfly neckerchief, **11**: 1315
    illustrating ties, **11**: 1312-13
    tree design tie, **11**: 1311-12
  preschool activities
    plants and painted pots, **13**:
    1632-33
  sand painting and layering
    fishbowl sand painting, **15**: 1894-96
    garden, layered-sand, **15**: 1896-99
    Navaho sand painting, **15**: 1890-91
    planter, sand-layered, **15**: 1891-94
  tie dyeing
    stitchery, tie-dye, **20**: 2479-81
    T-shirts, tie dyed, **20**: 2476-79
  tin painting
    freehand bronze tray, **20**: 2520-22
  vegetable dyes
    colorfast dyes, **21**: 2678-83
    wool yarn, dyeing, **21**: 2684-88

Paper Folding and Cutting
  airplanes, paper
    Barnaby, **1**: 35
    Dartmouth Dart, **1**: 33-34
    Falcon, **1**: 38-39
    Flying Tiger, **1**: 36-37
    Pegasus, **1**: 40-41
  boxes
    organizer, kitchen-matchbox drawer,
    3: 267
    wall sculpture, **3**: 268
  cardboard
    whirligig weathervane, **3**: 369-71
  Christmas celebrations
    gift wrapping, **4**: 462
  costumes
    paper costumes, **5**: 528-29
  flowers, artificial
    crepe paper flowers, **6**: 694-96
    foil flowers, **6**: 690-91
    tissue paper flowers, **6**: 689
  foam forms
    decorations, foam cup, **6**: 702-3

Outdoor Activities
cryptography

Ç

Paper Folding and Cutting, continued

greeting cards
pressed flower cards, **7**: 838
ribbon bookmark card, **7**: 837

mobiles
cardboard snail mobile, **10**: 1223

napkin folding
artichoke fold, **11**: 1306
band fold, **11**: 1305
candle fold, **11**: 1303
fan fold, **11**: 1307
fleur-de-lis fold, **11**: 1307
lily fold, **11**: 1304
palm leaf fold, **11**: 1301-2
pocket fold, **11**: 1304
sailboat fold, **11**: 1302

origami
carrier pigeon, **11**: 1382
crane, **11**: 1375, 1383
dog face and cat face, **11**: 1376-77
drinking cup, **11**: 1378
house, **11**: 1378
jumping frog, **11**: 1384-85
penguin, **11**: 1380
samurai hat, **11**: 1381
uses of origami, **11**: 1385

quilling
bird, quillwork, **14**: 1681-83
butterflies, quillwork, **14**: 1678-79
Christmas tree ornaments, **14**: 1675-77
eggs, decorated, **14**: 1680-81

silhouettes
pictures, silhouette, **16**: 2046-48
silhouettes, **16**: 2044-46

valentines
gift box, valentine, **21**: 2674-75
lovebird valentine, **21**: 2674
playing card valentine, **21**: 2673
two-heart valentine, **21**: 2672-73

wycinanki
animal chain cutout, **23**: 2890-91
applied wycinanki, **23**: 2898-99
disk mobile, **23**: 2896-97
stars, paper, **23**: 2892-93
tree-of-life, **23**: 2894-95

zoetrope toys
flipbook, **23**: 2942-44
moving-picture wheels, **23**: 2930-33
thaumatropes, **23**: 2926-29
zoetropes, **23**: 2934-41

Performing Arts
costumes
makeup, **5**: 536-37

dulcimers
fretboard dulcimer, **5**: 625-26

masks
clown hoop mask, **10**: 1184-85
lion hoop mask, **10**: 1186-87
newspaper bird mask, **10**: 1188-91

puppetry
foam puppets, **13**: 1643
paper marionettes, **13**: 1646-47
pop-up, finger, and junk puppets, **13**: 1638-40

skin painting
stage face makeup, **17**: 2072-73

tea
Japanese tea ceremony, **20**: 2447-51

Toys and Games

bean-bags
games, bean-bag, **2**: 162-63
paperweights, felt, **2**: 161
toss toy, **2**: 160

birthday celebrations
party games, **2**: 208-9

cardboard
train, toy, **3**: 366, 368

cryptography
codes, **5**: 559-60
signal communications, **5**: 564-65

dolls and doll clothes
apple-head doll, **5**: 609
cloth doll, **5**: 612-13
clothespin doll, **5**: 608
cornhusk doll, **5**: 610
pieces doll, **5**: 608
walnut and egg dolls, **5**: 606-7

flowers, artificial
pencil posy, **6**: 688

kaleidoscopes
Hue View kaleidoscope, **8**: 962-63

kites
Greek kite, **8**: 992-95
Indian fighter kite, **8**: 989, 998-99
sled kite, **8**: 991
Thai dragon kite, **8**: 996-97

papier-mâché
puppet heads, **11**: 1405-7

piñatas
doll piñata, **12**: 1534
rabbit-foot piñata, **12**: 1529
sailboat piñata, **12**: 1535-36
star piñata, **12**: 1524-28
wishing-well piñata, **12**: 1530-34

preschool activities
hand puppets, **13**: 1635
stuffed giraffe, **13**: 1622-24

puzzles
counter puzzle, **13**: 1658-59
crossword puzzles, **13**: 1655-57
jigsaw puzzle, **13**: 1663-64
tangrams, **13**: 1659-60

rockers and cradles
doll's cradle, **14**: 1780-81
rocker boat, **14**: 1777-78

soapbox and skate vehicles
cart crate, **17**: 2089-90
scooter, skate, **17**: 2088-89

spool toys
auto race, spool, **17**: 2157
balance toys, **17**: 2160-61
knitting, spool, **17**: 2158
parachute toy, **17**: 2159
pull-along toys, **17**: 2156
ring-toss game, **17**: 2160-61
rocking toys, **17**: 2157
streamers, spool, **17**: 2160-61
wind-up toys, **17**: 2159

street games
association football, **18**: 2265
box ball, **18**: 2267
Chinese handball, **18**: 2262
double dutch, **18**: 2269
follow-the-leader, **18**: 2268
hit-the-penny, **18**: 2265
hopscotch, **18**: 2266
kickball, **18**: 2264
kick-the-can, **18**: 2261
ring-a-levio, **18**: 2268
running bases, **18**: 2264
skullies, **18**: 2260
stickball, street, **18**: 2263
stoopball, **18**: 2267

table games
Anagrams, **19**: 2373-74
Jungle Game, **19**: 2366-67, 2370-72
Lasca, **19**: 2374-75
Mancala, **19**: 2368
Mill, **19**: 2369-70
Quick Trip, **19**: 2376-77

toys
bull roarer, **20**: 2550
gee-haw whimmy-diddle, **20**: 2550-51
jumping jack, **20**: 2552-53
moonwinder, **20**: 2548
sports car, **20**: 2553
stern-wheel boat, **20**: 2554-55

yard toys
playhouse, cable-spool, **23**: 2906-7
trampoline, **23**: 2900-1

yo-yos
drawer-pull yo-yo, **23**: 2918-20
sink-strainer yo-yo, **23**: 2920

Weaving, Braiding, Knotting

basketry
hanging basket, **1**: 116-17
Indian coil basket, **1**: 115
pencil holder, **1**: 114
shopping basket, **1**: 118-19

braided rugs
coasters, braided, **3**: 275

inkle weaving
hat band and bag handle, **8**: 932
pick-up pattern belt, **8**: 935
wall-hanging, inkle, **8**: 929, 934-35
watchband and vase cover, **8**: 933

lace
  collar and cuffs, bobbin lace, **8:** 1019-21
  sash, bobbin lace, **8:** 1017-18
macramé
  adjustable belt, **9:** 1120-21
  micromé hanging, **9:** 1126-27
  willow tree sculpture, **9:** 1125-26
ojo de dios
  evening star ojo de dios, **11:** 1357-58
  flat ojo de dios, **11:** 1351-53
  galaxy ojo de dios, **11:** 1358-59
  necklace, ojo de dios, **11:** 1355
  snowflake ojo de dios, **11:** 1356
  woven ojo de dios, **11:** 1354-55
raffia and straw
  giraffes, straw, **14:** 1713-14
rope knotting
  carrick bend chain, **14:** 1788
  hot-plate pad, **14:** 1789
  planter hanging, knotted, **14:** 1790-92
sprang
  belt, sprang, **17:** 2168
  sampler, sprang, **17:** 2163-66
  scarf, sprang, **17:** 2169
  wall hanging, sprang, **17:** 2172-73
tablet and frame weaving
  belt, tablet-woven, **19:** 2398
  branch weaving, **19:** 2402
tatting
  child's vest, **19:** 2426-27
  flowerpot holder, **19:** 2429-30
  handkerchief edging, **19:** 2421, 2424
  shell-cluster collar, **19:** 2424-25
  sunflower place mat, **19:** 2427-28
woven tapestries
  apple-tree tapestry, **23:** 2870-71
  field-of-flowers tapestry, **23:** 2872-73
  frame loom, **23:** 2861-63
wrapped and coiled work
  bread tray, raffia, **23:** 2886-87
  necklace, wrapped, **23:** 2880-82

 The projects that follow are of medium cost, about $10.

Carving and Molding
  carving
    wax reliefs, carving, **4:** 417
  diorama
    portable diorama, **5:** 583-91
  pewtersmithing
    cast figurine, **12:** 1476, 1478-79
  pipe making
    briar pipe, **13:** 1556-60
  sand casting
    candle, sand-casted, **15:** 1875-77
    weed pot, **15:** 1878-81
  scrimshaw
    bone hair piece, **15:** 1917-18
    color-engraved scrimshaw, **15:** 1919-20
  walking sticks
    spiral-design cane, **22:** 2718-19
Ceramics
  ceramics
    clay bowl, **4:** 440
    clay tiles, **4:** 434-49
    coiled bowl, **4:** 441-43
  kilns
    sawdust kiln, **8:** 980-82
  pottery
    hand-built pottery, **13:** 1609-11
  sculpture
    clay figure, **16:** 1926-29
Designs and Decorations
  Christmas celebrations
    Christmas-tree trims, **4:** 460-61
  collages and assemblages
    cigar box assemblage, **4:** 484-85
    scrap lumber collage, **4:** 482-83
  decoupage
    tortoise-shell base, **5:** 575-76
    wooden cabinet, **5:** 577
  models and mock-ups
    garden structures, **10:** 1232, 1241-44
    mock-ups, **10:** 1245
  mosaics
    mirror frame, mosaic, **10:** 1272-73
  pin striping
    boat helm, **13:** 1547
    car customizing, **13:** 1548-50
    door panel, **13:** 1546
    restoring antique automobiles, **13:** 1542, 1551
  pod and cone art
    wired tree, **13:** 1593-95
  rosemaling
    Telemark box, **15:** 1810-13
  ship models
    ship in bottle, **16:** 2038-41
  stamp decoupage
    container decoupage, **18:** 2237-39
  stenciling
    floors, stenciled, **18:** 2250-51
    place mats, stenciled, **18:** 2246-47
    walls and ceilings, stenciled, **18:** 2248-49
Environmental Projects
  beachcombing
    aquarium tank, **2:** 138
    driftwood constructions, **2:** 142-43
  birds and birdhouses
    bird feeder, **2:** 194-95
    purple-martin house, **2:** 196-97
  insects
    collecting insects, **8:** 942-47
    trapping insects, **8:** 940-42
  vivariums
    chameleon lizards, **22:** 2710-11
    English hooded rat, **22:** 2708
    guinea pigs, **22:** 2706-7
    snakes, **22:** 2711-13
  wind harps
    simple wind harp, **22:** 2786-90
Fragrances
  perfumes
    cologne, **12:** 1462-63
    homemade perfumes, **12:** 1457
    recipes, perfume, **12:** 1458-60
  potpourris and pomanders
    pillow potpourri, **13:** 1600
Furniture and Finishes
  antiquing furniture
    marbleizing, **1:** 79
  boxes
    decorative cigar boxes, **3:** 270-71
    toy-chest bench, **3:** 262, 269
  caning and rushing
    chair, recaning, **3:** 348-50
    chair seat, splint, **3:** 344-47
  cardboard
    furniture, cardboard, **3:** 372-74
    headboard, **3:** 367, 375
  framing
    box frame, **6:** 725
    metal frame, **6:** 721
    stick frame, **6:** 722-23
    wood frame, **6:** 719-21
  structural furnishings
    table, wall-hanging, **18:** 2286-87
  tables and benches
    plant table, **19:** 2382-83
Glass and Plastics
  bean-bags
    wall hanging, **2:** 167
  bottle cutting
    basic cutting, **2:** 244-48
  glass working
    glass rod sculpture, **7:** 779
    lead glass beads, **7:** 776-77
    swizzle sticks, **7:** 778-79
  lamps and shades
    potichomania lamp, **9:** 1036-37
  leaded glass
    candle box or planter, **9:** 1064-65
    window panel, **9:** 1063
  mosaics
    light sculpture, mosaic, **10:** 1274-75
  stained glass
    leaded stained-glass panel, **18:** 2229-31
    slab-glass casting, **18:** 2223-24
Graphic Arts
  batik
    floor pillow, **1:** 128
  block printing
    linoleum prints, **2:** 216-19
  cameras
    camera obscura, **3:** 322-26
    pinhole camera, **3:** 327-29
  flags and banners
    felt banner, **6:** 668, 674-75

$

Graphic Arts, continued

gold leafing
lettering signs in gold, **7:** 795-97

greeting cards
birth announcement, **7:** 846

music making
visual instruments, **11:** 1287, 1292

serigraphy
poster print, **16:** 1963-65

string art
conics in box, **18:** 2271, 2280-81
helios, **18:** 2276-77
raised ellipse, **18:** 2278-79
three adjacent hexagons, **18:** 2272-73
triple stellate forms, **18:** 2274-76

Greenery and Growing Things

bonsai
cascade bonsai, **2:** 227
driftwood bonsai, **2:** 223-25
miniature bonsai, **2:** 229
rock-grown bonsai, **2:** 228
tropical bonsai, **2:** 226

bottle gardens
lab-bottle garden, **2:** 256
water-cooler bottle garden, **2:** 252-56

herbs
hanging garden, **7:** 882

terrariums
cactus terrarium, **20:** 2460-61
fern terrarium, **20:** 2457-59

trellises
fan trellises, **21:** 2616-18

Jewelry, Lapidary, and Metalwork

jewelry
stone pendant and neck ring, **8:** 956-57

mobiles
copper shapes mobile, **10:** 1225-26

pewtersmithing
fabricated pewter box, **12:** 1484-87
handwrought pewter bowl, **12:** 1480-83

seashells
lampshade, shell, **16:** 1950-51

tin and pierced work
candle sconce and snuffer, **20:** 2504-7
fruit bowl, **20:** 2508-9

Kitchen Favorites and Celebrations

cheeses and churning
cheeses, **4:** 450-52

hibachi and hot-pot cookery
hibachi cooking, **7:** 892-93
hot-pot cooking, **7:** 894-96

pasta
homemade pasta, **12:** 1428-31
macaroni recipes, **12:** 1436-37
stuffed pasta, **12:** 1432-35

sashimi and sushi
chirashi sushi, **15:** 1911
nigiri sushi, **15:** 1905-7
norimake sushi, **15:** 1908-10
sashimi, **15:** 1903-5

soups
chicken soup, **17:** 2127
vichyssoise, **17:** 2130-31

terrines and timbales
terrines, **20:** 2463-66
timbales, **20:** 2467-69

vinegars
wine vinegar, **22:** 2696-97

wok cookery
Chinese meal, **23:** 2845

Leathercrafts

belts and buckles
cowboy belt, **2:** 168, 170-71

carryalls
leather tote bag, **4:** 396-99

leather working
appliquéd pillow, **9:** 1070-71
envelope briefcase, **9:** 1077-79
sculpture, leather, **9:** 1068, 1079

sandal making
Italia sandal, **15:** 1867
Riviera sandal, **15:** 1867-68
Seville sandal, **15:** 1864-66
T-tie sandal, **15:** 1868

Needlecrafts

bean-bags
furniture, bean-bag, **2:** 164-66

carryalls
back pack, canvas, **4:** 395
tote bag, vinyl, **4:** 392-94

crochet
beaded bag, **5:** 553
evening dress, **5:** 554-55

flags and banners
boat pennant, nylon, **6:** 672-73
club banner, **6:** 670-71

granny squares
cap and scarf, **7:** 812
shoulder tote bag, **7:** 814-15

hardanger embroidery
red place mat and napkin, **7:** 861-62
white place mat and napkin, **7:** 863-65

machine stitchery
personalized place mat, **9:** 1111-12

mittens and mukluks
mittens, **10:** 1210-15
mukluks, **10:** 1216-19

neckties
recycled tie skirt, **11:** 1316-17

needlepoint
belt, signature, **11:** 1324
mirror frame, needlepoint, **11:** 1328-29
pencil holder, gingham, **11:** 1322-23

patchwork
reversible vest, **12:** 1449-50

quilting
rainbow-cloud quilt, **14:** 1707-9

vest and skirt, quilted, **14:** 1706-7
wall hanging, quilted, **14:** 1690, 1697-98

raffia and straw
cap, crocheted raffia, **14:** 1718-19
purse, pine-straw, **14:** 1723
shoulder bag, raffia, **14:** 1718

rag dolls
making rag dolls, **14:** 1726-31

ribboncraft
evening bag, ribbon, **14:** 1771
pillow, parquet ribbon, **14:** 1766-67
pillow, patchwork and ribbon, **14:** 1768-69
serving tray, **14:** 1772
tennis racket cover, **14:** 1769-70

rya and flossa
pillow, needlepoint and rya, **15:** 1824, 1829-30
pillow, rya, **15:** 1824, 1828-29

sandal making
needlepoint clogs, **15:** 1869-71
ribbon clogs, **15:** 1871

sewing without pattern
bias-cut apron-shawl, **16:** 1974-76
caftan, **16:** 1977, 1978-80
kimono coat, **16:** 1977-78

smocking
dress, cotton, **17:** 2085
dress, silk, **17:** 2083-84
pillow, smock, **17:** 2078-81
shirt, man's, **17:** 2081-82

soft sculpture
abstraction, soft sculpture, **17:** 2110-11
airplane, soft sculpture, **17:** 2107-9

Swedish huck work
handbag, huck work, **19:** 2341-42
pillow, huck work, **19:** 2342-43

tambour
dragonfly, tambour, **19:** 2417-19
pillow, tambour, **19:** 2416-17
wall-hanging, tambour, **19:** 2415-16
white-on-white curtain, **19:** 2412

traditional knitting motifs
bias-knit scarf, **21:** 2578-79

trapunto
batik handbag, **21:** 2586
face pillow, trapunto, **21:** 2588-89
sheet and pillow cases, trapunto, **21:** 2582-84

Outdoor Activities

shelters and tents
tarp tents and lean-tos, **16:** 2014-18

tying flies
Rat-Faced MacDougall fly, **21:** 2648-49
Royal Coachman fly, **21:** 2650-51
TW Special fly, **21:** 2645-47

Paint and Color
  acrylics
    painting Volkswagen, **1**: 21-23
  folk art
    Senufo wall hanging, **6**: 714-15
  oil painting
    cityscape, **11**: 1344-45
    portraits, **11**: 1346-47
    still life, **11**: 1342-43
  tie dyeing
    wall hanging, block-dyed, **20**: 2484-87
    table throw, velvet, **20**: 2482-84
  tin painting
    antique stenciled tin box, **20**: 2523-27
    canister, painted, **20**: 2518-19
    country tin painting, **20**: 2513-17

Performing Arts
  music making
    marimbas, **11**: 1287, 1294-99
  puppetry
    clown marionette, **13**: 1645, 1648-51
    felt puppets, **13**: 1640-42
  shadow theater
    color silhouettes, **16**: 1991
    paper shadow puppets, **16**: 1996-97
    plastic jellyfish, **16**: 1989, 1992
    plastic puppets, **16**: 1992-93
    shadow play, **16**: 1993
    silhouette puppets, **16**: 1988-89
  whistles and flutes
    flutes, **22**: 2778-79
    shepherd's pipe, bamboo, **22**: 2780-83

Toys and Games
  kaleidoscopes
    cubes, kaleidoscopic, **8**: 960-61
    kaleidoscope, **8**: 965-67
    teleidoscope, **8**: 963-65
  music making
    percussion instruments, **11**: 1287-91
  preschool activities
    busyboard, **13**: 1625-27
  toys
    elephant toy chest, **20**: 2549, 2556-58
    hammer man, **20**: 2559-60
  whistles and flutes
    dowel whistle, **22**: 2776-77
    hardwood whistle, **22**: 2778
  yard games
    spiral staircase, **23**: 2908-9
    tire and box toys, **23**: 2902-3
    utility pole animals, **23**: 2904-5

Weaving, Braiding, Knotting
  braided rugs
    place mats, braided, **3**: 276-77
  leather working
    magic braid belt, **9**: 1072-73
  macramé
    dress yoke and sash, **9**: 1122-23
  raffia and straw
    hat, straw, **14**: 1714-15
    oval tray, **14**: 1722
    round tray, **14**: 1720-22
  sprang
    tote bag, sprang, **17**: 2167
  swings
    baby swing, **19**: 2354-57
  tablet and frame weaving
    bag, tablet-woven, **19**: 2399-2401
    geometric frame weaving, **19**: 2403-4
    hoop weaving, **19**: 2393, 2405
    landscape frame weaving, **19**: 2404-5
  tatting
    openwork tablecloth, **19**: 2431-32
  weaving
    pillow, plaid, **22**: 2755-63
    pillow, twill, **22**: 2767
    scarf, leno-weave, **22**: 2765-67
    tote-bag, weft-faced, **22**: 2770-71
    wall-hanging, woven, **22**: 2772-73
  woven tapestries
    frame loom, tapestry, **23**: 2864-65
    pillow, geometric, **23**: 2866-67
  wrapped and coiled work
    plant holder, **23**: 2882-84
    sisal basket, **23**: 2884-86

 The projects that follow are high in cost, above $15.

Carving and Molding
  casting
    plaster-cast head, **4**: 424-29
    tin belt buckle, **4**: 430-33
  folk art
    reindeer weathervane, **6**: 716-17
  sculpture
    alabaster sculpture, **16**: 1935-37
    rosewood serving tray, **16**: 1930-33

Ceramics
  enameling metal
    dish, copper, **6**: 664
    pendant, copper, **6**: 661-63
  kilns
    raku kiln, **8**: 983-85
  pottery
    wheel-thrown pottery, **13**: 1614-21

Designs and Decorations
  collages and assemblages
    free-form assemblages, **4**: 486-87
  mosaics
    grouted mosaics, **10**: 1277-78
    tile mural, **10**: 1278-80

ship models
  "Philadelphia" ship model, **16**: 2025-37
soft sculpture
  gorilla, soft sculpture, **17**: 2114, 2116-19

Environmental Projects
  astronomy
    telescope, **1**: 101-5
  greenhouse construction
    cold frame, **7**: 818, 819
    curved fiberglass greenhouse, **7**: 822-35
    hotbed, **7**: 818-19
    pit greenhouse, **7**: 820-21
  papermaking
    handmade rag paper, **11**: 1394-99
  pet habitats
    birdcage, five-story, **12**: 1472-75
    doghouse, barrel, **12**: 1464, 1466-67
    two-pet tote, **12**: 1470-72
  spinning
    flax on wheel, spinning, **17**: 2151-53
    wool on wheel, spinning, **17**: 2146-50
  wind harps
    Aeolian harp, **22**: 2791-93

Furniture and Finishes
  folk art
    hope chest, **6**: 710-11
  gold leafing
    chair, gilded, **7**: 792
    shadow-box, gilt-edge, **7**: 790-91
  marquetry
    chessboard, marquetry, **10**: 1179
    geometric design, **10**: 1167-76
    special effects, **10**: 1177-78
  plywood and foam furnishings
    banquette and bench, **13**: 1579-83
    chair and ottoman, **13**: 1572-75
    platform seating, **13**: 1576-78
  Shaker furniture
    candle sconce, **16**: 2000-3
    dovetailed candle box, **16**: 2009-11
    side table, **16**: 2003-5
    utility bench, **16**: 2006-8
  structural furnishings
    lofts, **18**: 2284, 2288-93
    platforms, **18**: 2294-98
  tables and benches
    modular tables and benches, **19**: 2384-87
    nesting tables, **19**: 2388-91
  upholstery
    bench, cushioned, **21**: 2654-57

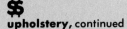

upholstery, continued

chair seat, padded, **21:** 2658
easy chair, stuffed, **21:** 2659-65

Glass and Plastics
acrylics
room divider, **1:** 11-14
glass working
glass beads, **7:** 786
hanging ornament, **7:** 787
lampblown glass bottle, **7:** 774, 780-85
gold leafing
gilding glass, **7:** 793-95
leaded glass
lampshade, **9:** 1066-67
plastic pipe constructions
bookshelves, **13:** 1567-69
easy chair and footrest, **13:** 1564-66
sculptural lamp, **13:** 1570-71

Graphic Arts
bookbinding
leather-bound diary, **2:** 236-42
enameling metal
steel tiles, **6:** 665-67
photographic printing
contact prints, **12:** 1494-96
developing negatives, **12:** 1491-94
enlargements, making, **12:** 1496-99
serigraphy
garden print, **16:** 1960, 1971-72
printing on plastic, **16:** 1970-71
wall-hanging catchalls, **16:** 1968-70

Greenery and Growing Things
Christmas celebrations
wheat-and-flower wreath, **4:** 463
lighted indoor gardens
bookcase shelf garden, **9:** 1086
corner garden, **9:** 1087-88
nursery, indoor, **9:** 1085
skylight floor garden, **9:** 1090-91
wall garden, **9:** 1081, 1091-93
window garden, **9:** 1088-89
topiary
privet hedge, **20:** 2533-35
trellises
doorway trellis, **21:** 2614, 2622-25
freestanding trellis, **21:** 2619-21

Jewelry, Lapidary, and Metalwork
jewelry
bracelet, wrapped wire, **8:** 957
lapidary
cabochons, gemstone, **9:** 1048-51
eggs, gemstone, **9:** 1045-48

flats, gemstone, **9:** 1052-53
tumbling gemstones, **9:** 1042-44
mineralogy
decorative mineral projects, **10:** 1206-9
mobiles
steel fin mobile, **10:** 1227-31
repoussé and chased metal
necklace, metal, **14:** 1751-53
silversmithing
butter knife, silver, **17:** 2056-57
spoon, silver, **17:** 2059-61

Kitchen Favorites and Celebrations
Christmas celebrations
recipes, Christmas, **4:** 466-67

Needlecrafts
afghan stitch
afghan, **1:** 29
crochet
sisal rug, **5:** 557
embroidery
circles, **6:** 653
Florentine stitch
pillow, **6:** 686-87
granny squares
floral afghan, **7:** 811
popcorn stitch afghan, **7:** 813
traditional afghan, **7:** 807-8
knitting to fit
hooded parka sweater, **8:** 1010-11
sweater and skirt, knit, **8:** 1007-9
needlepoint
pillow, needlepoint, **11:** 1330-31
rug, needlepoint, **11:** 1332-33
patchwork
crib quilt, **12:** 1447-48
pillow, patchwork, **12:** 1443-46
tote bag, patchwork, **12:** 1451-52
traditional quilt, **12:** 1439, 1452-53
quilting
Dresden-plate quilt, **14:** 1702-5
ribboncraft
pillow, woven ribbon, **14:** 1764-66
rya and flossa
designing ryas, **15:** 1832-34
wall hanging, wool, **15:** 1826-28
sewing without pattern
hooded cape, **16:** 1980-81
quilted coverlet, **16:** 1975, 1983-84
soft sculpture
palm tree, soft sculpture, **17:** 2114-16
tennis shoes, soft sculpture, **17:** 2112-14
tambour
wool rug, **19:** 2413-15
traditional knitting motifs
Norwegian-pattern sweater, **21:** 2574-77
trapunto
wall hanging, trapunto, **21:** 2590-91
yoked dress, **21:** 2580, 2584-85

Outdoor Activities
sail making and repair
Marconi dinghy sail, **15:** 1844-47
shelters and tents
tepees, **16:** 2020-23
swings
monkey swing, **19:** 2351-52
pulley-and-cable glides, **19:** 2348-51
rope swing, **19:** 2344, 2346
tire swings, **19:** 2345-48
tree houses
outdoor platform, **21:** 2596-99

Paint and Color
supergraphics
child's bedroom supergraphic, **19:** 2327
dark background supergraphic, **19:** 2328
diagonal stripes supergraphic, **19:** 2330-31
fabric design supergraphic, **19:** 2334-45
flowers supergraphic, **19:** 2330-31
free-form supergraphic, **19:** 2332
furniture framing supergraphic, **19:** 2327-28
geometric supergraphic, **19:** 2324-26
Indian motif supergraphic, **19:** 2333
reversed colors supergraphic, **19:** 2329
sunrise supergraphic, **19:** 2323, 2330

Paper Folding and Cutting
boxes
desk and seat, milk-crate, **3:** 262-65

Performing Arts
dulcimers
Appalachian dulcimer, **5:** 624, 626-33
stagecraft
set design, **18:** 2196-2201
stage lighting, **18:** 2206-13

Toys and Games
dioramas
train diorama, **5:** 579-82
puzzles
block puzzle, **13:** 1661-62
soapbox and skate vehicles
lay-back racer, **17:** 2091-97

Weaving, Braiding, Knotting
braided rugs
petal-design rug, **3:** 278-79
traditional braided rug, **3:** 276-77
hammocks and slings
canvas log sling, **7:** 850-51
naval hammock, **7:** 851-53
hooked rugs
geometric rug, **8:** 904-5
"love" hooked rug, **8:** 907-9

owl rug, **8**: 906
macramé
room-divider screen, **9**: 1116-24
rya and flossa
cat, woven rya, **15**: 1834-37
sprang
hammock, sprang, **17**: 2174-76
weaving
twill jackets, **22**: 2768-69

Estimated Time Required

 The projects that follow can be completed in hours.

Carving and Molding
candlemaking
confectionary candles, **3**: 336-37
dried-flower candles, **3**: 341
hand-dipped candles, **3**: 330-33
honeycomb candles, **3**: 334-35
molded candles, **3**: 338-40
carving
soap fish, carved, **4**: 415-16
wax reliefs, carving, **4**: 417
casting
tin belt buckle, **4**: 430-33
pipe making
briar pipe, **13**: 1556-60
corncob pipe, **13**: 1555-56
sand casting
candle, sand-casted, **15**: 1875-77
sea animals, cast, **15**: 1874-75
totem poles
miniature totem pole, **20**: 2543
wall plaque, totem-mask, **20**: 2541-42
treen ware
kitchen utensils, **21**: 2604-9
party table accessories, **21**: 2610-13
walking sticks
spiral-design cane, **22**: 2718-19
winter sculpture
ice sculptures, **22**: 2812-16

Ceramics
enameling metal
dish, copper, **6**: 664
pendant, copper, **6**: 661-63
kilns
raku kiln, **8**: 983-85
sawdust kilns, **8**: 980-82
pottery
hand-built pottery, **13**: 1609-11
wheel-thrown pottery, **13**: 1614-21
sculpture
clay figure, **16**: 1926-29

Designs and Decorations
Christmas celebrations
candy wreaths, **4**: 464
Christmas-tree trims, **4**: 460-61

handmade Christmas-tree ornaments, **4**: 459
patchwork Christmas-tree ornaments, **4**: 458
collages and assemblages
pure-paper collage, **4**: 480-81
herbs
note cards, herb, **7**: 884
models and mock-ups
bedroom redecorating model, **10**: 1235-40
garden structures, **10**: 1232, 1241-44
mock-ups, **10**: 1245
mosaics
button mosaics, **10**: 1270-71
pin striping
boat helm, **13**: 1547
car customizing, **13**: 1548-50
door panel, **13**: 1546
restoring antique automobiles, **13**: 1542, 1551
pod and cone art
alligator, pod and cone, **13**: 1585, 1589
candle holder, **13**: 1590-91
Christmas wreath, **13**: 1591
lion, pine-cone, **13**: 1584, 1587-88
llama, pine-cone, **13**: 1584, 1586
ostrich, pine-cone, **13**: 1588
shadow box, **13**: 1592
turkey, pine-cone, **13**: 1590
wired tree, **13**: 1593-95
preschool activities
junk sculpture, **13**: 1630-31
kitchen clay, **13**: 1628-29
woodworking **13**: 1634
raffia and straw
mosaics, split-straw, **14**: 1712-13
rosemaling
bread board, **15**: 1805-7
hand mirror, **15**: 1803-4
Telemark plate, **15**: 1808-10
seashells
collage, seashell, **16**: 1944
figurines, shell, **16**: 1948-49
jewelry, seashell, **16**: 1945
skin painting
body painting, **17**: 2066, 2074-75
heavenly-nights face makeup, **17**: 2068-69
leopard face makeup, **17**: 2068-69
primitive face makeup, **17**: 2070-71
spool toys
constructions, spool, **17**: 2155-56
stamp decoupage
pieced pictures, **18**: 2235-36
stenciling
personalized note paper, **18**: 2244-45
place mats, stenciled, **18**: 2246-47
stone painting
animals, stone, **18**: 2256-57
assemblages, painted stone, **18**: 2253-54
time telling
candle clock, **20**: 2494-95
noon light show, **20**: 2490-93

wood assemblages
heraldic standards, **23**: 2852-55
sculpture, wood, **23**: 2850-52
wall illusion, **23**: 2846-49
yarn painting
bottle yarn painting, **23**: 2917
clown face, yarn, **23**: 2912-14
landscape with feathers, **23**: 2916-17
landscape, yarn, **23**: 2915
paper-plate mask, **23**: 2914-15

Environmental Projects
ant farms
ant farm, **1**: 66-69
ant house, Mason-jar, **1**: 65-66
astronomy
telescope, **1**: 101-5
beachcombing
aquarium tank, **2**: 138
lobster-man and shell paperweight, **2**: 140-41
birds and birdhouses
bluebird house, **2**: 192
wren house, **2**: 193
greenhouse construction
cold frame greenhouse, **7**: 818, 819
hotbed greenhouse, **7**: 818-19
masks
African rope mask, **10**: 1192-95
papermaking
blender-made paper, **11**: 1390-93
handmade rag paper, **11**: 1394-99
pet habitats
cat cabaña, **12**: 1468-69
doghouse, barrel, **12**: 1464, 1466-67
quill pens
making quill pens, **14**: 1686-89
spinning
drop spindle spinning, **17**: 2143-45
flax on wheel, spinning, **17**: 2151-53
wool on wheel, spinning, **17**: 2146-50
sundials
Egyptian sundial, **19**: 2313-14
horizontal sundial, **19**: 2316-21
portable sundial, **19**: 2315
vivariums
chameleon lizards, **22**: 2710-11
English hooded rat, **22**: 2708
guinea pigs, **22**: 2706-7
snakes, **22**: 2711-13
walking sticks
hiking stick, **22**: 2716-18
weather forecasting
making weather instruments, **22**: 2740-45
wind harps
Aeolian harp, **22**: 2791-93
simple wind harp, **22**: 2786-90

Fragrances
cosmetics
astringent, **5**: 523
cold creams, **5**: 520-22

cosmetics, continued
powder and shadow, **5:** 524-25
perfumes
cologne, **12:** 1462-63
homemade perfumes, **12:** 1457
recipes, perfume, **12:** 1458-60
potpourris and pomanders
pillow potpourri, **13:** 1600
pomander buds, **13:** 1601
potpourris, **13:** 1596-98
seasonal potpourris, **13:** 1599
soaps and bath products
cleansing creams and masks, **17:** 2104-5
quick soaps, **17:** 2098-2102
shaving soaps and bath oils, **17:** 2103

Furniture and Finishes
antiquing furniture
distressing, **1:** 74-77
gilding, **1:** 81
hardware, antiquing, **1:** 80
boxes
curio cabinet, beverage-case, **3:** 266
decorative cigar boxes, **3:** 270-71
toy-chest bench, **3:** 262, 269
caning and rushing
rush chair seat, **3:** 351-53
splint chair seat, **3:** 344-47
cardboard
furniture, cardboard, **3:** 372-74
headboard, **3:** 367, 375
framing
barn siding background frame, **6:** 723
box frame, **6:** 725
metal frame, **6:** 721
stick frame, **6:** 722-23
wood frame, **6:** 719-21
plywood and foam furnishings
chair and ottoman, **13:** 1572-75
platform seating, **13:** 1576-78
rockers and cradles
rocking chair, child's, **14:** 1776
rocking cradle, **14:** 1778-79
Shaker furniture
candle sconce, **16:** 2000-3
structural furnishings
table wall-hanging, **18:** 2286-87
tables and benches
plant table, **19:** 2382-83
sawhorse stool, **19:** 2379-81

Glass and Plastics
acrylics
poured acrylics, **1:** 15-20
beachcombing
mosaic, beach glass, **2:** 139

bean-bags
wall hanging, **2:** 167
bottle cutting
basic cutting, **2:** 244-48
decorating bottles, **2:** 249-51
foam forms
cup constructions, **6:** 700-1
packing pieces sculpture, **6:** 699
glass working
beads, glass, **7:** 786
hanging ornament, **7:** 787
lampblown glass bottle, **7:** 774, 780-85
lead glass beads, **7:** 776-77
rod sculpture, glass, **7:** 779
swizzle sticks, **7:** 778-79
leaded glass
window panel, **9:** 1063
plastic pipe constructions
bookshelves, **13:** 1567-69
easy chair and footrest, **13:** 1564-66
lamp, sculptural, **13:** 1570-71
stained glass
casting, slab-glass, **18:** 2223-24
mosaic, glass, **18:** 2225-26
panel, laminated, **18:** 2217, 2222-23
time telling
sandglass, **20:** 2495-96

Graphic Arts
block printing
eraser prints, **2:** 214-15
vegetable prints, **2:** 210-13
calligraphy
chancery cursive, **3:** 316-18
cameras
camera obscura, **3:** 322-26
pinhole camera, **3:** 327-29
cartooning
comic strips, **4:** 410-11
figures and hands, **4:** 406-7
heads, faces, expressions, **4:** 404-5
self-starter cartoons, **4:** 412-13
single-panel cartoons, **4:** 408-9
gold leafing
lettering signs in gold, **7:** 795-97
greeting cards
birth announcement, **7:** 845
cardboard printing, **7:** 844-45
stained-glass-window card, **7:** 840-41
linoleum and wood cuts
block-printed scarf, **9:** 1096-98
greeting cards, **9:** 1099-1101
two-color wall hanging, **9:** 1102-3
monoprinting
calligraphic T-shirt, **10:** 1265-66
greeting cards, fingerprint, **10:** 1259-60
litho-monoprint, **10:** 1263-64
placemat, Janus, **10:** 1267
reverse silhouettes, **10:** 1261-63
stationery, fingerprint, **10:** 1258-59
music making
gongs and chimes, **11:** 1287, 1292
photographic printing
contact prints, **12:** 1494-96

developing negatives, **12:** 1491-94
enlargements, making, **12:** 1496-99
rubbings
brass rubbings, **15:** 1818-19
high reliefs, reproducing, **15:** 1823
inking raised designs, **15:** 1820-21
tombstone rubbings, **15:** 1815-17
serigraphy
poster print, **16:** 1963-65
string art
children's string designs, **18:** 2282-83
helios, **18:** 2276-77
raised ellipse, **18:** 2278-79
three adjacent hexagons, **18:** 2272-73
triple stellate forms, **18:** 2274-76

Greenery and Growing Things
bottle gardens
lab-bottle garden, **2:** 256
water-cooler bottle garden, **2:** 252-56
Christmas celebrations
traditional wreath, **4:** 465
wheat-and-flower wreath, **4:** 463
herbs
gift basket, herb, **7:** 884
hanging garden, **7:** 882
ikebana
avant-garde ikebana, **8:** 926-27
cascading nageire, **8:** 924-25
upright moribana, **8:** 922-23
lighted indoor gardens
nursery, indoor, **9:** 1085
seed sprouting
growing sprouts, **16:** 1952-59
terrariums
cactus terrarium, **20:** 2460-61
fern terrarium, **20:** 2457-59
tropical terrarium, **20:** 2454-55
trellises
doorway trellis, **21:** 2614, 2622-25
fan trellises, **21:** 2616-18
freestanding trellis, **21:** 2619-21

Jewelry, Lapidary, and Metalwork
American Indian crafts
chain, beaded daisy, **1:** 45
loom beading, **1:** 47
medallion, **1:** 46
ring, beaded, **1:** 44
beadwork
bead-making, **2:** 145-47
breechcloth, **2:** 151
earrings, pearl, **2:** 156-57
fruits, beaded, **2:** 152-53
necklace, safety-pin, **2:** 154
ring, bead, **2:** 154-55
stringing beads, **2:** 148-50
jewelry
coconut shell jewelry, **8:** 951
feather jewelry, **8:** 948-51
hardware bracelets, **8:** 954

spoon ring and fork bracelet, **8**: 955
stone pendant and neck ring, **8**: 956-57
wrapped wire bracelet, **8**: 957
lamps and shades
canister lamp, **9**: 1035
tin lantern, **9**: 1030-32
lapidary
cabochons, gemstones, **9**: 104-51
eggs, gemstone, **9**: 1045-48
flats, gemstone, **9**: 1052-53
mineralogy
decorative mineral projects, **10**: 1206-9
mobiles
balsa wood mobile, **10**: 1224-25
copper shapes mobile, **10**: 1225-26
pewtersmithing
bowl, handwrought pewter, **12**: 1480-83
box, fabricated pewter, **12**: 1484-87
repoussé and chased metal
box tops, ornamented, **14**: 1746-48
mirror frame, foil, **14**: 1748-50
seashells
lampshade, shell, **16**: 1950-51
silversmithing
bowl, copper, **17**: 2063-65
butter knife, **17**: 2056-57
spoon, silver, **17**: 2059-61
stone painting
key-chain fob, **18**: 2255-56
tin and pierced work
candle sconce and snuffer, **20**: 2504-7
cookie cutters, **20**: 2502-3
fruit bowl, **20**: 2508-9
wire sculpture
basket, wire, **23**: 2832-33
belt and bracelet, forged, **23**: 2828-29
figures, wire, **23**: 2822, 2834-35
flowers, wire, **23**: 2831-32
necklace, forged, **23**: 2829-31
necklace, loop-link, **23**: 2823-25

Kitchen Favorites and Celebrations
baby foods
breakfast cookies, **1**: 110-11
preparing baby foods, **1**: 107-9
birthday celebrations
baking for children, **2**: 206-7
cake, **2**: 202-5
breads
sourdough bread, **3**: 284-89
trail breads, **3**: 282-83
carving
vegetables and fruits, carving, **4**: 418-21

cheeses and churning
cheeses, **4**: 450-52
churning, **4**: 453
yogurts and sour cream, **4**: 446-49
Christmas celebrations
recipes, Christmas, **4**: 466-67
confections and comfits
brittles and fudges, **4**: 510-11
coated chocolates, **4**: 512
hard candies, **4**: 509
quick candies, **4**: 508
egg decoration
Imperial Easter eggs, **5**: 638-40
margutis and pysanka eggs, **5**: 634-37
flowers, artificial
fabric flowers, **6**: 696-97
feather flowers, **6**: 692-93
gingerbread
cookies, gingerbread, **6**: 767-68
herbs
cooking with herbs, **7**: 885-86
hibachi and hot-pot cookery
hibachi cooking, **7**: 892-93
hot-pot cooking, **7**: 894-96
ice cream, sherbet, and ices
flavored ice creams, **8**: 915-16
ices, **8**: 917
sherbet, **8**: 917
vanilla ice cream, **8**: 914-15
marmalades and preserves
chutney, **10**: 1165
curd, **10**: 1163
jam, **10**: 1160-62
jelly, **10**: 1164
marmalade, **10**: 1162-63
masks
paper-plate masks, **10**: 1182-83
pasta
homemade pasta, **12**: 1428-31
macaroni recipes, **12**: 1436-37
stuffed pasta, **12**: 1432-35
pickled and canned foods
fruit recipes, **12**: 1511
pickle recipes, **12**: 1506
tomato recipes, **12**: 1507-8
vegetable recipes, **12**: 1509-10
sashimi and sushi
chirashi sushi, **15**: 1911
nigiri sushi, **15**: 1905-7
norimaki sushi, **15**: 1908-10
sashimi, **15**: 1903-5
soups
chicken julienne, **17**: 2126
chicken soup, **17**: 2127
cupboard soups, **17**: 2131-29
vichyssoise, **17**: 2130-31
sugar shapes
brown-sugar shapes, **18**: 2304
ladybugs, sugar, **18**: 2303
place cards, sugar, **18**: 2304
schoolhouse, sugar, **18**: 2302-3
wedding bells, sugar, **18**: 2303
winter scene, sugar, **18**: 2300, 2302

syrups
beverages and desserts, **19**: 2358-63
main dishes, syrup-flavored, **19**: 2364-65
tea
brewing tea, **20**: 2442-43
terrines and timbales
terrines, **20**: 2463-66
timbales, **20**: 2467-69
vinegars
cider vinegar, **22**: 2698
wok cookery
beef with broccoli, **23**: 2839-41
cabbage, spicy, **23**: 2839
chicken, Tai Chien, **23**: 2844
fish, steamed, **23**: 2841-42

Leathercrafts
American Indian crafts
moccasins, Apache, **1**: 49-53
belts and buckles
beaded belt, **2**: 172-73
cowboy belt, **2**: 168, 170-71
elastic belts, **2**: 174-75
carryalls
leather tote bag, **4**: 396-99
lamps and shades
suede shade, **9**: 1038-39
leather working
bracelet, painted, **9**: 1069-70
briefcase, envelope, **9**: 1077-79
pillow, appliquéd, **9**: 1070-71
sculpture, leather, **9**: 1068, 1079
sandal making
Italia sandal, **15**: 1867
Riviera sandal, **15**: 1867-68
Seville sandal, **15**: 1864-66
T-tie sandal, **15**: 1868
Needlecrafts
animal dolls
alligator, stuffed, **1**: 62-63
elephant, stuffed, **1**: 56-59
lion, stuffed, **1**: 60-62
appliqué
machine appliqué, **1**: 87-89
people pillows, **1**: 90
bean-bags
furniture, bean-bag, **2**: 164-66
buttons
hand-painted buttons, **3**: 310-11
seashell buttons, **3**: 306-7
carryalls
back pack, canvas, **4**: 395
tote bag, vinyl, **4**: 392-94
costumes
basic dress pattern, **5**: 533
caftans, **5**: 534
circular patterns, **5**: 531
drapes and wraparounds, **5**: 530
historic costumes, **5**: 527, 532
period dress, **5**: 535

Needlecrafts, continued

crochet
bag, beaded, **5**: 553
pincushion, **5**: 556
tie, **5**: 552

embroidery
black work tissue covers, **6**: 654-55
flower appliqué, **6**: 652

flags and banners
boat pennant, nylon, **6**: 672-73
club banner, **6**: 670-71

Florentine stitch
eyeglass case, **6**: 680-81
plastic box cover, **6**: 683-84
tote bag pocket, **6**: 681-82

fur recycling
coat, shortening, **6**: 744-45
fling, fur, **6**: 749
pillows, fur, **6**: 742-43

granny squares
place mat, **7**: 810

greeting cards
needlepoint cards, **7**: 838-39

hardanger embroidery
bookmark, **7**: 858
cocktail mat, **7**: 859-60

knitting to fit
tassel cap, **8**: 1006-7

lace
window hanging, needle lace, **8**: 1013, 1021-23

lamps and shades
shade cover, **9**: 1039

machine stitchery
appliquéd wall hanging, **9**: 1109-11
embroidered pillowcase, **9**: 1115
folk art hanging, **9**: 1107-8
free embroidery work shirt, **9**: 1106-7
personalized place mat, **9**: 1111-12
ribbon pillow, **9**: 1114
trapunto bag, **9**: 1113-14

mittens and mukluks
mittens, **10**: 1210-15
mukluks, **10**: 1216-19

mobiles
felt auto-mobile, **10**: 1222

neckties
skirt, recycled tie, **11**: 1316-17

needlepoint
belt, signature, **11**: 1324
mirror frame, needlepoint, **11**: 1328-29
pencil holder, gingham, **11**: 1322-23

patchwork
pillow, patchwork, **12**: 1443-46

quilting
quilt, rainbow-cloud, **14**: 1707-9
shoulder bag, quilted, **14**: 1694-96

wall hanging, quilted, **14**: 1690, 1697-98

raffia and straw
belt, crocheted raffia, **14**: 1716
cap, crocheted raffia, **14**: 1718-19
earrings, raffia, **14**: 1719
purse, pine-straw, **14**: 1723
shoulder bag, raffia, **14**: 1718

rag dolls
making rag dolls, **14**: 1726-31

recycling clothes
appliquéd child's dress, **14**: 1741-42
casual top, **14**: 1739
denim skirt and knit top, **14**: 1733-35
halter, **14**: 1740
lengthening dress, **14**: 1742-43
raglan top, **14**: 1736-38

reverse appliqué
pillow, reverse appliqué, **14**: 1758-59
tote bag, **14**: 1759-60

ribboncraft
evening bag, ribbon, **14**: 1771
pillow, parquet ribbon, **14**: 1766-67
pillow, patchwork and ribbon, **14**: 1768-69
pillow, woven ribbon, **14**: 1764-66
serving tray, **14**: 1772
tennis racket cover, **14**: 1769-70
T-shirt, appliquéd, **14**: 1772-73

rya and flossa
needlepoint and rya pillow, **15**: 1824, 1829-30
rya pillow, **15**: 1824, 1828-29

samplers
cross-stitch denim patch, **15**: 1857-58
hoop-framed samplers, **15**: 1855-57
pegboard sampler, **15**: 1854

sandal making
needlepoint clogs, **15**: 1869-71
ribbon clogs, **15**: 1871

sewing without pattern
apron shawl, bias-cut, **16**: 1974-76
caftan, **16**: 1977, 1978-80
cape, hooded, **16**: 1980-81
coat, kimono, **16**: 1977-78
coverlet, quilted, **16**: 1975, 1983-84
pillow cover, ruffled, **16**: 1985
skirt, wraparound, **16**: 1982
tablecloth, round, **16**: 1985

smocking
man's shirt, **17**: 2081-82

soft sculpture
abstraction, soft sculpture, **17**: 2110-11
airplane, soft sculpture, **17**: 2107-9
palm tree, soft sculpture, **17**: 2114-16

Swedish huck work
handbag, huck work, **19**: 2341-42
hand towel, huck work, **19**: 2340
pillow, huck work, **19**: 2342-43

traditional knitting motifs
shoulder bag, **21**: 2570

trapunto
dress, yoked, **21**: 2580, 2584-85
face pillow, trapunto, **21**: 2588-89
handbag, batik, **21**: 2586

sheet and pillowcases, trapunto, **21**: 2582-84
T shirt, lion, **21**: 2587-88
wall hanging, trapunto, **21**: 2590-91

Outdoor Activities
cryptography
ciphers, **5**: 561-64, 565

maps and pathfinding
compass, making and using, **9**: 1146-48
maps, making and using, **9**: 1141-44
natural guides, **9**: 1148-52

sail making and repair
Marconi dinghy sail, **15**: 1844-47

shelters and tents
tepees, **16**: 2020-23

swings
pulley-and-cable glides, **19**: 2348-51
rope swing, **19**: 2344, 2346

time telling
star dial, **20**: 2497-99

tree houses
grove tree house, **21**: 2594-96

tying flies
Rat-Faced MacDougall fly, **21**: 2648-49
Royal Coachman fly, **21**: 2650-51
TW Special fly, **21**: 2645-47

winter sculpture
snow sculptures, **22**: 2806-11

Paint and Color
acrylics
painting Volkswagen, **1**: 21-23

folk art
fraktur traufscheine, **6**: 708-9

neckties
butterfly neckerchief, **11**: 1315
illustrating ties, **11**: 1312-13
tree design tie, **11**: 1311-12

sand painting and layering
fishbowl sand painting, **15**: 1894-96
garden, layered-sand, **15**: 1896-99
Navaho sand painting, **15**: 1890-91
planter, sand-layered, **15**: 1891-94

tie dyeing
table throw, velvet, **20**: 2482-84
T-shirts, tie dyed, **20**: 2476-79
wall hanging, block-dyed, **20**: 2484-87

vegetable dyes
colorfast dyes, **21**: 2678-83
wool yarn, dyeing, **21**: 2684-88

Paper Folding and Cutting
airplanes, paper
Barnaby, **1**: 35

toys, continued
 gee-haw whimmy-diddle, **20:** 2550-51
 hammer man, **20:** 2559-60
 jumping jack, **20:** 2552-53
 moonwinder, **20:** 2548
 sports car, **20:** 2553
 stern-wheel boat, **20:** 2554-55
 yard toys
 trampoline, **23:** 2900-1
 yo-yos
 drawer-pull yo-yo, **23:** 2918-20
 sink-strainer yo-yo, **23:** 2920

Weaving, Braiding, Knotting
 basketry
 hanging basket, **1:** 116-17
 Indian coil basket, **1:** 115
 pencil holder, **1:** 114
 shopping basket, **1:** 118-19
 braided rugs
 coasters, braided, **3:** 275
 hammocks and slings
 canvas log sling, **7:** 850-51
 naval hammock, **7:** 851-53
 inkle weaving
 hat band and bag handle, **8:** 932
 pick-up pattern belt, **8:** 935
 watchband and vase cover, **8:** 933
 leather working
 belt, magic braid, **9:** 1072-73
 ojo de dios
 evening star ojo de dios, **11:** 1357-58
 flat ojo de dios, **11:** 1351-53
 galaxy ojo de dios, **11:** 1358-59
 necklace, ojo de dios, **11:** 1355
 snowflake ojo de dios, **11:** 1356
 woven ojo de dios, **11:** 1354-55
 raffia and straw
 giraffes, straw, **14:** 1713-14
 hat, straw, **14:** 1714-16
 oval tray, **14:** 1722
 round tray, **14:** 1720-22
 rope knotting
 carrick bend chain, **14:** 1788
 hot-plate pad, **14:** 1789
 planter hanging, knotted, **14:** 1790-92
 sprang
 belt, sprang, **17:** 2168
 sampler, sprang, **17:** 2163-66
 scarf, sprang, **17:** 2169
 tote bag, sprang, **17:** 2167
 wall hanging, sprang, **17:** 2172-73
 swings
 baby swing, **19:** 2354-57
 tablet and frame weaving
 belt, tablet-woven, **19:** 2398
 branch weaving, **19:** 2402

 geometric frame weaving, **19:** 2403-4
 hoop weaving, **19:** 2393, 2405
 landscape frame weaving, **19:** 2404-5
 tatting
 handkerchief edging, **19:** 2421, 2424
 weaving
 leno-weave scarf, **22:** 2765-67
 plaid pillow, **22:** 2755-63
 twill pillow, **22:** 2767
 woven tapestries
 frame loom, **23:** 2861-63
 frame loom, tapestry, **23:** 2864-65
 wrapped and coiled work
 basket, sisal, **23:** 2884-86
 necklace, wrapped, **23:** 2880-82
 plant hanger, **23:** 2882-84

 The projects that follow can be completed in a matter of days.

Carving and Molding
 casting
 head, plaster-cast, **4:** 424-29
 dioramas
 portable diorama, **5:** 583-91
 foam forms
 fish impression, **6:** 706-7
 giraffe, synthetic stone, **6:** 704-5
 folk art
 reindeer weathervane, **6:** 716-17
 molding methods
 hand mold and cast, **10:** 1248-49
 latex molding, **10:** 1251-52
 pop-art candle, **10:** 1253-55
 pewtersmithing
 figurine, cast, **12:** 1476, 1478-79
 sand casting
 weed pot, **15:** 1878-81
 scrimshaw
 bone hair piece, **15:** 1917-18
 color-engraved scrimshaw, **15:** 1919-20
 sculpture
 rosewood serving tray, **16:** 1930-33
 totem poles
 full-sized totem pole, **20:** 2546-47
 walking sticks
 sculptured walking stick, **22:** 2720-21

Ceramics
 ceramics
 clay bowl, **4:** 440
 clay tiles, **4:** 434-39
 coiled bowl, **4:** 441-43

Designs and Decorations
 collages and assemblages
 cigar box assemblage, **4:** 484-85
 free-form assemblages, **4:** 486-87
 scrap lumber collage, **4:** 482-83
 decoupage
 box, switch, lamp, **5:** 573
 techniques, decoupage, **5:** 568-72
 tin-can decoupage, **5:** 574

 mosaics
 grouted mosaics, **10:** 1277-78
 mirror frame, mosaic, **10:** 1272-73
 mural, tile, **10:** 1278-80
 papier-mâché
 bottle people, **11:** 1401, 1403-4
 dinosaur, papier-mâché, **11:** 1407-8
 rosemaling
 Telemark box, **15:** 1810-13
 seashells
 flowers, seashell, **16:** 1946-47
 soft sculpture
 gorilla, soft sculpture, **17:** 2114, 2116-19
 stenciling
 floors, stenciled, **18:** 2250-51
 walls and ceilings, stenciled, **18:** 2248-49

Environmental Projects
 beachcombing
 aquarium tank, **2:** 138
 driftwood constructions, **2:** 142-43
 birds and birdhouses
 birdbath, concrete, **2:** 198-99
 bird feeder, **2:** 194-95
 purple-martin house, **2:** 196-97
 greenhouse construction
 curved fiberglass greenhouse, **7:** 822-35
 pit greenhouse, **7:** 820-21
 insects
 trapping insects, **8:** 940-42
 pet habitats
 two-pet tote, **12:** 1470-72

Furniture and Finishes
 antiquing furniture
 glaze antiquing, **1:** 70-73
 marbleizing, **1:** 79
 caning and rushing
 chair, recaning, **3:** 348-50
 folk art
 hope chest, **6:** 710-11
 gold leafing
 chair, gilded, **7:** 792
 shadow-box, gilt-edge, **7:** 790-91
 marquetry
 chessboard, marquetry, **10:** 1179
 geometric marquetry design, **10:** 1167-76
 special marquetry effects, **10:** 1177-78
 plywood and foam furnishings
 banquette and bench, **13:** 1579-83
 Shaker furniture
 dovetailed candle box, **16:** 2009-11
 side table, **16:** 2003-5
 utility bench, **16:** 2006-8
 structural furnishings
 lofts, **18:** 2284, 2288-93

platforms, **18:** 2294-99
tables and benches
modular tables and benches, **19:**
2384-87
nesting tables, **19:** 2388-91
upholstery
bench, cushioned, **21:** 2654-57
chair seat, padded, **21:** 2658

Glass and Plastics
acrylics
room divider, acrylic, **1:** 11-14
gold leafing
gilding glass, **7:** 793-95
lamps and shades
potichomania lamp, **9:** 1036-37
leaded glass
candle box or planter, **9:** 1064-65
lampshade, **9:** 1066-67
mosaics
light sculpture, mosaic, **10:** 1274-75
stained glass
necklace, copper-foiled, **18:** 2226-29
panel, leaded stained-glass, **18:**
2229-31

Graphic Arts
batik
floor pillow, **1:** 128
table mat, **1:** 127
wall hanging, **1:** 126
block printing
linoleum prints, **2:** 216-19
bookbinding
denim bookcover, **2:** 233-35
calligraphy
hand illumination, **3:** 312, 319-21
enameling metal
steel tiles, **6:** 665-67
flags and banners
felt banner, **6:** 668, 674-75
serigraphy
garden print, **16:** 1960, 1971-72
printing on plastic, **16:** 1970-71
wall-hanging catchalls, **16:** 1968-70
string art
conics in box, **18:** 2271, 2280-81

Greenery and Growing Things
dried flowers
bouquet, dried-spice, **5:** 622-23
herbs
harvesting and drying herbs, **7:**
822-83
lighted indoor gardens
bookcase shelf garden, **9:** 1086
corner garden, **9:** 1087-88
skylight floor garden, **9:** 1090-91
wall garden, **9:** 1081, 1091-93

window garden, **9:** 1088-89
tea
herb cultivation, **20:** 2439-42

Jewelry, Lapidary, and Metalwork
mobiles
steel fin mobile, **10:** 1227-31
repoussé and chased metal
necklace, metal, **14:** 1751-53

Kitchen Favorites and Celebrations
gingerbread
house, gingerbread, **6:** 762-66
vinegars
cider vinegar, **22:** 2698
flavored vinegars, **22:** 2699-2703
wok cookery
Chinese meal, **23:** 2845
duck, deep-fried, **23:** 2843

Needlecrafts
afghan stitch
afghan, **1:** 29
pillow tic-tac-toe, **1:** 28
vest and child's skirt, **1:** 24-28
appliqué
hand appliqué, **1:** 82-85
tablecloth, **1:** 91
buttons
clay buttons, **3:** 308-9
cuff links, button, **3:** 305
crochet
evening dress, **5:** 554-55
embroidery
black work owl, **6:** 656-57
circles, **6:** 653
fur recycling
collar and cuffs, fur, **6:** 746-48
granny squares
cap and scarf **7:** 812
shoulder tote bag, **7:** 814-15
hardanger embroidery
red place mat and napkin, **7:** 861-62
white place mat and napkin, **7:** 863-65
lace
necklace, lace, **8:** 1023-24
needlepoint
pillow, needlepoint, **11:** 1330-31
rug, needlepoint, **11:** 1332-33
patchwork
crib quilt, **12:** 1447-48
reversible vest, **12:** 1449-50
tote bag, patchwork, **12:** 1451-52
traditional quilt, **12:** 1439, 1452-53
quilting
Dresden-plate quilt, **14:** 1702-5
reverse appliqué
hanging, reverse appliqué, **14:**
1760-61
rya and flossa
designing ryas, **15:** 1832-34
wall hanging, wool, **15:** 1826-28
samplers
designing samplers, **15:** 1858-59
perforated paper sampler, **15:**
1860-61

smocking
cotton dress, **17:** 2085
pillow, smock, **17:** 2078-81
silk dress, **17:** 2083-84
soft sculpture
tennis shoes, soft sculpture, **17:**
2112-14
tambour
dragonfly, tambour, **19:** 2417-19
pillow, tambour, **19:** 2416-17
wall hanging, tambour, **19:** 2415-16
white-on-white curtain, **19:** 2412
traditional knitting motifs
bias-knit scarf, **21:** 2578-79
Irish-knit top, child's, **21:** 2571-74

Outdoor Activities
shelters and tents
tarp tents and lean-tos, **16:** 2014-18
swings
monkey swing, **19:** 2351-52
tire swings, **19:** 2345-48
tree houses
outdoor platform, **21:** 2596-99
traditional tree house, **21:** 2593,
2600-1

Paint and Color
folk art
Senufo wall hanging, **6:** 714-15
preschool activities
plants and painted pots, **13:** 1632-33
supergraphics
child's bedroom supergraphic, **19:**
2327
dark background supergraphic, **19:**
2328
diagonal stripes supergraphic, **19:**
2330-32
fabric design supergraphic, **19:**
2334-35
flowers supergraphic, **19:** 2330-31
free-form supergraphic, **19:** 2332
furniture framing supergraphic, **19:**
2327-28
geometric supergraphic, **19:** 2324-26
Indian motif supergraphic, **19:** 2333
reversed colors supergraphic, **19:**
2329
sunrise supergraphic, **19:** 2323, 2330

Paper Folding and Cutting
boxes
desk and seat, milk-crate, **3:** 262-65
cardboard
whirligig weathervane, **3:** 369-71
quilling
bird, quillwork, **14:** 1681-83
butterflies, quillwork, **14:** 1678-79

, continued

Performing Arts
  dulcimers
    Appalachian dulcimer, **5**: 624, 626-33
    fretboard dulcimer, **5**: 625-26
  whistles and flutes
    flutes, **22**: 2778-79
    shepherd's pipe, bamboo, **22**: 2780-83

Toys and Games
  dioramas
    train diorama, **5**: 579-82
  dolls and doll clothes
    apple-head doll, **5**: 609
  kites
    Indian fighter kite, **8**: 989, 998-99
    Thai dragon kite, **8**: 996-97
  papier-mâché
    puppet heads, **11**: 1405-7
  preschool activities
    hand puppets, **13**: 1635
  puzzles
    block puzzle, **13**: 1661-62
  whistles and flutes
    dowel whistle, **22**: 2776-77
    hardwood whistle, **22**: 2778

Weaving, Braiding, Knotting
  braided rugs
    place mats, braided, **3**: 276-77
  hooked rugs
    geometric rugs, **8**: 904-5
  inkle weaving
    wall hanging, inkle, **8**: 934-35
  lace
    collar and cuffs, bobbin lace, **8**: 1019-21
    sash, bobbin lace, **8**: 1017-18
  macramé
    adjustable belt, **9**: 1120-21
    dress yoke and sash, **9**: 1122-23
    willow tree sculpture, **9**: 1125-26
  rya and flossa
    cat, woven rya, **15**: 1834-37
  sprang
    hammock, sprang, **17**: 2174-76
  tablet and frame weaving
    bag, tablet-woven, **19**: 2399-2401
  tatting
    child's vest, **19**: 2426-27
    flowerpot holder, **19**: 2429-30
    shell-cluster collar, **19**: 2424-25
    sunflower place mat, **19**: 2427-28
  weaving
    tote bag, weft-faced, **22**: 2770-71
    twill jackets, **22**: 2768-69
    wall hanging, woven, **22**: 2772-73
  woven tapestries
    apple-tree tapestry, **23**: 2870-71
    field-of-flowers tapestry, **23**: 2872-73
    pillow, geometric, **23**: 2866-67

1 30 The projects that follow will take several weeks to complete.

Carving and Molding
  sculpture
    alabaster, **16**: 1935-37

Designs and Decorations
  decoupage
    wooden cabinet, **5**: 577
  ship models
    "Philadelphia" ship model, **16**: 2025-37
    ship in bottle, **16**: 2038-41
  stamp decoupage
    container decoupage, **18**: 2237-39

Environmental Projects
  astronomy
    telescope, **1**: 101-5
  insects
    collection, insect, **8**: 942-47
  pet habitats
    five-story birdcage, **12**: 1472-75

Fragrances
  potpourris and pomanders
    pendant, pomander-ball, **13**: 1605
    pomander balls, **13**: 1602-4

Furniture and Finishes
  upholstery
    stuffed easy chair, **21**: 2659-65

Graphic Arts
  bookbinding
    leather-bound diary, **2**: 236-42

Greenery and Growing Things
  bonsai
    cascade bonsai, **2**: 227
    driftwood bonsai, **2**: 223-25
    miniature bonsai, **2**: 229
    rock-grown bonsai, **2**: 228
    tropical bonsai, **2**: 226
  topiary
    geometric topiary, **20**: 2530-31
    privet hedge, **20**: 2533-35
    three-ball ivy topiary, **20**: 2532

Jewelry, Lapidary, and Metalwork
  lapidary
    tumbling gemstones, **9**: 1042-44

Kitchen Favorites and Celebrations
  brewing
    ginger beer, **3**: 298-301
    root beer and sarsaparilla, **3**: 294-97
  vinegars
    wine vinegars, **22**: 2696-97

Needlecrafts
  crewel
    embroidery sampler, **5**: 538-41, 546-49
  crochet
    sisal rug, **5**: 557
  Florentine stitch
    pillow, **6**: 684-87
  granny squares
    floral afghan, **7**: 811
    popcorn stitch afghan, **7**: 813
    traditional afghan, **7**: 807-8
  knitting to fit
    hooded parka sweater, **8**: 1010-11
    sweater and skirt, knit, **8**: 1007-9
  tambour
    wool rug, **19**: 2413-15
  traditional knitting motifs
    Norwegian-pattern sweater, **21**: 2574-77

Paint and Color
  oil painting
    cityscape, **11**: 1344-45
    portraits, **11**: 1346-47
    still life, **11**: 1342-43
  tin painting
    antique stenciled tin box, **20**: 2523-27
    canister, painted, **20**: 2518-19
    country tin painting, **20**: 2513-17
    freehand bronze tray, **20**: 2520-22

Performing Arts
  stagecraft
    lighting, stage, **18**: 2206-13
    set design, **18**: 2196-2201

Toys and Games
  soapbox and skate vehicles
    lay-back racer, **17**: 2091-97
  yard toys
    cable-spool playhouse, **23**: 2906-7
    spiral staircase, **23**: 2908-9
    tire and box toys, **23**: 2902-3
    utility pole animals, **23**: 2904-5

Weaving, Braiding, Knotting
  braided rugs
    petal-design rug, **3**: 278-79
    traditional braided rug, **3**: 276-77
  hooked rugs
    "love" hooked rug, **8**: 907-9
    owl rug, **8**: 906
  macramé
    micromé hanging, **9**: 1126-27
    room-divider screen, **9**: 1116, 1124
  tatting
    openwork tablecloth, **19**: 2431-32

wrapped and coiled work
bread tray, raffia, **23**: 2886-87

Level of Skill Required

The projects that follow can be completed by a child working alone.

Carving and Molding
 sand casting
  sea animals, cast, **15**: 1874-75

Designs and Decorations
 Christmas celebrations
  patchwork Christmas-tree ornaments, **4**: 458
 mosaics
  mirror frame, mosaic, **10**: 1272-73
 preschool activities
  junk sculpture, **13**: 1630-31

Glass and Plastics
 mosaics
  light sculpture, mosaic, **10**: 1274-75

Graphic Arts
 cartooning
  comic strips, **4**: 410-11
  figures and hands, **4**: 406-7
  heads, faces, expressions, **4**: 404-5
  self starter cartoons, **4**: 412-13
  single panel cartoons, **4**: 408-9

Jewelry, Lapidary, and Metalwork
 beadwork
  fruit, beaded, **2**: 152-53
  necklace safety pin, **2**: 154

Kitchen Favorites and Celebrations
 egg decoration
  margutis and pysanka eggs, **5**: 634-37

Needlecrafts
 buttons
  cuff links, button, **3**: 305
 costumes
  drapes and wraparounds, **5**: 530

Paper Folding and Cutting
 costumes
  paper costumes, **5**: 528-29
 origami
  dog face and cat face, **11**: 1376-77

Toys and Games
 bean-bags
  paperweights, felt, **2**: 161
 spool toys
  auto race, spool, **17**: 2157
  balance toys, **17**: 2160-61

constructions, spool, **17**: 2155-56
  parachute toy, **17**: 2159
  pull-along toys, **17**: 2156
  ring-toss game, **17**: 2160-61
  rocking toys, **17**: 2157
  streamers, spool, **17**: 2160-61
 table games
  Jungle Game, **19**: 2366-67, 2370-72
  Mancala, **19**: 2368
  Mill, **19**: 2369-70

The projects that follow can be completed by a child working under the supervision of an adult or they can be family projects.

Carving and Molding
 candlemaking
  hand dipped candles, **3**: 330-33
 carving
  soap carved fish, **4**: 415-16
 dioramas
  portable diorama, **5**: 583-91
 foam forms
  fish impressions, **6**: 706-7
  giraffe, synthetic stone, **6**: 704-5
 molding methods
  hand mold and cast, **10**: 1248-49
  latex molding, **10**: 1251-52
  pop-art candle, **10**: 1253-55
 sand casting
  candle, sand-castle, **15**: 1875-77
  weed pot, **15**: 1878-81
 totem poles
  wall plaque, totem-mask, **20**: 2541-42
Ceramics
 enameling metal
  dish, copper, **6**: 664
  pendant, copper, **6**: 661-63
 kilns
  sawdust kiln, **8**: 980-82
 pottery
  hand-built pottery, **13**: 1609-11
  wheel-thrown pottery, **13**: 1614-21
 sculpture
  clay figure, **16**: 1926-29

Designs and Decorations
 Christmas celebrations
  candy wreaths, **4**: 464
  Christmas-tree trims, **4**: 460-61
  handmade Christmas-tree ornaments, **4**: 459
 collages and assemblages
  pure-paper collage, **4**: 480-81
  scrap lumber collage, **4**: 482-83
 decoupage
  box, switch, lamp, **5**: 573
  techniques, decoupage, **5**: 568-72
  tin-can decoupage, **5**: 574
  tortoise-shell base, **5**: 575-76
  wooden cabinet, **5**: 577

herbs
  note cards, herb, **7**: 884
mosaics
  button mosaics, **10**: 1270-71
papier-mâché
  bottle people, **11**: 1401, 1403-4
pod and cone art
  alligator, pod and cone, **13**: 1585
  lion, pine-cone, **13**: 1584, 1587-88
  llama, pine-cone, **13**: 1584, 1585
  ostrich, pine-cone, **13**: 1588
preschool activities
  kitchen clay, **13**: 1628-29
  woodworking, **13**: 1634
raffia and straw
  mosaics, split-straw, **14**: 1712-13
rosemaling
  hand mirror, **15**: 1803-4
seashells
  collage, seashell, **16**: 1944
stamp decoupage
  pieced pictures, **18**: 2235-36
stone painting
  animals, stone, **18**: 2556-57
  assemblages, painted stone, **18**: 2253-54
time telling
  candle clock, **20**: 2494-95
  noon light show, **20**: 2490-93
yarn painting
  clown face, yarn, **23**: 2912-14
  paper-plate mask, **23**: 2914-15

Environmental Projects
 ant farms
  ant farm, **1**: 66-69
  ant house, Mason-jar, **1**: 65-66
 astronomy
  telescope, **1**: 101-5
 beachcombing
  lobster-man and shell paperweight, **2**: 140-41
 birds and birdhouses
  bird feeder, **2**: 194-95
  bluebird house, **2**: 192
  wren house, **2**: 193
 insects
  collection, insect, **8**: 942-47
  trapping insects, **8**: 940-42
 masks
  African rope mask, **10**: 1192-95
 papermaking
  blender-made paper, **11**: 1390-93
 pet habitats
  cat cabaña, **12**: 1468-69

Environmental Projects, continued

quill pens
making quill pen, **14:** 1686-89
spinning
drop spindle spinning, **17:** 2143-45
sundials
Egyptian sundial, **19:** 2313-14
horizontal sundial, **19:** 2316-21
portable sundial, **19:** 2315
vivariums
chameleon lizards, **22:** 2710-11
English hooded rat, **22:** 2708
guinea pigs, **22:** 2706-7
snakes, **22:** 2711-13
walking sticks
hiking stick, **22:** 2716-18
weather forecasting
making weather instruments, **22:** 2740-45

Fragrances
cosmetics
powder and shadow, **5:** 524-25
potpourris and pomanders
balls, pomander, **13:** 1602-4
buds, pomander, **13:** 1601
pendant, pomander-ball, **13:** 1605
pillow potpourri, **13:** 1600
potpourris, **13:** 1596-98
seasonal potpourris, **13:** 1599
soaps and bath products
quick soaps, **17:** 2098-2102
shaving soaps and bath oils, **17:** 2103

Furniture and Finishes
framing
barn siding background frame, **6:** 723
metal frame, **6:** 721

Furniture and Refinishing
caning and rushing
rush chair seat, **3:** 351-53
splint chair seat, **3:** 344-47

Glass and Plastics
acrylics
poured acrylics, **1:** 15-20
beachcombing
mosaic, beach glass, **2:** 139
bottle cutting
basic cutting, **2:** 244-48
decorating bottles, **2:** 249-51
foam forms
sculpture, packing pieces, **6:** 699
glass working
beads, lead glass, **7:** 776-77
sculpture, glass rod, **7:** 779
swizzle sticks, **7:** 778-79
plastic pipe constructions
bookshelves, **13:** 1567-69

easy chair and footrest, **13:** 1564-66
stained glass
mosaic, glass, **18:** 2225-26
panel, laminated, **18:** 2217, 2222-23
slab-glass cutting, **18:** 2223-24
time telling
sandglass, **20:** 2495-96

Graphic Arts
batik
table mat, **1:** 127
wall hanging, **1:** 126
block printing
eraser prints, **2:** 214-15
vegetable prints, **2:** 210-13
calligraphy
chancery cursive, **3:** 316-18
cameras
camera obscura, **3:** 322-26
pinhole camera, **3:** 327-29
enameling metal
tiles, steel, **6:** 665-67
greeting cards
cardboard printing, **7:** 844-45
linoleum and woodcuts
greeting cards, **9:** 1099-1101
scarf, block-printed, **9:** 1096-98
monoprinting
greeting cards, fingerprint, **10:** 1259-60
litho-monoprint, **10:** 1263-64
place mat, Janus, **10:** 1267
silhouettes, reverse, **10:** 1261-63
stationery fingerprint, **10:** 1258-59
T-shirt, calligraphic, **10:** 1265-66
music making
gongs and chimes, **11:** 1287, 1292
rubbings
brass rubbings, **15:** 1818-19
inked raised designs, **15:** 1820-21
reproducing high reliefs, **15:** 1823
tombstone rubbings, **15:** 1815-17
string art
children's string designs, **18:** 2282-83

Greenery and Growing Things
dried flowers
bouquet, dried-spice, **5:** 622-23
herbs
gift basket, herb, **7:** 884
terrariums
cactus terrarium, **20:** 2460-61
fern terrarium, **20:** 2457-59
tropical terrarium, **20:** 2454-55
topiary
geometric topiary, **20:** 2530-31
three-ball ivy topiary, **20:** 2532

Jewelry, Lapidary, and Metalwork
American Indian crafts
ring, beaded, **1:** 44
beadwork
making beads, **2:** 145-47
ring, bead, **2:** 154-55
stringing beads, **2:** 148-50

jewelry
bracelets, hardware, **8:** 954
lamps and shades
tin lantern, **9:** 1030-32
lapidary
tumbling gemstones, **9:** 1042-44
mobiles
balsa wood mobile, **10:** 1224-25
repoussé and chased metal
ornamented box tops, **14:** 1746-48
silversmithing
butter knife, silver, **17:** 2056-57
stone painting
key-chain fob, **18:** 2255-56
wire sculpture
basket, wire, **23:** 2832-33
belt and bracelet, forged, **23:** 2828-29
figure, wire, **23:** 2822, 2834-35
flowers, wire, **23:** 2831-32
necklace, forged, **23:** 2829-31
necklace, loop-link, **23:** 2823-25

Kitchen Favorites and Celebrations
baby foods
breakfast cookies, **1:** 110-11
preparing baby foods, **1:** 107-9
birthday celebrations
baking for children, **2:** 206-7
cheeses and churning
cheeses, **4:** 450-52
churning, **4:** 453
yogurts and sour cream, **4:** 446-49
confections and comfits
quick candies, **4:** 508
egg decoration
Imperial Easter eggs, **5:** 638-40
gingerbread
cookies, gingerbread, **6:** 767-68
hibachi and hot-pot cookery
hibachi cooking, **7:** 892-93
ice cream, sherbet, and ices
flavored ice creams, **8:** 915-16
ices, **8:** 917
sherbet, **8:** 917
vanilla ice cream, **8:** 914-15
marmalades and preserves
chutney, **10:** 1165
curd, **10:** 1163
jam, **10:** 1160-62
jelly, **10:** 1164
marmalade, **10:** 1162-63
masks
paper-plate masks, **10:** 1182-83
pasta
macaroni recipes, **12:** 1436-37
stuffed pasta, **12:** 1432-35
soups
chicken julienne, **17:** 2126
chicken soup, **17:** 2127
cupboard coups, **17:** 2131
fruit soups, **17:** 2128-29
vichyssoise, **17:** 2130-31

sugar shapes
brown-sugar shapes, **18:** 2304
ladybugs, sugar, **18:** 2303
place cards, sugar, **18:** 2304
schoolhouse, sugar, **18:** 2302-3
wedding bells, sugar, **18:** 2303
winter scene, sugar, **18:** 2300, 2302
syrups
beverages and desserts, **19:** 2358-63
main dishes, syrup-flavored, **19:** 2364-65

Leathercrafts
belts and buckles
beaded belt, **2:** 172-73
cowboy belt, **2:** 168, 170-71
elastic belts, **2:** 174-75
leather working
sculpture, leather, **9:** 1068, 1079

Needlecrafts
afghan stitch
vest and child's skirt, **1:** 24-28
animal dolls
alligator, stuffed, **1:** 62-63
elephant, stuffed, **1:** 56-59
appliqué
people pillows, **1:** 90
buttons
buttons, seashell, **3:** 306-7
costumes
basic dress pattern, **5:** 533
caftans, **5:** 534
circular patterns, **5:** 531
historic costumes, **5:** 527, 532
period dress, **5:** 535
crochet
beaded bag, **5:** 553
evening dress, **5:** 554-55
pincushion, **5:** 556
sisal rug, **5:** 557
tie, **5:** 552
embroidery
flower appliqué, **6:** 652
flags and banners
club banner, **6:** 670-71
Florentine stitch
eyeglass case, **6:** 680-81
granny squares
cap and scarf, **7:** 812
place mat, **7:** 810
hardanger embroidery
bookmark, **7:** 858
knitting to fit
tassel cap, **8:** 1006-7
lace
window hanging, needle lace, **8:** 1013, 1021-23
mobiles
felt auto-mobile, **10:** 1222
needlepoint
belt, signature, **11:** 1324
pencil holder, gingham, **11:** 1322-23
raffia and straw
belt, crocheted raffia, **14:** 1716

cap, crocheted raffia, **14:** 1718-19
earrings, raffia, **14:** 1719
shoulder bag, raffia, **14:** 1718
rag dolls
making rag dolls, **14:** 1726-31
ribboncraft
serving tray, **14:** 1772
samplers
cross-stitch denim patch, **15:** 1857-58
hoop-framed samplers, **15:** 1855-57
pegboard sampler, **15:** 1854
soft sculpture
palm tree, soft sculpture, **17:** 2114-16
Swedish huck work
hand towel, huck work, **19:** 2340
traditional knitting motifs
shoulder bag, **21:** 2570

Outdoor Activities
cryptography
ciphers, **5:** 561-64, 565
maps and pathfinding
compass, making and using, **9:** 1146-48
maps, making and using, **9:** 1141-44
natural guides, **9:** 1148-52
shelters and tents
tarp tents and lean-tos, **16:** 2014-18
tepees, **16:** 2020-23
swings
monkey swing, **19:** 2351-52
rope swing, **19:** 2344, 2346
time telling
star dial, **20:** 2497-99
tree houses
grove tree house, **21:** 2594-96
outdoor platform, **21:** 2596-99
traditional tree house, **21:** 2593, 2600-1
tying flies
Rat-faced MacDougall fly, **21:** 2648-49
Royal Coachman fly, **21:** 2650-51
TW Special fly, **21:** 2645-47
winter sculpture
snow sculpture, **22:** 2806-11

Paint and Color
acrylics
painting Volkswagen, **1:** 21-23
folk art
Senufo wall hanging, **6:** 714-15
preschool activities
plants and painted pots, **13:** 1632-33
sand painting and layering
fishbowl sand painting, **15:** 1894-96
garden, layered-sand, **15:** 1896-99
Navajo sand painting, **15:** 1890-91
planter, sand-layered, **15:** 1891-94
tie dyeing
T-shirts, tie dyed, **20:** 2476-79

Paper Folding and Cutting
airplanes, paper
Barnaby, **1:** 35
Dartmouth Dart, **1:** 33-34
Falcon, **1:** 38-39

Flying Tiger, **1:** 36-37
Pegasus, **1:** 40-41
boxes
drawer organizer, kitchen-matchbox, **3:** 267
Christmas celebrations
gift wrapping, **4:** 462
greeting cards
pressed flower cards, **7:** 838
ribbon bookmark card, **7:** 837
mobiles
cardboard snail mobile, **10:** 1223
napkin folding
artichoke fold, **11:** 1306
band fold, **11:** 1305
candle fold, **11:** 1303
fan fold, **11:** 1307
fleur-de-lis fold, **11:** 1307
lily fold, **11:** 1304
palm leaf fold, **11:** 1301-2
pocket fold, **11:** 1304
sailboat fold, **11:** 1302
origami
drinking cup, **11:** 1378
house, **11:** 1378
penguin, **11:** 1380
quilling
Christmas tree ornaments, **14:** 1675-77
decorated eggs, **14:** 1680-81
silhouettes
silhouettes, **16:** 2044-46
valentines
gift box, valentine, **21:** 2674-75
lovebird valentine, **21:** 2674
playing card valentine, **21:** 2673
two-heart valentine, **21:** 2672-73
wycinanki
animal chain cutout, **23:** 2890-91
applied wycinanki, **23:** 2898-99
disk mobile, **23:** 2896-97
stars, paper, **23:** 2892-93
tree-of-life, **23:** 2894-95
zoetrope toys
flipbook, **23:** 2942-44
moving-picture wheel, **23:** 2930-33
thaumatropes, **23:** 2926-29
zoetropes: **23:** 2934-41

Performing Arts
costumes
makeup, **5:** 536-37
masks
bird mask, newspaper, **10:** 1188-91
clown hoop mask, **10:** 1184-85
lion hoop mask, **10:** 1186-87
music making
marimbas, **11:** 1287, 1294-99
puppetry
clown marionette, **13:** 1645, 1648-51
felt puppets, **13:** 1640-42
foam puppets, **13:** 1643
paper marionettes, **13:** 1646-47
pop-up, finger, and junk puppets, **13:** 1638-40

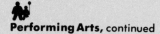

Performing Arts, continued

shadow theater
color silhouettes, **16:** 1991
paper shadow puppets, **16:** 1996-97
plastic jellyfish, **16:** 1989, 1992
plastic puppets, **16:** 1992-93
shadow play, **16:** 1993
silhouette puppets, **16:** 1988-89
whistles and flutes
shepherd's pipe, bamboo, **22:** 2780-83

Toys and Games
bean-bags
games, bean-bag, **2:** 162-63
toss toys, **2:** 160
birthday celebrations
party games, **2:** 208-9
cardboard
train, toy, **3:** 366,368
cryptography
codes, **5:** 559-60
signal communications, **5:** 564-65
dioramas
train diorama, **5:** 579-82
dolls and doll clothes
apple-head doll, **5:** 609
cloth doll, **5:** 612-13
clothespin doll, **5:** 608
cornhusk doll, **5:** 610
pieces doll, **5:** 608
walnut and egg dolls, **5:** 606-7
flowers, artificial
pencil posy, **6:** 688
kaleidoscopes
cubes, kaleidoscopic, **8:** 960-61
Hue View kaleidoscope, **8:** 962-63
kaleidoscope, **8:** 965-67
teleidoscope, **8:** 963-65
kites
Greek kite, **8:** 992-95
sled kite, **8:** 991
music making
percussion instruments, **11:** 1287-91
papier-mâché
puppet-heads, **11:** 1405-7
piñatas
doll piñata, **12:** 1534
rabbit-foot piñata, **12:** 1529
sailboat piñata, **12:** 1535-36
star piñata, **12:** 1524-28
wishing-well piñata, **12:** 1530-34
preschool activities
hand puppets, **13:** 1635
puzzles
crossword puzzles, **13:** 1655-57
tangrams, **13:** 1659-60
soapbox and skate vehicles
cart, crate, **17:** 2089-90

racer, lay-back, **17:** 2091-97
scooter, skate, **17:** 2088-89
spool toys
knitting, spool, **17:** 2158
wind-up toys, **17:** 2159
street games
association football, **18:** 2265
boxball, **18:** 2267
Chinese handball, **18:** 2262
double dutch, **18:** 2269
follow-the-leader, **18:** 2268
hit-the-penny, **18:** 2265
hopscotch, **18:** 2266
Johnny-on-the-pony, **18:** 2258-59
kickball, **18:** 2264
kick-the-can, **18:** 2261
ring-a-levio, **18:** 2268
running bases, **18:** 2264
skullies, **18:** 2260
stickball, street, **18:** 2263
stoopball, **18:** 2267
toys
bull roarer, **20:** 2550
jumping jack, **20:** 2552-53
moonwinder, **20:** 2548
whistles and flutes
dowel whistle, **22:** 2776-77
yard toys
trampoline, **23:** 2900-1
yo-yos
drawer-pull yo-yo, **23:** 2918-20
sink-strainer yo-yo, **23:** 2920

Weaving, Braiding, Knotting
basketry
pencil holder, **1:** 114
braided rugs
coasters, braided, **3:** 275
hooked rugs
geometric rugs, **8:** 904-5
"love" hooked rug, **8:** 907-9
owl rug, **8:** 906
ojo de dios
evening star ojo de dios, **11:** 1357-58
flat ojo de dios, **11:** 1351-53
galaxy ojo de dios, **11:** 1358-59
necklace, ojo de dios, **11:** 1355
snowflake ojo de dios, **11:** 1356
woven ojo de dios, **11:** 1354-55
raffia and straw
giraffes, straw, **14:** 1713-14
hat, straw, **14:** 1714-16
rope knotting
carrick bend chain, **14:** 1788
hot-plate pad, **14:** 1789
planter hanging, knotted, **14:** 1790-92
tablet and frame weaving
belt, tablet-woven, **19:** 2398
branch weaving, **19:** 2402
hoop weaving, **19:** 2393, 2405
landscape frame weaving, **19:** 2404-5
tatting
handkerchief edging, **19:** 2421, 2424
wrapped and coiled work
bread tray, raffia, **23:** 2886-87
plant hanger, **23:** 2882-84

The projects that follow can
be completed by an adult
without special skills or training.

Carving and Molding
candlemaking
confectionary candles, **3:** 336-37
dried-flower candles, **3:** 341
honeycomb candles, **3:** 334-35
molded candles, **3:** 338-40
carving
wax reliefs, carving, **4:** 417
casting
plaster-cast head, **4:** 424-29
tin belt buckle, **4:** 430-33
pewtersmithing
figurine, cast, **12:** 1476, 1478-79
pipe making
briar pipe, **13:** 1556-60
corncob pipe, **13:** 1555-56
scrimshaw
bone hair piece, **15:** 1917-18
color-engraved scrimshaw, **15:** 1919-20
sculpture
rosewood serving tray, **16:** 1930-33
totem poles
full-sized totem pole, **20:** 2546-47
miniature totem pole, **20:** 2543
treen ware
kitchen utensils, **21:** 2604-9
party table accessories, **21:** 2610-13
walking sticks
spiral-design cane, **22:** 2718-19
winter sculpture
ice sculptures, **22:** 2812-16

Ceramics
ceramics
bowl, clay, **4:** 440
bowl, coiled, **4:** 441-43
tiles, clay, **4:** 434-39
kilns
raku kiln, **8:** 983-85

Designs and Decorations
collages and assemblages
cigar box assemblage, **4:** 484-85
free-form assemblage, **4:** 486-87
models and mock-ups
bedroom redecorating model, **10:** 1235-40
garden structures, **10:** 1232, 1241-44
mock-ups, **10:** 1245
papier-mâché
dinosaur, papier-mâché, **11:** 1407-8

pin striping
boat helm, **13:** 1547
car customizing, **13:** 1548-50
door panel, **13:** 1546
restoring antique automobiles, **13:** 1542, 1551

pod and cone art
candle holder, **13:** 1590-91
Christmas wreath, **13:** 1591
shadow box, **13:** 1592
turkey, pine-cone, **13:** 1590
wired tree, **13:** 1593-95

rosemaling
box, Telemark, **15:** 1810-13
bread board, **15:** 1805-7
plate, Telemark, **15:** 1808-10

seashells
figurines, shell, **16:** 1948-49
flowers, seashell, **16:** 1946-47
jewelry, seashell, **16:** 1945

ship models
"Philadelphia" ship model, **16:** 2025-37
ship in bottle, **16:** 2038-41

skin painting
body painting, **17:** 2066, 2074-75
heavenly-nights face makeup, **17:** 2068-69
leopard face makeup, **17:** 2068-69
primitive face makeup, **17:** 2070-71

soft sculpture
gorilla, soft sculpture, **17:** 2114, 2116-19

stamp decoupage
container decoupage, **18:** 2237-39

stenciling
floors, stenciled, **18:** 2250-51
note paper, personalized, **18:** 2244-45
place mats, stenciled, **18:** 2246-47
walls and ceilings, stenciled, **18:** 2248-49

wood assemblages
heraldic standards, **23:** 2852-55
sculpture, wood, **23:** 2850-52
wall illusion, **23:** 2846-49

yarn painting
bottle yarn painting, **23:** 2917
landscape with feathers, **23:** 2916-17
landscape, yarn, **23:** 2915

Environmental Projects
beachcombing
driftwood constructions, **2:** 142-43
birds and birdhouses
birdbath, concrete, **2:** 198-99
purple-martin house, **2:** 196-97
greenhouse construction
cold frame greenhouse, **7:** 818, 819
curved fiberglass greenhouse, **7:** 822-35
hotbed, **7:** 818-19
pit greenhouse, **7:** 820-21

papermaking
handmade rag paper, **11:** 1394-99
pet habitats
birdcage, five-story, **12:** 1472-75
doghouse, barrel, **12:** 1464, 1466-67
tote, two-pet, **12:** 1470-72
spinning
flax on wheel, spinning, **17:** 2151-53
wool on wheel, spinning, **17:** 2146-50
wind harps
Aeolian harp, **22:** 2791-93
simple wind harp, **22:** 2786-90

Fragrances
cosmetics
astringent, **5:** 523
cold cream, **5:** 520-22
perfumes
cologne, **12:** 1462-63
homemade perfumes, **12:** 1457
recipes, perfume, **12:** 1458-60
soaps and bath products
cleansing creams and masks, **17:** 2104-5

Furniture and Finishes
antiquing furniture
distressing, **1:** 74-77
gilding, **1:** 81
glaze antiquing, **1:** 70-73
hardware, antiquing, **1:** 80
marbleizing, **1:** 79
boxes
curio cabinet, beverage-case, **3:** 266
decorative cigar boxes, **3:** 270-71
toy-chest bench, **3:** 262, 269
caning and rushing
chair, recaning, **3:** 348-50
cardboard
furniture, cardboard, **3:** 372-74
headboard, **3:** 367, 375
folk art
hope chest, **6:** 710-11
framing
box frame, **6:** 725
stick frame, **6:** 722-23
wood frame, **6:** 719-21
gold leafing
chair, gilded, **7:** 792
shadow-box, gilt-edge, **7:** 790-91
marquetry
chessboard, marquetry, **10:** 1179
geometric marquetry design, **10:** 1167-76
special marquetry effects, **10:** 1177-78
plywood and foam furnishings
chair and ottoman, **13:** 1572-75
platforms, seating, **13:** 1576-78
rockers and cradles
child's rocking chair, **14:** 1776
cradle, rocking, **14:** 1778-79
Shaker furniture
candle sconce, **16:** 2000-3
structural furnishings
lofts, **18:** 2284-93
platforms, **18:** 2294-99
table, wall-hanging, **18:** 2286-87

tables and benches
modular tables and benches, **19:** 2384-87
nesting tables, **19:** 2388-91
plant table, **19:** 2382-83
sawhorse stool, **19:** 2379-81
upholstery
bench, cushioned, **21:** 2654-57
chair seat, padded, **21:** 2658
easy chair, stuffed, **21:** 2659-65

Glass and Plastics
acrylics
room divider, **1:** 11-14
bean-bags
wall hanging, **2:** 167
foam forms
cup constructions, **6:** 700-1
gold leafing
glass, gilding, **7:** 793-95
lamps and shades
potichomania lamp, **9:** 1036-37
leaded glass
candle box or planter, **9:** 1064-65
window panel, **9:** 1063
plastic pipe constructions
lamp, sculptural, **13:** 1570-71
stained glass
necklace, copper-foiled, **18:** 2226-29
panel, leaded stained-glass, **18:** 2229-31

Graphic Arts
batik
floor pillow, **1:** 128
block printing
linoleum prints, **2:** 216-19
bookbinding
denim bookcover, **2:** 233-35
leather-bound diary, **2:** 236-42
calligraphy
hand illumination, **3:** 312, 319-21
flags and banners
felt banner, **6:** 668, 674-75
gold leafing
lettering signs in gold, **7:** 795-97
greeting cards
birth announcement, **7:** 845
stained-glass-window card, **7:** 840-41
linoleum and woodcuts
two-color wall hanging, **9:** 1102-3
photographic printing
contact prints, **12:** 1494-96
developing negatives, **12:** 1491-94
enlargements, making, **12:** 1496-99
serigraphy
garden print, **16:** 1960, 1971-72
poster print, **16:** 1963-65
printing on plastic, **16:** 1970-71
wall-hanging catchalls, **16:** 1968-70

Graphic Arts, continued
string art
conics in box, **18:** 2271, 2280-81
helios, **18:** 2276-77
raised ellipse, **18:** 2278-79
three adjacent hexagons, **18:** 2272-73
triple stellate forms, **18:** 2274-76

Greenery and Growing Things
bonsai
cascade bonsai, **2:** 227
driftwood bonsai, **2:** 223-25
miniature bonsai, **2:** 229
rock-grown bonsai, **2:** 228
tropical bonsai, **2:** 226
bottle gardens
lab-bottle garden, **2:** 256
water-cooler bottle garden, **2:** 252-56
Christmas celebrations
traditional wreath, **4:** 465
wheat-and-flower wreath, **4:** 463
herbs
hanging garden, **7:** 882
harvesting and drying, **7:** 882-83
ikebana
avant-garde ikebana, **8:** 926-27
cascading nageire, **8:** 924-25
upright moribana, **8:** 922-23
lighted indoor gardens
bookcase shelf garden, **9:** 1086
corner garden, **9:** 1087-88
nursery, indoor, **9:** 1085
skylight floor garden, **9:** 1090-91
wall garden, **9:** 1081, 1091-93
window gardens, **9:** 1088-89
seed sprouting
growing sprouts, **16:** 1952-59
tea
herb cultivation, **20:** 2439-42
topiary
privet hedge, **20:** 2533-35
trellises
doorway trellis, **21:** 2614, 2622-25
fan trellises, **21:** 2616-18
freestanding trellis, **21:** 2619-21

Jewelry, Lapidary, and Metalwork
American Indian crafts
chain, beaded daisy, **1:** 45
loom beading, **1:** 47
medallion, **1:** 46
beadwork
breechcloth, **2:** 151
earrings, pearl, **2:** 156-57
jewelry
bracelet, wrapped wire, **8:** 957
coconut shell jewelry, **8:** 951
feather jewelry, **8:** 948-51
pendant and neck ring, stone, **8:** 956-57
ring, spoon, and bracelet, fork, **8:** 955

lamps and shades
canister lamp, **9:** 1035
lapidary
cabochons, gemstone, **9:** 1048-51
eggs, gemstone, **9:** 1045-48
flats, gemstone, **9:** 1052-53
mineralogy
decorative mineral projects, **10:** 1206-9
mobiles
copper shapes mobile, **10:** 1225-26
pewtersmithing
bowl, handwrought pewter, **12:** 1480-83
box, fabricated pewter, **12:** 1484-87
repoussé and chased metal
mirror frame, foil, **14:** 1748-50
silversmithing
bowl, copper, **17:** 2063-65
spoon, silver, **17:** 2059-61
tin and pierced work
candle sconce and snuffer, **20:** 2504-7
cookie cutters, **20:** 2502-3
fruit bowl, **20:** 2508-9

Kitchen Favorites and Celebrations
birthday celebrations
cake, **2:** 202-5
breads
sourdough bread, **3:** 284-89
trail breads, **3:** 282-83
brewing
ginger beer, **3:** 298-301
root beer and sarsaparilla, **3:** 294-97
Christmas celebrations
recipes, Christmas, **4:** 466-67
confections and comfits
brittles and fudges, **4:** 510-11
coated chocolates, **4:** 512
hard candies, **4:** 509
flowers, artificial
fabric flowers, **6:** 696-97
feather flowers, **6:** 692-93
gingerbread
house, gingerbread, **6:** 762-66
herbs
cooking with herbs, **7:** 885-86
hibachi and hot-pot cookery
hot-pot cookery, **7:** 894-96
pasta
homemade pasta, **12:** 1428-31
pickled and canned foods
fruit recipes, **12:** 1511
pickle recipes, **12:** 1506
tomato recipes, **12:** 1507-8
vegetable recipes, **12:** 1509-10
sashimi and sushi
chirashi sushi, **15:** 1911
nigiri sushi, **15:** 1905-7
norimaki sushi, **15:** 1908-10
sashimi, **15:** 1903-5
tea
brewing tea, **20:** 2442-43
terrines and timbales
terrines, **20:** 2463-66
timbales, **20:** 2467-69

vinegars
cider vinegar, **22:** 2698
flavored vinegars, **22:** 2699-2703
wine vinegar, **22:** 2696-97
wok cookery
beef with broccoli, **23:** 2839-41
cabbage, spicy, **23:** 2839
chicken, Tai Chien, **23:** 2844
Chinese meal, **23:** 2845
duck, deep-fried, **23:** 2843
fish, steamed, **23:** 2841-42

Leathercrafts
American Indian crafts
moccasins, Apache, **1:** 49-53
carryalls
tote bag, leather, **4:** 396-99
lamps and shades
suede shade, **9:** 1038-39
leather working
appliquéd pillow, **9:** 1070-71
envelope briefcase, **9:** 1077-79
painted bracelet, **9:** 1069-70
sandal making
Italia sandal, **15:** 1867
Riviera sandal, **15:** 1867-68
Seville sandal, **15:** 1864-66
T-tie sandal, **15:** 1868

Needlecrafts
afghan stitch
afghan, **1:** 29
pillow, tic-tac-toe, **1:** 28
animal dolls
lion, stuffed, **1:** 60-62
appliqué
hand appliqué, **1:** 82-85
machine appliqué, **1:** 87-89
tablecloth, **1:** 91
buttons
clay buttons, **3:** 308-9
hand-painted buttons, **3:** 310-11
carryalls
back pack, canvas, **4:** 395
tote bag, vinyl, **4:** 392-94
crewel
sampler, embroidery, **5:** 538-41, 546-49
tissue covers, black work, **6:** 654-55
embroidery
circles, **6:** 653
owl, black work, **6:** 656-57
flags and banners
boat pennant, nylon, **6:** 672-73
Florentine stitch
plastic box cover, **6:** 683-84
tote bag pocket, **6:** 681-82
fur recycling
fling, fur, **6:** 749
pillows, fur, **6:** 742-43
shortening coat, **6:** 744-45

granny squares
floral afghan, **7:** 811
popcorn stitch afghan, **7:** 813
tote bag, shoulder, **7:** 814-15
traditional afghan, **7:** 807-8
greeting cards
needlepoint cards, **7:** 838-39
hardanger embroidery
cocktail mat, **7:** 859-60
red place mat and napkin, **7:** 861-62
white place mat and napkin, **7:** 863-65
knitting to fit
sweater and skirt, knit, **8:** 1007-9
sweater, hooded parka, **8:** 1010-11
lace
necklace, lace, **8:** 1023-24
lamps and shades
shade cover, **9:** 1039
machine stitchery
bag, trapunto, **9:** 1113-14
folk art hanging, **9:** 1,107-8
pillowcase, embroidered, **9:** 1115
pillow, ribbon, **9:** 1114
place mat, personalized, **9:** 1111-12
wall hanging, appliquéd, **9:** 1109-11
work shirt, free embroidery, **9:** 1106-7
mittens and mukluks
mittens, **10:** 1210-15
mukluks, **10:** 1216-19
needlepoint
mirror frame, needlepoint, **11:** 1328-29
pillow, needlepoint, **11:** 1330-31
rug, needlepoint, **11:** 1332-33
patchwork
crib quilt, **12:** 1447-48
pillow, patchwork, **12:** 1443-46
reversible vest, **12:** 1449-50
tote bag, patchwork, **12:** 1451-52
traditional quilt, **12:** 1439, 1452-53
quilting
Dresden-plate quilt, **14:** 1702-5
rainbow-cloud quilt, **14:** 1707-9
shoulder bag, quilted, **14:** 1694-96
vest and skirt, quilted, **14:** 1706-7
wall hanging, quilted, **14:** 1690, 1697-98
raffia and straw
purse, pine-straw, **14:** 1723
recycling clothes
appliquéd child's dress, **14:** 1741-42
casual top, **14:** 1739
denim skirt and knit top, **14:** 1733-35
halter, **14:** 1740
lengthening dress, **14:** 1742-43
raglan top, **14:** 1736-38
reverse appliqué
pillow appliqué, **14:** 1758-59
tote bag, **14:** 1759-60
ribboncraft
evening bag, ribbon, **14:** 1771
parquet ribbon pillow, **14:** 1766-67
patchwork and ribbon pillow, **14:** 1768-69
tennis racket cover, **14:** 1769-70

T-shirt, appliquéd, **14:** 1772-73
woven ribbon pillow, **14:** 1764-66
rya and flossa
designing ryas, **15:** 1832-34
needlepoint and rya pillow, **15:** 1824, 1829-30
rya pillow, **15:** 1824, 1828-29
wool wall hanging, **15:** 1826-28
samplers
designing samplers, **15:** 1858-59
perforated-paper sampler, **15:** 1860-61
sandal making
needlepoint clogs, **15:** 1869-71
ribbon clogs, **15:** 1871
sewing without pattern
apron-shawl, bias-cut, **16:** 1974-76
caftan, **16:** 1977, 1978-80
cape, hooded, **16:** 1980-81
coat, kimono, **16:** 1977-78
coverlet, quilted, **16:** 1975, 1983-84
pillow cover, ruffled, **16:** 1985
skirt, wraparound, **16:** 1982
tablecloth, round, **16:** 1985
smocking
cotton dress, **17:** 2085
man's shirt, **17:** 2081-82
pillow, smock, **17:** 2078-81
silk dress, **17:** 2083-84
soft sculpture
abstraction, soft sculpture, **17:** 2110-11
airplane, soft sculpture, **17:** 2107-9
tennis shoes, soft sculpture, **17:** 2112-14
Swedish huck work
handbag, huck work, **19:** 2341-42
pillow, huck work, **19:** 2342-43
tambour
curtain, white-on-white, **19:** 2412
dragonfly, tambour, **19:** 2417-19
pillow, tambour, **19:** 2416-17
rug, wool, **19:** 2413-15
wall hanging, tambour, **19:** 2415-16
traditional knitting motifs
bias-knit scarf, **21:** 2578-79
Irish-knit top, child's, **21:** 2571-74
Norwegian-pattern sweater, **21:** 2574-77
trapunto
dress, yoked, **21:** 2580, 2584-85
face pillow, trapunto, **21:** 2588-89
handbag, batik, **21:** 2586
sheet and pillowcases, trapunto, **21:** 2582-84
T-shirt, lion, **21:** 2587-88
wall hanging, trapunto, **21:** 2590-91

Outdoor Activities
sail making and repair
Marconi dinghy sail, **15:** 1844-47

swings
pulley-and-cable glides, **19:** 2348-51
tire swings, **19:** 2345-48

Paint and Color
folk art
fraktur traufscheine, **6:** 708-9
neckties
butterfly neckerchief, **11:** 1315
illustrating ties, **11:** 1312-13
tree design tie, **11:** 1311-12
oil painting
cityscape, **11:** 1344-45
portraits, **11:** 1346-47
still life, **11:** 1342-43
supergraphics
child's bedroom supergraphic, **19:** 2327
dark background supergraphic, **19:** 2328
diagonal stripes supergraphic, **19:** 2330-31
fabric design supergraphic, **19:** 2334-35
flowers supergraphic, **19:** 2330-31
free-form supergraphic, **19:** 2332
furniture framing supergraphic, **19:** 2327-28
geometric supergraphic, **19:** 2324-26
Indian motif supergraphic, **19:** 2333
reversed colors supergraphic, **19:** 2329
sunrise supergraphic, **19:** 2323, 2330
tie dyeing
stitchery, tie-dye, **20:** 2479-81
table throw, velvet, **20:** 2482-84
wall hanging, block dyed, **20:** 2484-87
tin painting
antique stenciled tin box, **20:** 2523-27
canister, painted, **20:** 2518-19
country tin painting, **20:** 2513-17
freehand bronze tray, **20:** 2520-22
vegetable dyes
colorfast dyes, **21:** 2678-83
wool yarn, dyeing, **21:** 2684-88

Paper Folding and Cutting
boxes
desk and seat, milk-crate, **3:** 262-65
wall sculpture, **3:** 268
cardboard
whirligig weathervane, **3:** 369-71
flowers, artificial
crepe paper flowers, **6:** 694-96
foil flowers, **6:** 690-91
tissue paper flowers, **6:** 689
origami
samurai hat, **11:** 1381
uses of origami, **11:** 1385
quilling
bird, quillwork, **14:** 1681-83
butterflies, quillwork, **14:** 1678-79
silhouettes
pictures, silhouette, **16:** 2046-48

, continued

Performing Arts
dulcimers
Appalachian dulcimer, **5**: 624, 626-33
fretboard dulcimer, **5**: 625-26
skin painting
stage face makeup, **17**: 2072-73
stagecraft
lighting, stage, **18**: 2206-13
set design, **18**: 2196-2201
tea
Japanese tea ceremony, **20**: 2447-51
whistles and flutes
flutes, **22**: 2778-79

Toys and Games
kites
Indian fighter kite, **8**: 989, 998-99
Thai dragon kite, **8**: 996-97
preschool activities
busy board, **13**: 1625-27
giraffe, stuffed, **13**: 1622-24
puzzles
block puzzle, **13**: 1661-62
counter puzzle, **13**: 1658-59
jigsaw puzzle, **13**: 1663-64
rockers and cradles
boat, rocker, **14**: 1777-78
doll's cradle, **14**: 1780-81
table games
Anagrams, **19**: 2373-74
Lasca, **19**: 2374-75
Quick Trip, **19**: 2376-77
toys
elephant toy chest, **20**: 2549, 2556-58
gee haw whimmy diddle, **20**: 2550-51
hammer man, **20**: 2559-60
sports car, **20**: 2553
stern-wheel boat, **20**: 2554-55
yard toys
cable-spool playhouse, **23**: 2906-7
spiral staircase, **23**: 2908-9
tire and box toys, **23**: 2902-3
utility pole animals, **23**: 2904-5

Weaving, Braiding, Knotting
basketry
hanging basket, **1**: 116-17
Indian coil basket, **1**: 115
shopping basket, **1**: 118-19
braided rugs
petal-design rug, **3**: 278-79
place mats, braided, **3**: 276-77
traditional braided rug, **3**: 276-77
hammocks and slings
log sling, canvas, **7**: 850-51
naval hammock, **7**: 851-53
inkle weaving
hat band and bag handle, **8**: 932

pick-up pattern belt, **8**: 935
wall hanging, inkle, **8**: 929, 934-35
watchband and vase cover, **8**: 933
lace
collar and cuffs, bobbin lace, **8**: 1019-21
sash, bobbin lace, **8**: 1017-18
leather working
belt, magic braid, **9**: 1072-73
macramé
belt, adjustable, **9**: 1120-21
dress yoke and sash, **9**: 1122-23
sculpture, willow tree, **9**: 1125-26
raffia and straw
oval tray, **14**: 1722
round tray, **14**: 1720-22
rya and flossa
cat, woven rya, **15**: 1834-37
sprang
belt, sprang, **17**: 2168
hammock, sprang, **17**: 2174-76
sampler, sprang, **17**: 2163-66
scarf, sprang, **17**: 2169
tote bag, sprang, **17**: 2167
wall hanging, sprang, **17**: 2172-73
swings
baby swing, **19**: 2354-57
tablet and frame weaving
bag, tablet-woven, **19**: 2399-2401
geometric frame weaving, **19**: 2403-4
tatting
collar, shell-cluster, **19**: 2424-25
flowerpot holder, **19**: 2429-30
place mat, sunflower, **19**: 2427-28
tablecloth, openwork, **19**: 2431-32
vest, child's, **19**: 2426-27
weaving
leno-weave scarf, **22**: 2765-67
plaid pillow, **22**: 2755-63
twill jackets, **22**: 2768-69
twill pillow, **22**: 2767
woven tapestries
apple-tree tapestry, **23**: 2870-71
field-of-flowers tapestry, **23**: 2872-73
frame loom, **23**: 2861-63
frame loom, tapestry, **23**: 2864-65
pillow, geometric, **23**: 2866-67
wrapped and coiled work
basket, hanging, **23**: 2884-86
necklace, wrapped, **23**: 2880-82

 The projects that follow can be completed only by an adult who has had specialized prior training.

Carving and Molding
folk art
reindeer weathervane, **6**: 716-17
sculpture
alabaster sculpture, **16**: 1935-37
walking sticks
sculptured walking stick, **22**: 2720-21

Designs and Decorations
mosaics
grouted mosaics, **10**: 1277-78
tile mural, **10**: 1278-80

Furniture and Finishes
plywood and foam furnishings
banquette and bench, **13**: 1579-83
Shaker furniture
dovetailed candle box, **16**: 2009-11
side table, **16**: 2003-5
utility bench, **16**: 2006-8

Glass and Plastics
glass working
glass beads, **7**: 786
hanging ornament, **7**: 787
lampblown glass bottle, **7**: 774, 780-85
leaded glass
lampshade, **9**: 1066-67

Jewelry, Lapidary, and Metalwork
mobiles
steel fin mobile, **10**: 1227-31
repoussé and chased metal
necklace, metal, **14**: 1751-53
seashells
lampshade, shell, **16**: 1950-51

Needlecrafts
bean-bags
furniture, bean-bag, **2**: 164-66
Florentine stitch
pillow, **6**: 684-87
fur recycling
collar and cuffs, fur, **6**: 746-48
neckties
recycled tie skirt, **11**: 1316-17
reverse appliqué
hanging, reverse appliqué, **14**: 1760-61

Paper Folding and Cutting
origami
carrier pigeon, **11**: 1382
crane, **11**: 1375, 1383
jumping frog, **11**: 1384-85

Toys and Games
whistles and flutes
hardwood whistle, **22**: 2778

Weaving, Braiding, Knotting
macramé
micromé hanging, **9**: 1126-27
room-divider screen, **9**: 1116, 1124
weaving
tote bag, weft-faced, **22**: 2770-71
wall hanging, woven, **22**: 2772-73